Understanding and Evaluating Educational Research

James H. McMillan

Jon F. Wergin

Virginia Commonwealth University

 MERRILL,
an imprint of Prentice Hall
Upper Saddle River, New Jersey   Columbus, Ohio

Library of Congress Cataloging-in-Publication Data

McMillan, James H.

    Understanding and evaluating educational research / by James H. McMillan, Jon F. Wergin.

      p. cm.

    Includes index.

    ISBN 0-13-193541-0

    1. Education—Research—Methodology. 2. Education—Research—Evaluation. 3. Action research in education. I. Wergin, Jon F. II. Title.

LB1028.M366   1998

370'.7—dc21   97-30618

                                                            CIP

Cover art: © Harvey Sibley/Super Stock 1994
Editor: Kevin M. Davis
Production Editor: Linda Hillis Bayma
Production Coordinator: WordCrafters Editorial Services, Inc.
Design Coordinator: Karrie M. Converse
Cover Designer: Susan Unger
Production Buyer: Laura Messerly
Director of Marketing: Kevin Flanagan
Marketing Manager: Suzanne Stanton
Advertising/Marketing Coordinator: Julie Shough
Illustrations: Carlisle Communications, Ltd.

This book was set in Garamond by Carlisle Communications, Ltd., and was printed and bound by The Banta Company. The cover was printed by Phoenix Color Corp.

10 9 8 7 6 5 4 3 2 1

ISBN 0-13-193541-0

Prentice-Hall International (UK) Limited, *London*
Prentice-Hall of Australia Pty. Limited, *Sydney*
Prentice-Hall of Canada Inc., *Toronto*
Prentice-Hall Hispanoamericana, S.A., *Mexico*
Prentice-Hall of India Private Limited, *New Delhi*
Prentice-Hall of Japan, Inc., *Tokyo*
Simon & Schuster Asia Pte. Ltd., *Singapore*
Editora Prentice-Hall do Brasil, Ltda., *Rio de Janeiro*

Preface

The purpose of this book is to help students become better and more informed consumers of published research studies. For most students enrolled in introductory research classes in education, this is the only research course they will take. Many students will approach the course with dread or, at best, resignation. "Why should I have to take a course in research methods, if I'm never going to do this kind of work myself?" they ask. Our response is simple. Practicing professionals, whether teachers, principals, or counselors, need to be able to read, understand, and evaluate research studies. They need to approach research data with a critical eye—to discriminate sound arguments from specious ones, to discern appropriate uses of statistics from those meant to mislead or obfuscate. As professionals they should not have to depend on others' assessments of the validity or usefulness of research; they should be able to read, critique, and evaluate research information *themselves*.

Our approach in this book is to provide students with a systematic approach for first identifying whether an article or report should be considered "research," then understanding the type of research, and, finally, utilizing criteria by which studies of each type should be judged. This approach is illustrated with published articles from various journals. We include questions with each article which we hope will help students learn how to apply appropriate criteria, both for the case at hand and for other studies of its type, and provide answers to illustrate the thinking of informed consumers. By the end of the book we hope that students will have developed a *way of thinking* about published research and a greater sense of confidence in their ability to read it profitably.

Understanding and Evaluating Educational Research is not meant to supplant the main text for an introductory research class, but rather to serve as a supplement to it, especially in classes where a major focus is on understanding research. Research articles have been organized to be consistent with the methodological classification found in most introductory research texts. The writing uses nontechnical language for the research novice. Important terms and concepts are boldfaced. In the first chapter we lay out our typology, suggest how the reader might use it to classify research studies, and present criteria by which *all* educational research should be judged. Succeeding chapters present the research types one at a time, describe their peculiar characteristics, and present criteria by which each type ought to be evaluated. In the final chapter we discuss action-oriented research and practitioner research studies that transcend the categories and deserve particular criteria of their own.

Our criteria for selecting the published articles include the following:

1. *Publication date.* Most articles have been published within the past 5 years.

2. *Topic.* The articles represent the diversity of topics found in education (e.g., educational administration, counseling, special education, curriculum, adult education, early childhood education).

3. *Relevance.* The articles are interesting, relevant, and useful.

4. *Level of difficulty.* The articles range from easily understood to moderate levels of difficulty.

We are most appreciative of the support and expertise of Merrill/Prentice Hall in preparing and publishing this book. We are also grateful to our students who have provided helpful suggestions on the choice of articles and on the introductory sections to each chapter. We also wish to thank our reviewers: John E. Bonfadini, George Mason University; Scott W. Brown, University of Connecticut; and Karen L. Ford, Ball State University.

Contents

Chapter 4   Qualitative Ethnographic Designs   89

Chapter 5   Action Research   151

Chapter 1

Introduction to Reading Educational Research

In this introduction we will summarize a series of steps that will help you identify if an article or report is empirical research, determine the type of research, and ask the kinds of questions that will facilitate an understanding of the study. In subsequent chapters we will provide more information about specific types of research designs and the kinds of questions to ask for each type. We refer to the first few steps as a "roadmap" for identifying different types of research (see Fig. 1).

What Is Educational Research?

Educational research is a systematic investigation, involving the collection of information (data), to solve an educational problem or contribute to our knowledge about an educational theory or practice. As systematic, disciplined inquiry, educational research relies on methods and principles that will produce credible and verifiable results. Defined in this way, research is not simply gathering information about something, such as going to the library and doing a "research paper." Rather, information is gathered from individuals, groups, documents, and other sources, more like a scientific study, in which a series of specific steps is followed:

1. Frame the initial question or problem.
2. Determine what previous research says about the question or problem.
3. Frame a research question, problem, or hypothesis.
4. Design a plan for collecting data to address the question, problem, or hypothesis.
5. Analyze the results of gathering data.
6. Generate conclusions.

The first step in understanding research is to be able to recognize that an article or report is, in fact, research. You will need to distinguish between empirical studies (research) and articles that summarize thinking about a topic or opinion. Here is a summary of what to look for in making this determination:

1. **Does the title suggest that data have been gathered?** The titles of research articles typically contain language that suggests the collection and analysis of data. The terms "study" and "investigation" denote research, as would phrases such as "an investigation of," "the relationship between," and "the effect of." Here are some examples:

   The relationship between cognitive style and student effort in learning mathematics problem solving.

   A study of teacher decision making concerning assessment and grading.

   Incentives for students: The effect of varying types of rewards on achievement.

   Effects of cooperative and individualized methods of instruction on student altruism.

   The title of an article is one clue as to whether it is research. If the above words or phrases are used, it probably is research, but some studies might not contain any of these words or phrases.

2. **Is there a question or problem that is investigated?** A distinguishing feature of research is that there must be some question or problem that is the focus of the study. Whereas literature that is not research may describe and summarize information, an empirical investigation is designed to answer a specific question or problem. The purpose of research is to answer the question. Doing "library" research, such as reading literature on factors affecting student self-concept, is not an empirical investigation because a specific question or problem is not answered as a result of collecting new information.

3. **Are new data collected?** Most research involves the collection of new information (some research reanalyzes information that has already been collected). This means that there will be reference to a procedure that was followed to collect the data. Usually there is a section that uses terms like "instruments," "measures," or "data collection."

4. **Is there a methodology or methods section?** In a research article or report there will be a "methodology" or "methods" section. The purpose of this section is to summarize the manner in which subjects or participants were obtained, the instrumentation utilized, procedures for collecting information, and any direct interventions on the subjects. This is usually a major heading.

5. **Is there a findings or results section?** Since the purpose of research is to collect information to answer a question, there will always be some kind of "results" or "findings" section that summarizes what the data that were collected shows. This section often includes tables or graphs to summarize the information.

What Are the Various Types of Educational Research?

While all educational research shares such attributes as a focus on empiricism and disciplined inquiry, there are many different ways or methods by which the research is carried out. Each of these methods has distinct purposes, advantages, and disadvantages. The second step toward becoming an intelligent consumer of educational research, then, is to recognize which method has been used. The third step is to assess the quality of the research according to criteria appropriate for that method.

For example, you would analyze a study of parental attitudes toward AIDS education very differently from a study reporting the results of an experimental curriculum. In the first case you would probably be most interested in questions like these: How were the parents chosen for this study, and how many participated? What method was used to collect data from parents, and how appropriate were the questions the researchers asked? What inferences were drawn from the results, and how valid were they? For the second case, in contrast, you would probably be most interested in questions like these: What precisely was different about the "experimental" curriculum? How was it implemented? What effects was it supposed to have, and how did the researchers choose to measure these effects? Did the researchers use a "control" group? How was it selected? Did the researchers find the effects they were looking for? Were these effects significant?

Types of educational research are categorized in Figure 1. It may be read, from left to right, as a decision tree. Here are the major distinctions to keep in mind as you work your way through it.

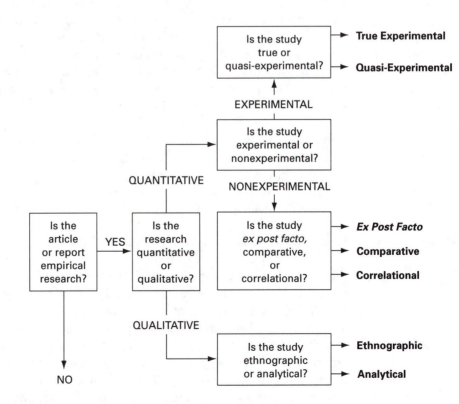

Figure 1.   Roadmap for identifying types of educational research

Quantitative/Qualitative Research

The most fundamental difference in methodology of research is whether it is quantitative or qualitative (or some combination of these two). **Quantitative** research involves the use of numerical indices to summarize, describe, and explore relationships among traits. There is a reliance on control, statistics, measurement, and experiments. In **qualitative** research, the emphasis is on conducting studies in natural settings using mostly verbal descriptions, resulting in stories and case studies rather than statistical reports. Both quantitative and qualitative approaches are viable in education. Until recently, almost all educational research was quantitative. Today, qualitative studies are reported with increasing frequency, and some studies combine both approaches.

Quantitative Research: Experimental/Nonexperimental

Once you have determined that a study is quantitative, it is helpful to determine if it is an experiment. An **experimental** study is one in which the researcher has control over one or more factors (variables) that may influence the responses of the subjects. There is "manipulation" of factors that may affect subjects' behavior. The purpose of this control is to determine whether one factor causes a change in another one. A **nonexperimental** study is one in which there is no control over what may influence subjects' responses. The investigator is interested in studying what occurs "naturally." Nonexperimental studies are generally used to describe phenomena and uncover relationships. For example, suppose that you were interested in looking at the relationship between students' participation in class discussion and teachers' verbal reinforcement of their comments. You could conduct a nonexperimental study by observing teacher and student behavior and noting when certain behaviors appear to occur together. If, however, you were interested in isolating more specific cause-effect relationships—that is, whether teacher reinforcement actually *causes* more student participation—you could conduct a more experimental-type study by systematically manipulating teacher behavior and noting its apparent effect on students. While this latter kind of study may appear more precise, it also introduces other kinds of problems, as we will see in Chapter 3. Experimental-type studies can be further broken down into two categories, true and quasi-experimental.

Experimental Research: True Experimental/Quasi-Experimental.
True experimental research involves something very specific, namely the use of comparison groups that have been **randomly assigned.** Random assignment means what it says: That assignment of subjects to comparison groups has been done completely at random, like flipping a coin or drawing names out of a hat. Random assignment strengthens the argument that any apparent effect of the "treatment" is not due to other factors, like inherent differences among the groups. **Quasi-experimental** research is that which manipulates "treatments" but does not use randomly assigned treatment groups. If, for example, you were interested in assessing the impact of a new

science curriculum on fifth graders, you might want to implement the new curriculum with one sample of students and then see how they do compared to another sample exposed to the "traditional" approach. Ideally you'd want to assign students to these two groups at random; practically this may be impossible, however, and so you use two *intact* fifth-grade classes instead, implementing the "new" curriculum with one and the "traditional" with the other. As you might imagine, what quasi-experiments gain in feasibility, they give up in explanatory power.

Nonexperimental Research: *Ex Post Facto*/**Comparative/Correlational.**   Once you determine that the study is nonexperimental, you will need to further classify it as *ex post facto,* comparative, or correlational. *Ex post facto* ("after the fact") research, also called causal-comparative research, is a nonexperiment dressed up to look like an experiment. *Ex post facto* studies examine a phenomenon that has already occurred and attempt to infer cause-effect relationships. These are examples of questions leading to *ex post facto* studies: Do children who have attended day care programs do better in kindergarten? Do couples who seek out marriage counselors have more stable marriages? Do people who smoke have higher rates of lung cancer than those who don't? In each case a "treatment" variable is identified— day care, marriage counselors, cigarette smoking—and those who have been exposed to it are compared to those who have not along some variable of interest—in these examples, academic performance, marital happiness, cancer incidence. Teasing out whether in fact any differences are due to the "treatment" variable is very difficult in *ex post facto* studies, as we will see later.

Comparative research investigates the relationship between two or more variables by examining the differences that exist between two or more groups of subjects. That is, the groups are compared to one another. For example, suppose a researcher is interested in whether a relationship exists between grade level and self-concept. Samples of subjects are obtained from several different grades, and the mean self-concept scores for the sample from each grade are calculated. The average scores from each grade are compared. For instance, if grades 4 through 10 are compared and the average self-concept scores for grades 8, 9 and 10 are higher than the scores for grades 4, 5, and 6, then a positive relationship exists between grade level and self-concept. Unlike *ex post facto* studies, comparative research makes no claim of causality.

Correlational designs investigate relationships among variables by calculating correlation coefficients, rather than looking at differences. To calculate a correlation, each subject presents scores from two variables. The correlation coefficient is calculated using these sets of scores to indicate the direction and strength of the relationship. The direction is either positive or negative; the strength varies from little or no relationship to moderate to strong. Here are some questions that would be investigated using a correlational design: How is teacher satisfaction related to the degree of autonomy on the job? Does a relationship exist between the degree of parental involvement with the school and socio-economic status? How well do SAT scores predict college grades? Correlational studies are common in education and generally use survey methods as a means of collecting data.

Qualitative Research: Ethnographic/Analytical

If the study you are examining is qualitative, examine it further to determine if it is ethnographic or analytical. **Ethnographic** studies involve direct engagement with the participants and environments being investigated. Since the intent is to understand, in depth, the phenomena being studied, the observations and interviews typically take place in naturally occurring settings and tend to be prolonged. Ethnographies collect observational and/or interview data and then summarize and analyze the data. Conclusions are based on a synthesis of the data that were collected. Some examples of ethnographic studies include the following:

> A study of the reasons gifted students give for not feeling challenged in the classroom.

> Inquiry into the motivations of African-American teacher education students.

> A study of the culture of sexual discrimination in middle schools.

> Research into the role of play in counseling elementary-level children.

> Case studies of the dynamics of school restructuring.

Qualitative research that is termed **analytical** investigates historical, legal, and policy concepts and events through an analysis of documents and relics. The data are not actively gathered by the researcher from observations or interviews. Rather, the data already exist in the form of written summaries, documents, and relics.

Ethnographic Research: Observation/Interview. Observations and/or interviews are conducted by the researchers in an ethnographic study. The investigator may observe carefully over an extended period of time, or may even become a "participant" in the setting to gain a deeper appreciation of what the role and culture are like. For example, a researcher may spend a great deal of time in elementary schools to understand how teachers make decisions concerning student assessment, or the researcher could even become a teacher for a period of time and experience first-hand the process of making these decisions. Interviews are typically open-ended and extensive. The researcher engages the participant in a conversation to discover how, in the participant's words, the concepts and ideas are expressed and understood.

What Criteria Are Useful for Understanding and Evaluating Research Articles?

As we have already noted, each type of research study has certain criteria for excellence that are indigenous to it, and we will focus on these criteria in exploring further each major type of research in subsequent chapters. Some criteria, however, pertain to *all* educational research, regardless of type, and we present these criteria here. Ultimately, it is important to meet these criteria for the research to be credible and useful.

Credibility is the extent to which the information is understandable, trustworthy, valid, and makes sense. If the article is well written, complete, and meets most of the criteria summarized below, then it is more likely to be credible and useful. You may find what could be called "fatal flaws" in some studies, deficiencies so serious that they render the article useless. More commonly, though, you will find that while the study may have some limitations, the information is helpful. Consequently, the intent is to help you become a critical reader, but not hypercritical.

In the following sections different parts of research articles are summarized, and questions are formulated for each part that you can ask as a guide to understanding and evaluating that part of the article.

Introduction

The purpose of the introduction is to set the context of the study and to indicate the research problem. This part of the article is usually one to several paragraphs. It may provide background to the study and indicate why it is significant to conduct the research. This is often accomplished with quotes or references to other studies that set a historical context. Most introductory sections will contain a general statement of the problem that will be investigated; in some studies the specific research questions will replace a general statement of purpose.

Questions to ask:

1. Is the general purpose of the study clear?

2. Is the study significant? Will it make a practical or theoretical contribution?

3. Is the introduction well organized and clear?

Review of Literature

The review of literature is one to several paragraphs in which previous studies of the same or similar problem are summarized and analyzed. The purpose of the review is to show how the current study is related to other studies. A good review is selective and goes beyond simply reporting what others have found. It is best if the review includes a critical analysis of previous studies and indicates implications of the analysis for the present study. The articles in the review should be closely related to the problem under investigation so that the problem is logically connected to what else has been done in the area. The review should use as many current articles as possible, organized by topic and not by date. The review should concentrate on other studies that are closely related to the current one, and should only mention briefly minor studies that are not very relevant.

Questions to ask:

1. Is the review comprehensive?

2. Is the review up to date?

3. Is there an emphasis on primary sources (i.e., actual studies, rather than other review articles)?

4. Is there a critical review or a summary of findings?

5. Is the review well organized?

6. Does the review clearly relate previous studies to the current research problem?

7. Does the review help establish the importance of the research?

Research Problem, Question, or Hypothesis

While a general problem statement is usually included in the introductory section, in quantitative studies it is necessary to indicate a specific research problem statement, question, and/or research hypothesis. Sometimes the specific problem statement or question is located at the end of the introduction, before the review of literature. More commonly, a specific research question or hypothesis follows the review. In fact, the review helps to establish the specific questions or hypotheses. (A **research hypothesis** is a statement that indicates the expected or predicted relationship between two or more variables.) The specific problem can be formulated as either a statement or a question. Regardless of the form, it is important for the specific problem to be clear, succinct, and researchable. It should give you an indication of the type of research method being used (e.g., experimental or nonexperimental), the independent and dependent variables, and the subjects.

In a qualitative study the research problem is formulated as the **foreshadowed question.** These are more general statements than specific questions or hypotheses found in quantitative studies, and are reformulated as data are collected. The emphasis is on what, where, and why, rather than on relationship among variables.

Questions to ask:

1. Is the problem or hypothesis clear and concise?

2. If there is a hypothesis, is it consistent with the review of literature?

3. If quantitative, does the problem or hypothesis communicate the variables, type of research, and population?

4. If qualitative, is the initial problem reformulated?

Methodology: Subjects or Participants

A **subject** or **participant** is a person from whom information is gathered to answer the research question. In most articles you will find a section of the methodology that will be labeled *subjects, sample, participants,* or *population.* In this section, the individuals from whom the data are collected will be described. It is important to know about the subjects since their backgrounds and characteristics may influence the results.

Questions to ask:

1. Is the population described adequately?
2. Is the sample clearly described?
3. Is the method of selecting the sample clear?
4. Could the method of selection affect the results?
5. Are subjects likely to be motivated to give biased responses?

Methodology: Instruments

Credibility of research depends on the quality of the measurement of the variables. If the measurement is weak, then so too are the results. **Instruments,** or **measures,** are devices and procedures that are used to gather information from subjects. Instruments can take a wide variety of forms, including tests, oral or written surveys, ratings, observation, and various archival and "unobtrusive" measures.

The credibility of the information gathered with these techniques depends on two kinds of evidence: validity and reliability. **Validity** refers to the appropriateness of the inferences made from the data collected. These are examples of validity questions: How useful are SAT scores as a measure of academic achievement in high school? How useful are they as a measure of likely academic achievement in college? To what extent do student responses on a survey that is meant to measure "self-esteem" really reflect self-esteem, and not some other variable like "verbal skill" or "social desirability"?

Evidence for validity should thus be presented in the context of how the results are to be used. Just because an instrument is "established" or standardized does not mean that it is valid; for example, it wouldn't make sense to use an intelligence test to measure musical ability. Validity is often established during a pilot test of the instrument.

Reliability refers to the degree of error that exists when obtaining a measure of a variable. No measure or instrument is perfect; each will contain some degree of error. The error can be because of the individual (general skills, attitudes, illness, motivation, etc.) or because of the way the instrument is designed and administered. Reliability is the estimate of the error in the assessment. Generally you will look for evidence of the instrument's consistency, whether across time or across raters, or within the instrument itself.

It will also be helpful to examine how the instrument was administered. Who gave it or who were the observers? Would they be biased? Were the observers trained? Did the subjects have sufficient time to answer the questions? If the instrument concerned attitudes, was it anonymous? Would the respondents want to give "socially desirable" answers?

The purpose of any data collection instrument is to provide accurate information about the variables being studied. Thus, each variable is actually "defined" by how it is measured and reported, as well as how it is labeled or defined conceptually by the researcher. There are advantages and disadvantages to using different procedures to collect information, but each should provide evidence of validity and reliability. Look for anything in the procedures or the instrument itself that could bias the results.

Questions to ask:

1. Is evidence for validity and reliability clearly presented and adequate?

2. Is there a clear description of the instrument and how it was used?

3. Is there a clear description of how the instrument was administered?

4. Is it likely that the subjects would fake their responses?

5. Are interviewers and observers trained?

6. If appropriate, how were standards of performance established?

7. If appropriate, what are the norms used to report percentile rank and other results?

Methodology: Procedures

The procedures subsection will indicate, depending on the study and journal, how subjects were selected, how instruments were developed and administered, and how experimental treatments, if any, were conducted. A qualitative study will describe procedures the researcher used to gain entry into the field, the nature and length of observations and interviews, and how participants were approached. In this section you will want to look for characteristics of the study design that might lead to erroneous interpretations of the data. For example, could the researcher's own biases and desires affect the results? Could the participants' awareness of being in a study affect their behavior when an observer is present?

Questions to ask:

1. Are there any clear weaknesses in the design of the study?

2. Are the procedures for collecting information described fully?

3. Is it likely that the researcher is biased?

Results

The results, or findings, section of the article presents a summary of the data analysis. This section is usually organized by the research question or hypothesis. It is helpful if the researcher first presents the findings without interpreting them. This will often involve the use of tables and charts. Basically the researcher is saying, "this is what I found."

With advances in computer technology, statistical analyses are usually done without mathematical error. It is another matter, however, to know if the appropriate statistics have been used and if the results are interpreted correctly. While it is beyond the scope of this book to cover different analysis techniques, some basic principles will help you to understand these sections.

In quantitative studies, researchers use **inferential statistics** to make probability statements about what is true. That is, how certain can we be that a statistical finding reflects reality? The degree of probability or certainty depends most on the amount of measurement and sampling error in the study. For example, when we select a sample from a population, inferential statistics tell us what is true about the population even though we only use a portion of the population in the study. "Statistical" significance is not related to practical significance, importance of the finding, or whether the study has a strong design. Some studies that use a very large number of subjects can report "statistically significant" results that are of little practical importance. Conversely, studies using a very small number of subjects may not be able even to establish statistical significance, due to the small sample size.

In qualitative research there is a need to document a systematic process of analyzing the data. Often ethnographers will code transcripts and rearrange examples of different kinds of evidence in an effort to identify trends or conclusions. **Triangulation** is used often, in which different sources of data pertaining to the same question are used to verify consistency of findings. The results are typically presented as they flow from the data, rather than in predetermined categories, and quotes from participants and specific events from observations are used to illustrate the findings.

Questions to ask:

1. Are the findings presented clearly?

2. Is there appropriate use of tables, charts, and figures?

3. Is the number of subjects taken into consideration when presenting the results?

4. Is there sufficient descriptive information to interpret the results?

5. Are the results presented in relation to the research question, or does it seem more like a "fishing expedition" to find something, anything, that is "statistically significant"?

6. If qualitative, are the results accompanied by illustrative quotes and specific instances?

Discussion and Conclusions

Once the results have been summarized, the researcher will present a discussion of their meaning. This interpretation is helpful in understanding why certain results were obtained. Usually the researcher evaluates the findings in light of the methodology to explain what the results mean and how they can be used. The researcher uses the research question and review of literature in this analysis. Essentially this is a statement of the judgment of the researcher given the research problem, review of literature, methodology, and results. Often limitations are summarized, due to subject selection, the nature of the instrument used, or a weakness in the procedures.

The final section of the article will present **conclusions**—summary statements of the findings and how the researcher interprets them. Conclusions should be supported by the data and logical analysis. It is helpful for the researcher to indicate limitations to the conclusions, based on subject characteristics, the context of the research, when the research is conducted, the nature of the treatments, and instruments used to collect information. An important research concept related to limitations is external validity. **External validity** refers to the extent to which the findings can be generalized to be true for other individuals, settings, times, treatments, and measures. That is, what is true for sixth graders who were involved in a study may not be true for ninth graders, or true for other sixth graders across town, and results demonstrated by one measure of creativity may not be replicated if a different measure of creativity is used. While it is possible to be overly strict in judging external validity, it is best to use reasonable professional judgment.

Questions to ask:

1. Is the discussion based on the research problem and results, or is there a tendency to discuss unrelated material or ideas?

2. Is there an adequate interpretation of the findings?

3. Is the interpretation separate from the results?

4. Are the results discussed in relation to previous studies?

5. Are limitations due to methodology included in the discussion?

6. Are the conclusions clearly stated and based on the results and discussion?

7. Are the conclusions reasonable? Do they go beyond the interpretation of the findings?

8. What is the external validity of the study? What factors would affect the external validity?

Chapter 2

Quantitative Nonexperimental Designs

Nonexperimental quantitative research is done to investigate relationships among variables (although some simple quantitative studies merely describe variables). The relationship is expressed as either a correlation or a comparison. A **correlational study** is one in which there are at least two measured variables for each subject. These variables are related by using one or more correlational analyses. A correlation is computed to show the direction and magnitude of the relationship. A **simple (bivariate)** correlation relates one variable to another one. It results in a number between -1 and $+1$. If the correlation is positive, then the relationship is positive (not necessarily "good"), which means that as the value of one variable increases, so does the value of the other variable. A negative, or inverse, relationship is designated by a negative correlation, and means that increases in one variable are associated with decreases in the other variable. The size of the correlation is important for interpreting the results. As the correlation approaches either -1 or $+1$ (depending on whether it is positive or negative), it becomes stronger. A correlation of .75 or above would be considered high, around .5 moderate, and below .3 low. A correlation of $-.86$ is stronger than a correlation of .78.

Another common type of correlational analysis is called a **multiple correlation** or **multiple regression.** In this type of study several independent variables are combined to see how well they predict one or more dependent variables. The resulting relationship shows how well the combined independent variables predict. For example, a researcher may want to see how well several variables from a sample of high school students, such as socio-economic status, family structure, and aptitude test scores, predict college grades. The analysis will tell the researcher how these three independent variables, together, predict grades, and also how much each of the three contributes to the overall correlation.

Another type of nonexperimental quantitative study is comparative. The purpose of **comparative research** is to provide an accurate description of how two or more groups differ on some phenomenon (dependent variable).

The variable that differentiates the groups is the independent variable. Thus, if a study compares the achievement of male students to female students, gender is the independent variable and achievement is the dependent variable. Comparative studies can examine the differences over time of the same or similar group of subjects, or can investigate how groups that are not the same compare. A **developmental** study investigates changes in subjects over time. If the same subjects are investigated, the study is **longitudinal.** If different groups of subjects who do not have the same age are studied at one time, the study is **cross-sectional.** While longitudinal developmental studies are stronger and more credible, they are more difficult to complete and require more time and resources. In a cross-sectional study, the researcher needs to be careful that differences between the subjects in different age categories in such characteristics as ability, motivation, background, and attitudes do not account for the results.

If groups that are different on the independent variable are compared, it is usually a straightforward study. For instance, the following questions suggest a comparative study: Do teachers with tenure have different attitudes about merit salary increases than untenured teachers? How does the self-concept of high-achieving students compare with the self-concept of low-achieving students? What is the difference in attitudes toward parking of commuter and noncommuter students? In each case there is a clearly defined independent variable with two or more levels.

In both correlational and comparative studies, the results rely heavily on the quality of the instrument, the nature of the sample, and the manner in which different groups have been identified. Thus, it is important to pay particular attention to these aspects of the study (e.g., Was the sample comprised of volunteers? Who administered the instrument? What were the circumstances of instrument administration? Were the scores from the instrument valid and reliable? What were the criteria for identifying subjects as being in different groups? How were subjects placed in each group?).

As with most nonexperimental designs, you need to be careful not to infer causation from correlations or comparative differences. A correlational study may show that students who have larger biceps are better readers, but that doesn't imply that students will read better if they are put on weight training! (Older students, with larger biceps, are better readers. This is a good example of the need to examine the nature of the sample carefully.)

Criteria for Evaluating Correlational and Comparative Studies

1. Is the general purpose of the study clear? Will the study provide a significant contribution?

2. Does the review of literature establish the relationship between previous studies and the current one? Is the review well organized and up to date?

3. Is the specific research hypothesis or question clearly and concisely stated?

4. Is the method of sampling clearly presented? Could the way the sample was obtained influence the results?

5. Is there anything in the procedures for collecting information, or in the instruments themselves, that could bias the results or weaken the study?

6. Is the magnitude of the correlation or difference between groups large enough to suggest practical significance or importance?

7. Do the conclusions and interpretations follow logically from the results presented? Are unwarranted causal conclusions made from correlational or comparison data? Are limitations indicated?

Another type of nonexperimental design is called ***ex post facto*** (or **causal-comparative**). In this type of study the researcher is able to identify past experiences of subjects that are consistent with a "treatment," and compares those subjects with others who have had a different treatment or no treatment. The goal of an *ex post facto* design is to establish a cause-and-effect relationship between the independent and dependent variables, much like an experiment. However, in an *ex post facto* study the independent variable has already occurred; it is not directly manipulated by the researcher. Since there is no manipulation of the independent variable, this design is technically nonexperimental, even though in all other respects it looks like an experiment—there is a treatment group, control or comparison group, a posttest, and sometimes a pretest. Since the treatment has already occurred, there can be no random assignment of subjects unless it was instituted prior to the treatment.

A good example of this design would be a study of the effect of attending a small or large high school on student achievement. While it is possible to conduct an experiment by identifying students starting high school and measuring their achievement three years later, an *ex post facto* study can investigate the question without waiting three years by identifying graduating students who have attended small high schools and comparing their achievement with students who have attended large high schools. Since the students would not have been randomly assigned to type of high school, it is important to see if the groups that are compared differ on variables that would affect the results. Also, there may be other factors that differentially influence achievement at each school. For example, small schools could differ from large ones in the type of curriculum offered, qualifications of teachers, or socio-economic status of the community. Each of these factors could affect achievement, in addition to size. Thus, when conducting an *ex post facto* study, it is important to think about whether differences other than the independent variable could affect the results.

Criteria for Evaluating *Ex Post Facto* Studies

1. Is the general purpose of the study clear? Will the study provide a significant contribution?

2. Does the review of literature establish the relationship between previous studies and the current one? Is the review well organized and up to date?

3. Is the specific research hypothesis or question clearly and concisely stated?

4. Is the method of sampling clearly presented? Could the way the sample was obtained influence the results?

5. Is there anything in the procedures for collecting information, or in the instruments themselves, that could bias the results or weaken the study?

6. Has the presumed treatment already occurred? Is the treatment well defined?

7. Are subjects in different groups similar except for the treatment?

8. Do the conclusions and interpretations follow logically from the results presented? Are causal conclusions made with caution? Are limitations indicated?

Differing Opinions on Testing between Preservice and Inservice Teachers

Kathy E. Green

University of Denver

❧

ABSTRACT

Studies of teachers' use of tests suggest that classroom tests are widely used and that standardized test results are rarely used. What is the genesis of this lack of use? A previous comparison of pre- and inservice teachers' attitudes toward assessment suggested no differences. This study assessed the different opinions among sophomores (n = 84), seniors (n = 152), and inservice teachers (n = 553) about the use of classroom and standardized tests. Significant differences were found; preservice teachers had less favorable attitudes toward classroom testing than teachers did and more favorable attitudes toward standardized testing.

This study assessed differences among college students entering a teacher education program, students finishing a teacher education program, and inservice teachers concerning their opinions of some aspects of classroom and standardized testing. Although numerous studies of inservice teachers' attitudes toward testing have been conducted, little research is available regarding preservice teachers' views of testing and of the genesis of teachers' views of testing.

Interest in this topic stemmed from research findings suggesting that the results of standardized tests are not used by most teachers. If standardized testing is to continue, the failure to use results is wasteful. Other studies have identified some of the reasons for the lack of use. This study's purpose was to determine whether opinions about the usefulness of standardized and other tests were negative for students before they even entered the teaching profession. When were those attitudes developed? Are attitudes fixed by students' educational experiences *prior* to entry into a teacher education program? Are preservice teachers socialized by their educational programs into resistance to testing? Do negative attitudes appear upon entry into the profession because of socialization into the school culture? Or do they appear after several years of service as a teacher because of personal experiences in the classroom?

I found only one study that addressed differences in opinions of pre- and inservice teachers (Reeves & Kazelskis, 1985). That study examined a broad range of issues salient to first-year teachers; only one item addressed testing specifically. Reeves and Kazelskis found no significant differences between pre- and inservice teachers' opinions about testing, as measured by that item. In this study, I sought more information pertinent to the development of opinions about testing.

Test use in U.S. schools has been and continues to be extensive. It has been estimated that from 10 to 15% of class time is spent dealing with tests (Carlberg, 1981; Newman & Stallings, 1982). Gullickson (1982) found that 95% of the teachers he surveyed gave tests at least once every 2 weeks. The estimated percentage of students' course grades that are based on test scores is 40 to 50%, ranging from 0 to 100% (Gullickson, 1984; McKee & Manning-Curtis, 1982; Newman & Stallings). Classroom tests, thus, are used frequently and may, at times, be used almost exclusively in determining students' grades.

In contrast, a review of past practice suggests minimal teacher use of *standardized* test results in making instructional decisions (Fennessey, 1982; Green & Williams, 1989; Lazar-Morrison, Polin, Moy, & Burry, 1980; Ruddell, 1985). Stetz and Beck (1979) conducted a national study of over 3,000 teachers' opinions about standardized tests. They noted that 41% of the teachers surveyed reported making little use of test results, a finding consistent with that of Goslin (1967) from several decades ago and that of Boyd, McKenna, Stake, and Yachinsky (1975). Test results were viewed as providing information that was supplemental to the wider variety of information that the teachers already possessed. Reasons offered for why standardized tests are given but results not always used by teachers include resistance to a perceived narrowing of the curriculum, resistance to management control, accountability avoidance (Darling-Hammond, 1985), and a limited understanding of score interpretation resulting from inadequate preservice training (Cramer & Slakter, 1968; Gullickson & Hopkins, 1987). Marso and Pigge (1988) found that teachers perceive a lower need for standardized testing skills than for classroom testing skills. They also found that teachers reported lower proficiencies in standardized test score use and interpretation than in classroom test score use and interpretation.

The results of those studies suggest that inservice teachers use classroom tests extensively but make little use of standardized test results. This suggests that inservice teachers, in general, hold positive attitudes toward classroom tests and less positive attitudes toward standardized tests. The literature does not lead to any predictions about preservice teachers' attitudes toward tests.

This study assessed differences between preservice and inservice teachers' opinions about testing and test use. The following research hypotheses were formulated to direct the study.

H1. There are significant differences in opinions about the testing and test use between preservice and inservice teachers.

H2. There are significant differences in opinions about testing between students beginning their preparation (sophomores) and students finishing their preparation (seniors).

H3. There are significant differences among inservice teachers with differing years of experience.

METHOD

Samples

Three samples were drawn for this study. They were samples of (a) practicing teachers, (b) college sophomores beginning a teacher education program, and (c) college seniors completing a teacher education program (but prior to student teaching). For the first sample, survey forms were mailed in a rural western state to 700 teachers randomly selected from the State Department of Education list of all licensed educators. During the spring semester of 1986, teachers were sent a letter explaining the nature of the study, a survey form, and a stamped return envelope. With two follow-up mailings, a total of 555 questionnaires were received, or 81% of the deliverable envelopes. (Twelve questionnaires were undeliverable, 4 persons refused to respond, and 133 persons did not reply.) No compulsory statewide standardized testing program was in place in the state.

The second sample was a convenience sample of three sections of an educational foundations class typically taken by college sophomores who have just enrolled in a teacher preparation program ($n = 84$). The course examines educational thought and practice in the United States. The classes were taught in an 8-week block, meeting for 50 min per day, 4 days per week. Survey forms were distributed in class and completed during class time.

The third sample was also a convenience sample of four sections of a tests and measurement class taken by college seniors ($n = 152$). The course is typically taken after coursework is almost complete, but prior to student teaching.

TABLE 1. Description of Samples

Item	Sophomores ($n = 84$)	Seniors ($n = 152$)	Teachers ($n = 553$)
Percentage female	84	152	553
Mean age	73.0	75.9	63.6
Age range	18–33	20–45	—
Mean years in teaching	—	—	12

The course provides instruction in basic statistics, classroom test construction and analysis, and standardized test use and interpretation. The course was also taught in an 8-week block, with the same schedule as the foundations course. Survey forms were distributed during the first week of class and completed during class time. Survey forms took from 10 to 30 min to complete. Responses were anonymous. Both sophomores and seniors were attending a public university in a small western town.

Table 1 presents descriptive information for the three samples.

Instruments

Three different forms with overlapping questions were used in this study. The survey form sent to the teachers contained questions regarding training in tests and measurement, subject and grades taught, tests given, and attitudes toward both standardized and classroom tests. The questionnaire was two pages in length, double-sided and contained 49 questions. The form given to the sophomores had 43 questions and was one page in length, double-sided. The form given to the seniors was three pages in length, single-sided. The latter two forms differed by the inclusion of an evaluation anxiety scale and items eliciting importance of contemporary measurement practices for the seniors. Although different formats may have affected responses to some extent, all the forms began with several demographic questions followed by the items relevant to this study. Any form differences would, then, likely be minimized for those initial items.

There were 18 items common to the three forms. Sixteen of the items were Likert items with a 1 to 6 (*strongly disagree* to *strongly agree*) response format. Likert-scale items were drawn from a previously developed measure of attitudes toward both standardized and classroom testing (Green & Stager, 1986). Internal consistency reliabilities of the measures ranged from .63 to .75. The remaining two items asked how many hours per week teachers spend in testing activities and how much of a student's grade should be based on test results. The study examined differences found among groups on those items. Item content is presented in Table 2, in which items are grouped by content (opinions about standardized tests, classroom tests, and about personal liking for tests).

Data were analyzed using multivariate analyses of variance, followed by univariate analyses of variance. If univariate results were significant, I used Tukey's HSD test to assess the significance of pairwise post hoc differences. Samples of both items and persons were limited; therefore, results may not be widely generalizable.

Results

Significant multivariate differences were found across opinion items (Wilks's lambda = .70, $p <$ .001) when the three samples were compared (Table 2). Hypothesis 1 was supported. Differences were found between teachers and students for all items, with significance levels varying from .02 to .001 for individual items. Opinions were not consistently more positive across all items for teachers or for students. For instance, whereas teachers were most likely to feel that standardized tests address important educational outcomes, teachers were least likely to find that standardized tests serve a useful purpose. In general, though, students favored use of standardized tests for student or teacher evaluation more than teachers did. Although the students were less likely to say that they do well on tests and that tests previously taken were good assessments of their ability, the students were also less likely to say that they disliked taking tests. Students' opinions

TABLE 2.   Means and Standard Deviations for Opinions About Testing by Group

Variable	Sophomores (*n* = 84)	Seniors (*n* = 152)	Teachers (*n* = 553)	*p*	1	2	3
Hours spent in testing/week	10.43 (6.72)	9.18 (6.43)	4.37 (4.05)	.001	*	*	—
Percentage grade based on test	49.63 (15.48)	46.94 (18.71)	41.31 (22.68)	.001	*	*	—
Standardized test items							
Standardized tests are the best way to evaluate a teacher's effectiveness.	2.79 (1.03)	2.83 (1.10)	2.12 (1.18)	.001	*	*	—
Teachers whose students score higher on standardized tests should receive higher salaries.	2.53 (1.07)	2.33 (1.17)	1.74 (1.01)	.001	*	*	—
Requiring *students* to pass competency tests would raise educational standards.	4.14 (1.13)	3.89 (1.09)	3.69 (1.26)	.001	*	*	—
Requiring *teachers* to pass competency tests would raise educational standards.	4.35 (.90)	4.09 (1.27)	3.30 (1.34)	.001	*	*	—
Standardized tests assess important educational outcomes.	3.47 (1.04)	3.54 (.87)	3.95 (.88)	.001	*	*	—
Standardized tests serve a useful purpose.	4.02 (.83)	3.97 (.81)	2.93 (.97)	.001	*	*	—
Standardized tests force teachers to "teach to the test."	3.05 (1.19)	2.74 (.98)	3.11 (1.22)	.02	—	*	—
Classroom test items							
Test construction takes too much teacher time.	4.57 (1.02)	4.36 (.85)	3.97 (.88)	.001	*	*	—
Test scores are a fair way to grade students.	3.42 (1.02)	3.32 (1.13)	4.04 (.84)	.001	*	*	—
Testing has a favorable impact on student motivation.	4.00 (.71)	3.88 (1.00)	4.16 (.88)	.01	—	*	—
Tests are of little value in identifying learning problems.	1.76 (.96)	1.43 (.84)	1.44 (1.05)	.01	*	—	*
It is relatively easy to construct tests in my subject area.	4.11 (1.25)	3.51 (1.34)	4.35 (.89)	.001	—	*	*
Tests measure only minor aspects of what students can learn.	2.92 (1.13)	3.01 (1.13)	3.24 (1.00)	.01	*	—	—
Personal reflections							
I do (did) well on tests.	4.05 (1.04)	4.00 (1.10)	4.46 (.94)	.001	*	*	—
I personally dislike taking tests.	3.13 (1.35)	3.12 (1.14)	3.46 (1.16)	.01	—	*	—
The tests I have taken were generally good assessments of my knowledge of an area.	3.65 (1.08)	3.41 (1.10)	4.09 (.82)	.001	*	*	—

Note. For opinion items, the scale ranged from *strongly disagree* (1) to *strongly agree* (6). Standard deviations are presented in parentheses. Asterisks (*) indicate significant ($p < .05$) differences between groups; 1 = teachers versus sophomores, 2 = teachers versus seniors, 3 = sophomores versus seniors.

about classroom testing were less favorable than were teachers' opinions for all but one item. Differences were also found between teachers and students in estimates of time spent in testing and in the percentage of students' grades based on test scores.

Hypothesis 2 was not supported. Only two significant differences in means were found between the sophomores and the seniors. One difference was found for the item "It is relatively easy to construct tests in my subject area." Sophomores tended to agree with that statement more than the seniors did. Because the seniors were required to complete a task involving test construction, the impending course requirement may have influenced their opinions. The second difference was found for the item "Tests are of little value in identifying learning problems," with more positive opinions expressed by seniors than by sophomores.

Hypothesis 3 was tested by dividing teachers into three groups: 0 to 1 years, 2 to 5 years, and 5 + years of experience as a teacher. No significant multivariate or univariate differences were found, so Hypothesis 3 was not supported. However, there were few teachers with 0 to 1 years of experience in the sample. Because of the small number of teachers with 0 to 1 years of teaching (46 teachers; 8.7% of the data file), groups were reformed as follows: 0 to 3 years, 4 to 6 years, and 6 + years of experience. Still, no significant multivariate or univariate differences were found. (In addition, no differences were found between teachers with 0 to 3 years of experience and those with 6 or more years of experience.)

DISCUSSION

This study was undertaken to examine whether differences in opinions about testing would be discerned between preservice and inservice teachers and whether those differences would suggest a progression. The differences found suggest that teacher education students are less favorable to classroom testing and more favorable to standardized testing

than teachers are. Differences were *not* found between sophomores and seniors, however. Nor were opinions about testing found to depend upon years of experience in teaching. Those results do not reflect a developmental progression. The shift in opinion seems to occur when beginning a teaching position, suggesting effects that result from job requirements or socialization as a teacher more than from a developmental trend. Differences between students and teachers, then, seem likely to be caused by direct teacher experience with creating, administering, and using tests or by acculturation into life as a teacher in a school. That conclusion suggests that if one wishes to affect teachers' opinions about testing, provision of inservice experiences may be a more profitable avenue than additional preservice education.

Test Use. The teachers sampled in this study reported spending an average of about 11% of their time in testing, which is consistent with estimates reported in the literature (10 to 15%). The finding in this study that an average of 41% of the students' grades was based on test results is also consistent with estimates reported in the literature (40 to 50%). Estimates of the time needed for testing activities obtained from students sampled in this study were much higher (23% and 26% for seniors and sophomores, respectively) than the estimates obtained from the teachers' reports. Although students' estimates of the percentage of grade based on test scores were significantly higher than those of teachers, they were within the range reported in the literature. Students, then, who lack an experiential base, seem either to have exaggerated views regarding the time that teachers spend on testing-related activities or think that it will take them longer to construct tests.

Beginning teachers also lack an experiential base. One might ask whether beginning teachers spend more time in test-related activities than do teachers with more experience, because beginning teachers may not have files of tests to draw upon. Mean reported time spent in testing was higher for first- and second-year teachers (means of 5.4 and 5.7 hours per week) than for teachers with more experience (mean for third year = 2.3, 4th year = 2.8, 5th year = 3.8). Thus, students may be accurate in their perception of the time needed by novices for testing-related activities.

Standardized Testing. The students' opinions ranged from neutral to positive regarding the use of standardized tests and were, on average, significantly more positive than the teachers' opinions. One explanation for the positive opinions may be that students have extremely limited personal experience with standardized tests (their own or their friends') and so have a limited basis upon which to judge test effectiveness. By college level, most students have taken a number of standardized tests but may not be aware of the results, may not have been directly affected by the results, or may have been affected by the results at a time when they were too young to understand or argue. Students may believe that the tests must be useful because "authorities and experts" sanction their administration. Students' opinions may, then, be shaped by the positive *public* value placed on tests, as well as by their educational programs. The tests and measurement course taken by many preservice teachers emphasizes how tests can be valuable if used properly. One can argue that most students view themselves as intending to use tests properly. In contrast, many teachers are required to give standardized tests, and they may also be required to take them.

Preservice-inservice differences might be even more extreme in states where the stakes attached to standardized test use are higher—where the teacher's job or salary depends upon test results. Teachers develop a broader base of experience with standardized testing, and they may be more aware of the limitations of the tests and of the controversy surrounding standardized testing. The measurement profession is unclear about the value of standardized testing; it is not surprising that teachers also have reservations.

Classroom Testing. Differences were also found between teachers and teacher education students for most classroom test items, though differences were not as pronounced for these items. The result is in contrast to Reeves and Kazelskis's (1985) finding of no differences between similar groups. The result of somewhat less favorable opinions of preservice than inservice teachers toward classroom testing may have stemmed from the frequent test taking by students versus the frequent use of tests by teachers. By the time students are seniors in college, they will have taken a larger number of classroom tests than standardized tests and thus will have considerably more experience in evaluating their effectiveness. Students undoubtedly encounter classroom tests and test questions that they consider to be unfair assessments of their knowledge. Such experiences may temper their opinions toward classroom tests. In contrast, because most teachers rely to some extent on test results in assigning grades and in evaluating instruction, opinions may change to conform with this behavior. Teachers' opinions may also be influenced by an experiential understanding of testing gained through learning how informative test results can be.

Because it is unlikely that the widespread use of classroom and standardized tests will diminish, teachers will continue to be called upon to use tests to make decisions that are important in the lives of students. Teachers need to be competent in test construction and interpretation. However, if tests are to be used effectively as part of the instructional process, teachers must perceive the positive aspects of test use. If a teacher finds that task impossible, that teacher should discontinue traditional test use and seek alternative assessment techniques, within the boundaries allowed by the district. Teachers should communicate positive feelings about the tests they give to their students. Teachers will probably be more likely to do so if they have positive opinions of tests. Tests are often viewed as evaluative; they may more effectively be viewed as informative and prescriptive.

If teacher educators wish to affect prospective teachers' views, they may need to both clarify their own views about the place of testing in instruction and clearly present arguments about testing, pro and con, to their classes. Well-constructed classroom assessments, whether paper-and-pencil, portfolio, or performance measures, provide diagnostic and prescriptive information about the students' progress and about the effectiveness of instruction. This information is valuable. Poorly constructed or standardized measures that do not address the curriculum provide little information of use in the classroom. The reasons for giving tests that do not provide information useful in instruction must be clearly explained. Such tests may be mandated to provide legitimate administrative, state, or national information.

But to what extent can teacher educators shape *prospective* teachers' views? The results of this study suggest that opinions held prior to and following preservice instruction may not survive the transition to the real world of the classroom. If this is the case, the preservice course—no matter how good it is—would be ineffective in influencing attitudes. (It may, however, be highly effective in influencing the quality of testing practices by providing basic skills in test construction and interpretation.) Inservice instruction may be a better vehicle to use to produce attitude change.

This study was cross-sectional in design. A longitudinal study that examined opinions over time (from preservice to inservice) is required to identify the extent to which opinions are shaped by school requirements. Additional information regarding school characteristics affecting preservice and inservice teachers' attitudes toward testing would be of interest, as would information about differences in testing skill levels between pre- and inservice teachers.

NOTES

An earlier version of this paper was presented at the 1990 annual meeting of the National Council on Measurement in Education, held April 1990 in Boston.

Appreciation is expressed to the *Journal of Educational Research* reviewers for their helpful suggestions.

REFERENCES

Boyd, J., McKenna, B. H., Stake, R. E., & Yachinsky, J. (1975). *A study of testing practices in the Royal Oak (MI) public schools.* Royal Oak, MI: Royal Oak City School District. (ERIC Reproduction Service No. 117 161)

Carlberg, C. (1981). South Dakota study report. Denver, CO: Midcontinent Regional Educational Laboratory.

Cramer, S., & Slakter, M. (1968). A scale to assess attitudes toward aptitude testing. *Measurement and Evaluation in Guidance, 1*(2).

Darling-Hammond, L., & Wise, A. E. (1985). Beyond standardization: State standards and school improvement. *Elementary School Journal, 85,* 315-336.

Fennessey, D. (1982). Primary teachers' assessment practices: Some implications for teacher training. Paper presented at the annual conference of the South Pacific Association for Teacher Education, Frankston, Victoria, Australia.

Goslin, D. A. (1967). *Teachers and testing.* New York: Russell Sage Foundation.

Green, K. E., & Stager, S. F. (1986-87). Testing: Coursework, attitudes, and practices. *Educational Research Quarterly, 11*(2), 48-55.

Green, K. E., & Stager, S. F. (1986). Measuring attitudes of teachers toward testing. *Measurement and Evaluation in Counseling and Development, 19,* 141-150.

Green, K. E., & Williams, E. J. (1989, March). Standardized test use by classroom teachers: Effects of training and grade level taught. Paper presented at the annual meeting of the National Council on Measurement in Education, San Francisco.

Gullickson, A. R. (1982). The practice of testing in elementary and secondary schools. (ERIC Reproduction Service No. ED 229 391)

Gullickson, A. R. (1984). Teacher perspectives of their instructional use of tests. *Journal of Educational Research, 77,* 244-248.

Gullickson, A. R., & Hopkins, K. D. (1987). The context of educational measurement instruction for preservice teachers: Professor perspectives. *Educational Measurement: Issues and Practice, 6,* 12-16.

Karmos, A. H., & Karmos, J. S. (1984). Attitudes toward standardized achievement tests and their relation to achievement test performance. *Measurement and Evaluation in Counseling and Development, 17,* 56-66.

Lazar-Morison, C., Polin, L., Moy, R., & Burry, J. (1980). A review of the literature on test use. Los Angeles: Center for the Study of Evaluation, California State University. (ERIC Reproduction Service No. 204 411)

Marso, R. N., & Pigge, F. L. (1988). Ohio secondary teachers' testing needs and proficiencies: Assessments by teachers, supervisors, and principals. *American Secondary Education, 17,* 2-9.

McKee, B. G., & Manning-Curtis, C. (1982, March). Teacher-constructed classroom tests: The stepchild of measurement research. Paper presented at the National Council on Measurement in Education annual conference, New York.

Newman, D. C., & Stallings, W. M. (1982). Teacher competency in classroom testing, measurement preparation, and classroom testing practices. Paper presented at the American Educational Research Association annual meeting, New York. (ERIC Reproduction Service No. ED 220 491)

Reeves, C. K., & Kazelskis, R. (1985). Concerns of preservice and inservice teachers. *Journal of Educational Research, 78,* 267-271.

Ruddell, R. B. (1985). Knowledge and attitudes toward testing: Field educators and legislators. *Reading Teacher, 38,* 538-543.

Stetz, F. P., & Beck, M. D. (1979). Comments from the classroom: Teachers' and students' opinions of achievement tests. Paper presented at the annual meeting of the National Council on Measurement in Education, San Francisco.

Evaluation Criteria

1. Is the general purpose of the study clear? Will the study provide a significant contribution?

The general purpose of the study is presented in the first sentence, and it is clear. However, a different "purpose" is stated in the second paragraph, which is confusing. Generally the lack of research in an area does not necessarily suggest that a study in the area is significant. While the goal of determining the "genesis" of attitudes toward testing is significant, the methodology in this study does not directly address this question. A longitudinal study would provide better data on the development and evolution of attitudes.

2. Does the review of literature establish the relationship between previous studies and the current one? Is the review well organized and up to date?

The literature reviewed is more helpful in establishing the importance of the study than summarizing previous research on the problem

Discussion Questions

1. How could a case be made for significance without depending so heavily on the fact that little research exists on the problem?

2. Are the studies presented analyzed as well as summarized? Are they explicitly related to the research problem?

that is investigated. While additional studies directly related to the problem may be lacking, it seems that there should be separate studies of preservice and inservice teachers that would be informative, and research of other differences between the two groups that could help inform the hypotheses. The review is adequately organized but does not seem to be completely up to date.

3. Is the specific research hypothesis or question clearly and concisely stated?

The hypotheses are clearly stated just before the Method section, but they do not suggest the direction of the difference, just that the attitudes will not be the same. A proper research hypothesis is directional. It would be better to state specific research questions rather than hypotheses for this study.

3. How could the research hypotheses be rewritten to be directional?

4. Is the method of sampling clearly presented? Could the way the sample was obtained influence the results?

The method of sampling is clearly presented, with good detail, in the Method section. The large sample of practicing teachers and high response rate are impressive. Because this is a cross-sectional study, it is possible that there are group differences unrelated to age or position. Students in the tests and measurements class, even though they completed the survey during the first week, could be expected to provide somewhat more positive responses, especially if prompted by the person who distributed the surveys. It would be helpful to know if the class was required.

4. What type of sample is used in the study? Examine Table 1 carefully. What is wrong with the numbers? What does this suggest about the overall credibility of the research? What other types of samples could be used to address the research question (e.g., new and experienced teachers; students while student teaching)?

5. Is there anything in the procedures for collecting information, or in the instruments themselves, that could bias the results or weaken the study?

The procedures for collecting information were fine, with the exception of not indicating who administered the surveys to the college students and what they were told. There is no evidence of validity presented.

5. What kind of evidence for validity would be appropriate for this study? How would the researcher conduct a pilot test to provide validity evidence?

The range for internal consistency was .63 to .75. Since there were only three forms, one had to be .63 and one had to be .75. It would have been better to indicate all three reliability estimates rather than give the range. Of all the reliability estimates, internal consistency is usually the highest. Those reported in this study are low.

6. Is the magnitude of the correlation or difference between groups large enough to suggest practical significance or importance?

Given the large sample size, it is easy in this type of study to obtain "statistically significant" differences which could be very small. There is little practical significance in the differences between students. Teachers show some important differences from students, particularly when the difference between the means is at least .5.

7. Do the conclusions and interpretations follow logically from the results presented? Are unwarranted causal conclusions made from correlational or comparison data? Are limitations indicated?

The conclusions are found at the end of the Discussion section. Many of these are not a reflection of the results, however. For example, the first conclusion, found at the end of the first paragraph in the Discussion section, suggests cause and effect, while the study only reports differences between the groups. Also, there is a suggestion at the end of the study that "opinions . . . may not survive the transition to the real world of teaching." Appropriately, the researcher points out the limitation of a cross-sectional design, but other limitations, such as the restricted nature of the student samples and low reliability, could also be included.

6. An interesting approach to determining "practical" significance is to divide the difference between two means by the average standard deviation. If the result is .3 or higher, we generally conclude that there is practical significance. What would these "effect sizes" be for some of the questions?

7. How could the conclusions that are embedded in the discussion section be more clearly presented? How should limitations to the external validity of the findings be stated?

Alienation from School: An Exploratory Analysis of Elementary and Middle School Students' Perceptions

Jerry Trusty
*University of Alabama
at Birmingham*

Katherine Dooley-Dickey
Mississippi State University

The dropout problem continues to be perceived as a threat to our social and economic systems. Many researchers have proposed that dropping out is the result of a slow, steadily developing process of alienation from school. The purpose of this study was to determine the extent to which the following variables: (a) gender, (b) race, (c) gender and race jointly, (d) socioeconomic status, (e) parent's educational level, (f) reading achievement, (g) mathematics achievement, (h) grade failure, (i) particular school attended, and (j) racial similarity of the student to his/her school's racial composition predicted feelings of alienation from school in students in each of Grades 4, 5, 6, 7, and 8. Data employed in the study were from 19 public schools in Mississippi. Gender and school variables emerged as the most consistent predictors of alienation from school. Analyses did not wholly support the theory that alienation from school is a steady developmental process. Alienation from school may not develop early in students' perceptions, and the effects of early negative school experiences may not be manifested until students reach high school.

Since the late 1970s national dropout rates have slowly and steadily declined for all major ethnic groups except Hispanics (Frase, 1989). Despite the long term decrease in the number of students failing to complete high school, there has been a general increase in concern over the dropout problem (Rumberger, 1987). Finn (1989) described this concern as a na-

tional obsession. The high level of interest in the dropout problem may be related to the prediction that negative social and economic consequences, for the individual and the nation, will result from premature exit from school (Wehlage & Rutter, 1986). Catterall (1985) proposed that even a conservative estimate of costs resulting from school dropout greatly exceeds the costs of resources devoted to dropout prevention.

Although specific consequences of dropping out are difficult to determine (Natriello, Pallas, & McDill, 1986), many factors have been found to be associated with school dropouts: (a) alcohol consumption (McCaul, Donaldson, Coladarci, & Davis, 1992), (b) illicit drug use (Mensch & Kandel, 1988), (c) criminal activity (Hartnagel & Krahn, 1989), (d) unemployment (Caliste, 1984), (e) lower lifetime earnings (Catterall, 1985), (f) social and political noninvolvement (McCaul et al., 1992), and (g) lower educational achievement (Ekstrom, Goertz, Pollack, & Rock, 1986). The above factors, however, may only be corollaries of school dropout. It seems rational that these negative experiences could be causally related to antecedent factors such as gender, socioeconomic status, or ethnic background (McCaul et al., 1992; Natriello et al., 1986).

The causes of dropout are also multifarious and complex (Baker, 1991). According to Rumberger (1987), research into the dropout problem should be directed toward understanding the underlying processes, and many of the factors implied or expressed as causes for dropping out of school could be symptoms

Trusty, Jerry, and Dooley-Dickey, Katherine. (1993). Alienation from school: An exploratory analysis of elementary and middle school students' perceptions. *Journal of Research and Development in Education, 26*(4), 232–242. Reprinted with permission.

of underlying factors. For example, Wehlage and Rutter (1986) found that race was not a factor in predicting dropouts when socioeconomic status was taken into account. Rumberger (1987) indicated that low socioeconomic status may be the most pervasive family background characteristic associated with dropping out of school.

Ekstrom et al. (1986) found that students who subsequently dropped out reported more disciplinary problems, higher absenteeism, lower self-concepts, and more external locus of control. Parents of dropouts were reported as spending less time monitoring their children and dropouts seemed to feel alienated from their schools. Researchers (Barrington & Hendricks, 1989; Lloyd, 1978) have found that school dropout could be fairly accurately predicted by achievement, attendance, and family data collected as early as students' third-grade year. Other authors have purported that school dropout is a developmental process that starts early in students' educational careers.

Mann (1986) suggested that the most effective way to keep students from dropping out in high school is to make elementary schools more successful, and Finn (1989) proposed that behaviors associated with complete withdrawal from school (dropping out) stem from an earlier withdrawal from school life. According to Wehlage, Rutter, Smith, Lesko, and Fernandez (1989) the alienated student has little motivation for learning and may eventually come to see dropping out of school as a viable alternative. Several authors (Bryk & Thum, 1989; Elliot & Voss, 1974; Finn, 1989; Firestone, Rosenblum, & Webb, 1987; Hendrix, Sederberg, & Miller, 1990; Newmann, 1981; Wehlage & Rutter, 1986; Wehlage et al., 1989) have proposed that alienation from school is a salient factor underlying the dropout process.

Adolescent alienation has been studied extensively (Fetro, 1987), and alienation from school has often been a component of adolescent alienation studies and measurement instruments (Fetro & Vitello, 1988). Alienation from school has been studied in high school

populations (e.g., Bryk & Thum, 1989; Elliot & Voss, 1974; Firestone et al., 1987; Fontes, 1988). However, no studies have been found that empirically investigate alienation from school in elementary and middle school students and the developmental properties of alienation from school in this age/grade group.

The complex web of factors that are associated with dropping out of school may have differing influences on various individuals in various situations (Mann, 1986) and therefore may be difficult to understand. Feelings of alienation from school may, however, be a common factor underlying the dropout process (Finn, 1989; Wehlage & Rutter, 1986). Furthermore, an understanding of alienation from school may help in understanding this process. According to Seldin (1989), most studies of alienation have confirmed that alienation exists; but few studies have offered guidance toward effective strategies to reduce alienation. An increased understanding of alienation from school and its development may lead to more effective prevention and intervention strategies for students at-risk of dropping out of school (Finn, 1989). Knowledge of student characteristics that are most highly associated with alienation from school may lead school personnel to school practices that reduce this alienation. Also, examination of the developmental properties of alienation from school may guide school personnel toward timely intervention and prevention strategies.

The purpose of this study was to examine possible predictors of feelings of alienation from school in students in each of Grades 4, 5, 6, 7, and 8. This study thereby explored the developmental properties of alienation from school through examination of predictors in the cross section of grade levels. Additionally, levels of alienation as a function of grade level were examined. This study did not seek to determine causal factors of alienation from school or school dropout, but was exploratory in nature. It is hoped that this study will provide a basis for subsequent study of the alienation/dropout paradigm.

Specifically, the major questions addressed by this study were:

1. To what extent do the variables (a) gender, (b) race, (c) gender and race jointly, (d) socioeconomic status, (e) educational level of the head of the household, (f) reading achievement, (g) mathematics achievement, (h) grade failure, (i) particular school attended, and (j) racial similarity of the student to her/his school's racial composition predict feelings of alienation from school in fourth-, fifth-, sixth-, seventh-, and eighth-grade students?

2. Do students differ in levels of feelings of alienation from school as a function of grade level?

RELATED LITERATURE

No studies of alienation from school in elementary and middle school students were found in review of the literature. However, there are a number of empirical and theoretical studies that have examined the following: (a) alienation from school in high school students, (b) general adolescent alienation, (c) alienation and school dropout, and (d) predictors of school dropout.

Alienation from School

The alienation construct is approximately 150 years old and has evolved through Christian and philosophical thought to contemporary sociology, and in turn, social psychology (Kanungo, 1979). Alienation from school is a relatively new construct and has recently become useful in understanding student behavior (Newmann, 1981).

Finn (1989) presented an effective argument for the central, developmental role of alienation from school in dropping out of school. He stated, "Research confirms that dropping out, absenteeism and truancy, disruptive behavior in class, and delinquency … may all be seen as outcomes of earlier patterns of withdrawal from the daily classroom and school routine" (p. 119). Several authors (Barrington & Hendricks, 1989; Calabrese,

1987, 1988; Evans & DiBenedetto, 1990; Finn, 1989; Lloyd, 1976; Rumberger, Ghatak, Poulos, Ritter, & Dornbusch, 1990; Stroup & Robins, 1972; Wehlage & Rutter, 1986; Wehlage et al., 1989) suggest that alienation from school is a developmental process that eventually results in school dropout. If such a process exists, then predictors of school dropout may also serve as predictors of alienation from school in elementary-school and middle-school students.

Possible Predictors of Alienation from School

Dropout rates for the last several years have been consistently higher for males (Frase, 1989; Rumberger, 1987). Furthermore, research points to different dropout characteristics for race and gender groups. Cairns, Cairns, and Neckerman (1989) indicated that race and gender groups dropped out at varying ages and grade levels depending on how many years they were behind in grade level (due to grade failures). Rumberger (1983) found differing effects of family background on dropout behavior for race and gender groups. However, Barrington and Hendricks (1989) found no differing dropout behavior associated with gender.

Several authors (Ekstrom et al., 1986; Frase, 1989; Howell & Frese, 1982; Lloyd, 1978; Rumberger, 1983; Rumberger et al., 1990; Stroup & Robins, 1972; Walters & Kranzler, 1970; Wehlage & Rutter, 1986), using either national, regional, or local data, have found socioeconomic status and/or parents' educational level to be strongly related to school dropout. Researchers have used parents' educational level as an index of socioeconomic status (e.g., Stroup and Robins, 1972; Rumberger, 1983), whereas other researchers have treated parents' educational level as a separate variable (e.g., Howell & Frese, 1982; Lloyd 1976).

Several authors (Laosa, 1982; Lloyd, 1976, 1978; Reitzammer, 1990; Stevens & Pihl, 1982; Vacca & Padak, 1990) indicate that lack of basic academic skills seriously impairs students' ability to progress through school and contributes to school dropout. Weber (1988), in a study of popular instruments and procedures designed to identify potential dropouts, found basic skills achievement to be one of the most frequently used variables in these instruments or procedures.

Similar evidence exists in the alienation literature. Newmann (1981) suggested concentration on learning fundamentals, reading and mathematics, as one of many strategies for reducing student alienation in high schools. Moyer and Motta (1982) found higher alienation scores were associated with lower grade point averages in students in Grades 10, 11, and 12. Alienation scores, for the students in their study, were a better predictor of academic achievement than intelligence test scores.

Grade failure has been found to be associated with school dropout (Cairns et al., 1989; Lloyd, 1976, 1978; Stroup & Robins, 1972; Walters & Kranzler, 1970). Cairns et al. (1989) found that students in the seventh grade characterized by high levels of aggression, combined with academic failures, were most likely to drop out of school early. A clear positive relationship between age in the seventh grade and dropping out was observed; and interestingly, white males generally dropped out earlier than African-American males even though more African-American males were behind in grade level than white males. The authors surmised that there may be less stigma attached to being behind in grade level for African-American males than for white males. Lloyd (1978) and Stroup and Robins (1972) found early grade failure to be an effective predictor of school dropout.

Many authors (e.g., Baker & Sansone, 1990; Bryk & Thum, 1989; Finn, 1989; Natriello et al., 1986; Wehlage & Rutter, 1986) have proposed that schools themselves contribute to the dropout problem. Likewise, several authors (Calabrese, 1987; Firestone et al., 1987; Hendrix et al., 1990; Newmann, 1981; Seldin, 1989; Weitzman et al., 1985; Wynne, 1989) propose that schools contribute to students' feelings of alienation from school. According to Calabrese (1987) schools and

other social institutions may be the cause of adolescent alienation.

Wehlage and Rutter (1986) observed that dropout research has traditionally focused upon social, family, and personal characteristics; but the authors suggested that new research should focus on understanding the characteristics of schools and how schools affect potential dropouts. In interviews with students who have dropped out of school (Pittman, 1986; Rumberger, 1987; Tidwell, 1988), reasons most often given for leaving school early were concerned with the students' personal relationships with their school. Research on dropout behavior has led to the contention that schools and students interact to produce dropouts (Baker, 1991; Bryk & Thum, 1989; Evans & DiBenetto, 1990; Natriello et al., 1986; Newmann, 1981; Wehlage & Rutter, 1986).

Research on alienation from school supports this contention. Firestone et al. (1987) through a study of 10 urban high schools, found teacher and student commitment to school to be mutually reinforcing. The relationship between student and teacher commitment may take on a positive (increasing student/teacher commitment) or negative (decreasing student/teacher commitment) function. Several school level and district level organizational factors appeared to affect student commitment to school. Additionally, Calabrese and Schumer (1986) and Bryk and Thum (1989) suggested that organizational and normative features of schools affect alienation and associated behavior.

The degree to which a particular student may or may not differ from the predominant racial group in his/her school may be pertinent to the manifested degree of feelings of alienation from school. Gottlieb and Tenhouten (1965) found that as the percentage of African Americans increased in high schools, the more alienated from school white students became. In racially balanced schools, alienation seemed to wane. In high schools with large numbers of African Americans, alienation was more pronounced in whites; and African Americans were more committed to school. It should be noted that this study was done shortly following desegregation of these schools.

No other studies, besides that by Gottlieb and Tenhouten (1965), were found which directly examine the relationship between the degree of a student's similarity to the predominant group in his/her school and school dropout or alienation from school. However, there are indirect indications of this possible relationship in studies that examine the effects of school racial composition on variables such as school attitudes and interracial hostility.

Longshore (1982b) studied students' attitudes toward school in a racial context, and his findings on racial composition and its effects differed from findings cited by Gottlieb and Tenhouten (1965). Longshore (1982b) found white elementary school students' attitudes toward desegregation were least favorable when schools were 40% to 50% African American. He suggested that when either whites or African Americans were clearly dominant in a school, whites' racial attitudes were more positive.

In a similar study, Longshore (1982a) found African Americans' attitudes toward desegregation were negative when their own racial group held a slight majority in the school. Those negative attitudes were more pronounced in low socioeconomic status schools and southern schools, where traditional racial norms may be stronger.

In contrast, Patchen (1982) suggested that African Americans tend to show higher levels of hostility toward whites in schools which have high percentages of African Americans. These findings support the ethnic community theory, which proposes that African-American ethnic group identification enhances group cohesion which leads to within-group power (Gutterbock & London, 1983). Research does not present a clear picture of the effects of racial composition of schools as it relates to students' attitudes, behavior, or feelings of alienation from school. Moreover, the relationships among racial attitudes, behavior, and alienation from school are not clear.

METHODS

Participants

Data used in this study were collected by the Program of Research and Evaluation for Public Schools (PREPS), Mississippi State University; and were from the PREPS At-risk Research Project. Data were collected in the Spring of 1991, and included 1,636 randomly selected students from 19 schools in Mississippi. Schools were not selected randomly; however, the resulting sample included students from small rural schools, intermediate size schools, and large semi-urban schools. Schools ranged from 25 students per grade to 245 students per grade and represented diverse geographical and sociocultural areas of Mississippi.

The schools included in this study have varied racial composition, ranging from 82% white to 1% white. Roughly 48% of the sample was white and 51% was African American. The sample had only 14 participants who are of a race other than African American or white, and all but two of these subjects are Native Americans. In each school district represented, approximately 50% of students were of economic status that allowed them to be eligible for the free school lunch program.

Design

A cross-sectional design was employed to study the developmental properties of alienation from school. Cross-sectional studies are descriptive in nature and afford the advantage of studying developmental phenomena by taking measurements at one single point in time. Cross-sectional studies, however, assume that groups of subjects differ only in age or grade level, and that chance differences between groups do not exist. Therefore, results may be biased (McMillan & Schumacher, 1989).

A longitudinal panel design, which involves taking measurements of a single group of participants at two or more points in time (Borg & Gall, 1989), may have been more appropriate for studying this developmental phenomenon. A disadvantage of longitudinal studies, however, is that it is difficult to keep track of subjects, and data are generally lost to some degree as those studies progress (McMillan & Schumacher, 1989).

Instruments

The criterion variable in this study was the School Affiliation scale of the Self Observational Scales (SOS) (Stenner & Katzenmeyer, 1979). The inverse of scores on this scale quantified levels of alienation from school. The SOS are a nationally normed measure of seven dimensions of the self-concept, and are in self-report, forced-choice format. The seven scales of the SOS were largely developed through exploratory and confirmatory factor analyses (Stenner & Katzenmeyer, 1979). Several authors (Ellis, Gehman, & Katzenmeyer, 1980; Stenner & Katzenmeyer, 1979; Stevens, 1975) found the School Affiliation scale highly invariant across gender/ethnic groups, socioeconomic status groups, and grade levels. The scale appears to exhibit constancy across the range of scores, but it may have an inadequate ceiling. Test-retest reliability coefficients, using a one-week interval, were .85 for the Intermediate Level (Grades 4, 5, and 6) and .83 for the Junior High Level (Grades 7 and 8) (Stenner & Katzenmeyer, 1979).

In presenting a model of school dropout, Finn (1989) characterized identification with school as having two fundamental elements, *belonging* and *valuing*. Belonging is the student's feeling, through psychological identification with the school, that he/she is part of the school environment. Valuing is the student's perceived relevance of school-related goals or norms.

Examples of School Affiliation scale items that assess the valuing component of school identification/alienation proposed by Finn (1989) are concerned with: (a) pride in school work, (b) a desire to change the nature of school, (c) desire to be a good student, (d) perceived relevance of school, (e) comparative value of school as compared to friends, and (f) perceived fairness of school. Items that assess the belonging aspect of school identifica-

tion/alienation are related to: (a) perceived caring of school personnel, (b) desire to stay home from school, (c) affinity to school, (d) pride in school, and (e) feelings at or about school (see Stenner & Katzenmeyer, 1979). Several items assess the degree that students *like* school. Use of this terminology may be necessitated by the relative young age of respondents. Instruments used to measure alienation from school have used similar terminology (e.g., Besag, 1966; Elliot & Voss, 1974).

Scores from the Stanford Achievement Tests (SAT) (Psychological Corporation, 1989) were used to represent achievement in this study. The Total Reading score, composed of Reading Vocabulary and Reading Comprehension subtests; and the Total Mathematics score, composed of Concepts of Number, Mathematics Computation, and Mathematics Applications subtests (Psychological Corporation, 1989) were employed as possible predictor variables. Predictor variables other than achievement were assessed by means of questionnaires completed by counselors and teachers of the student participants.

Analysis

Multiple regression procedures were employed to determine the best possible set of predictors of School Affiliation, the criterion variable. A separate analysis was performed at each grade level (Grade 4 through Grade 8). Possible predictor variables were: (a) gender, (b) race, (c) a gender/race joint term, (d) socioeconomic status, (e) educational level of the head of the household, (f) reading achievement, (g) mathematics achievement, (h) grade failure, (i) particular school attended, and (j) racial similarity of the student to her/his school's racial composition.

All predictor variables other than the school variable were selected through stepwise multiple regression procedures. After significant predictors were selected, the school variable was forced into the multiple regression equations. Race and school variables were dummy coded for analysis. In order to assess the predictability of the school variable as a whole, the school dummy vectors were forced into the multiple regression equation after stepwise selection had ended. Entering the school variable last helped ensure that racial and other differences among schools were controlled.

For validation purposes, a sample comprising roughly 40% of the subjects in each grade level was randomly selected for a hold-out sample. The remaining 60% of subjects' data were used to generate the multiple regression solutions. According to Kelly, Beggs and McNeil (1969), if the multiple R obtained from the hold-out sample is substantially smaller than the multiple R obtained from the primary sample, there is some unreliability or shrinkage in the data. Some authors suggest an even split of the sample for validation (e.g., Draper & Smith, 1981); however, 60% of the subjects were used for the primary sample in this study so that power in the original analyses would not be sacrificed.

In addition to multiple regression procedures, a one-way analysis of variance was used to determine any significant differences between scores on the School Affiliation scale of the SOS as a function of grade level. A priori contrasts were used to determine significant differences between adjacent grade levels. According to Howell (1987), a subset of all possible a priori comparisons, as opposed to post hoc comparisons, helps to keep Type I error rates at a minimum. The developmental properties of alienation from school were also examined through exploration of the predictive ability of variables and multiple regression solutions in the cross-section of grade levels.

RESULTS

Multiple Regressions by Grade Level

The discrepancies between the Multiple Rs of the primary sample and the hold-out sample were moderate in each grade-level analysis. Therefore, all multiple regression solutions appeared adequately reliable. The variables selected from the primary sample in these solutions were then entered directly—in the same order—using the entire sample from each grade level. Results from each entire-sample analysis are reported in Table 1.

Through examination of regression residual plots, support for assumptions of linear relationships, normality, homoscedasticity, and independence of residuals was generally found. A positive relationship between School Affiliation scale scores and standardized residuals, however, was evident to some degree in each analysis, indicating weak relationships between predictors and the criterion variable and pointing toward specification error. Multicollinearity diagnostics revealed no multicollinearity problems.

Alienation from School by Grade Level

One-way analysis of variance revealed that at least two grade levels differed significantly in School Affiliation scores. $F(4, 1631) = 11.28$, $p < .00005$. Results of contrasts are presented in Table 2. The contrasts revealed that School Affiliation scores dropped significantly from Grade 4 to Grade 5 and from Grade 5 to Grade 6. Scores appeared to stabilize at Grade 6.

DISCUSSION

In viewing the grade level analyses as a whole, gender had a consistent relationship with School Affiliation scale scores. This finding is consistent with literature on school dropout and alienation from school cited earlier in this paper. Males consistently exhibited lower School Affiliation scores and therefore appeared to be more alienated from school than females. The exclusion of gender in the Grade 4 analysis may have been a function of random selection of the primary and hold-out samples. That is, the zero-order correlation of gender and School Affiliation scores was considerably higher in the entire Grade 4 sample than in the Grade 4 primary (solution generating) sample. This points toward some degree of unreliability in the data.

TABLE 1.   Results of Multiple Regression Used to Predict School Affiliation Scores

Variable	Step	R	R2	F	p
		Grade 4			
Race	1	.222	.050	10.17	.000
Grade Failure	2	.246	.061	8.42	.000
Schools	3	.370	.137	3.75	.000
		Grade 5			
SES	1	.205	.042	16.88	.000
Gender	2	.283	.080	16.71	.000
Schools	3	.306	.094	2.56	.001
		Grade 6			
Gender	1	.267	.071	21.87	.000
Race	2	.316	.100	10.43	.000
RSM	3	.357	.127	10.29	.000
Schools	4	.483	.233	5.90	.000
		Grade 7			
Schools	1	.230	.053	2.07	.047
		Grade 8			
Gender	1	.255	.065	20.47	.000
Math	2	.295	.087	14.01	.000
Grade Failure	3	.318	.101	10.97	.000
Schools	4	.367	.135	4.46	.000

TABLE 2.   Differences in School Affiliation Scores as a Function of Grade Level

Contrast	t	p
Grade 4 vs. Grade 5	2.46	.014
Grade 5 vs. Grade 6	3.18	.001
Grade 6 vs. Grade 7	−0.65	.515
Grade 7 vs. Grade 8	0.26	.794

Note. Positive *t* values represent a decrease in School Affiliation scores, whereas negative *t* values represent an increase in School Affiliation scores.

The race variable yielded some unexpected results. White students had higher levels of alienation from school than African-American students. This finding is contrary to some of the dropout literature as well as literature on alienation (cf., Calabrese, 1988; Frase, 1989). This finding, however, is consistent with others, especially those by Howell and Frese (1982) and Tidwell (1988).

The association of race with alienation from school became steadily weaker in the seventh and eighth grades. Calabrese (1987) proposed that differences between African-American students' culture and the school's culture contribute to adolescent alienation. It may be that African-American students are not sensitive to the disparity between their culture and traditional school culture until adolescence, and results from these analyses may only reveal the beginning of a growing alienation by African-American students. In the Grade 7 and Grade 8 analyses, zero-order correlations between race and School Affiliation scores were small. Another possible explanation of this relationship is that these analyses revealed a group of schools and school districts that are sensitive and responsive to African-American students.

Results from this study did not support the existence of differences in levels of alienation from school for gender/race groups. The gender/race joint term did not enter into any of the grade level analyses. Gender and race were both associated with alienation from school, but their joint association with the criterion variable was weak.

Socioeconomic status entered only into the Grade 5 analysis. This relationship was also in the unexpected direction and is inconsistent with many previous findings on school dropout and opinions on alienation from school. In this study, lower socioeconomic status was consistently related to lower levels of alienation in the grade levels. Socioeconomic status and race were fairly closely related in the schools studied, and the relationships of both socioeconomic status and race to alienation from school were similar. One variable could have easily served as proxy for the other. Reasons for the presence of this unexpected relationship may be similar to reasons cited above regarding the unexpected race/alienation relationship. That is, students may not perceive socioeconomic or sociocultural incongruence between themselves and the school in the elementary school years. This counterintuitive relationship between socioeconomic status and alienation from school became weaker in higher grade levels. Also, it is possible that this group of schools may respond well to students of lower socioeconomic status. Higher socioeconomic students, at least in the earlier grades, may feel that the democratic, equalizing nature of schools is inconsistent with their culture. Additionally, there may be more pressure for academic achievement placed upon higher socioeconomic status students, and this pressure may translate into alienation from school. Findings from this study, however, did not either support or disconfirm either of these possibilities.

The relative educational levels of parents in this study were weakly associated with alienation from school. Zero-order correlations for these two variables were consistently weak even though parents' educational levels were moderately related to race and socioeconomic status. This finding is somewhat contrary to findings on school dropout (cf., Barrington &

Hendricks, 1989; Lloyd, 1976, 1978; Rumberger et al., 1990).

Reading and mathematics achievement were, surprisingly, not strongly related to alienation from school. A relationship between achievement and alienation was not found until the eighth grade. This relationship in the eighth grade was in the expected direction; that is, higher achievement was associated with lower levels of alienation from school. The reason that achievement did not appear as a predictor until the eighth grade may be that increased pressure for achievement generally comes in the higher grades.

The grade failure variable yielded results contrary to a parallelism of school dropout and alienation from school. If school dropout is the result of a steadily growing alienation from school, then it would be expected that these failures would be related to students' levels of alienation. Grade failure entered the regression equation in the expected direction in the Grade 4 sample and in the unexpected direction in the Grade 8 sample. It entered the Grade 8 analysis only when gender and mathematics variables were already in the equation. This finding is contrary to those findings by Cairns et al. (1989), Lloyd (1976, 1978), Stroup and Robins (1972), and Walters and Kranzler (1970).

Schools consistently contributed to the predictive ability in each grade level analysis. It should be noted that the school variable may have capitalized on chance variation. Some of the samples from particular schools were small. However, scores on the School Affiliation scale were examined in these small samples and no outliers were found. Much of the variability in the criterion variable was due to small schools. Smaller schools that represent homogeneous community areas generally produced higher School Affiliation scores and therefore lower levels of alienation from school.

The racial similarity variable entered into the Grade 6 analysis only. Higher levels of similarity were associated with higher School Affiliation scores. An additional multiple regression analysis was performed to further examine this variable. In Grade 6 data, examination of zero-order correlations between School Affiliation scores and particular schools revealed two schools with high correlations. These two schools are highly homogeneous with regard to racial composition. In order to determine if the variance in School Affiliation scores accounted for by racial similarity was independent of the variance accounted for by schools, an analysis was performed using these two variables. When differences in the criterion variable accounted for by schools were controlled, the racial similarity variable accounted for 2% of the variability in the criterion. In the stepwise multiple regression, racial similarity accounted for 3% of the variability in the criterion. Also, inspection of the zero-order correlations between racial similarity and scores on the School Affiliation scale revealed generally weak relationships between the two variables. These findings suggest that racial similarity may not be an effective predictor of alienation from school. It is noteworthy, however, that racial similarity appears to predict alienation from school at a point in students' development when alienation from school seems to become most intense, Grade 6.

Gender and school variables were the best predictors of alienation from school. None of the grade level multiple regression analyses accounted for over 24% of the variance in School Affiliation scores. Examination of the relationship of standardized residuals to School Affiliation scores pointed toward the exclusion of relevant predictors. It may be that more effective predictors would be school grade point average (Barrington & Hendricks, 1989), aggressiveness (Cairns et al., 1989), or parenting style (Rumberger et al., 1990).

Several authors (Finn, 1989; Newmann, 1981; Wehlage & Rutter, 1986; Wehlage et al., 1989) theorize that alienation from school is a developmental process that results in school dropout. These analyses do not wholly support this theory. However, there are some qualifications regarding this lack of support. Alienation from school involves the perceptions of stu-

dents, and these perceptions may not be reflective of reality. Students may not manifest the negative effects of low achievement, failure, or incongruence of their culture and the school's culture until their early high school years. Alienation from school may be a phenomenon that results from experiences in the elementary and middle school years, but these experiences may not come to bear on students' feelings of belonging with school or valuing of school until adolescence. Behavior of the achievement variables and the race variable support this notion.

IMPLICATIONS AND CONCLUSIONS

Variables that have repeatedly been shown to be related to school dropout (e.g., grade failure, socioeconomic status) may or may not be related to students' perceived alienation from school in early grades. Elementary students may not perceive that failure, low achievement, or lack of social and economic resources alienate them from the school. School personnel should capitalize on the positive attitudes that potentially marginal students have toward school in the late elementary school grades. Schools could inoculate students for alienation that may come later in their education.

It seems that schools themselves have an impact on levels of alienation in their students. It is therefore implied that programs and practices designed to reduce alienation from school could have a significant positive effect on students' levels of alienation.

Male students appear to be consistently more alienated than female students. Counselors, teachers, and administrators should formulate and implement programs and practices that positively impact male students' feelings of belonging and valuing with regard to the school. Traditional male stereotypes may possibly reinforce alienation from school. For example, significant others may value social identification with the school more for females and less for males.

Beginning in the eighth grade, reading and mathematics achievement appear to be related to alienation from school. Lower achievers at this grade level could benefit from efforts aimed at improving their relationship with the school. Also, differences in levels of alienation from school among races tend to grow smaller in the seventh and eighth grades, and alienation of African-American students may be beginning to become more serious.

Levels of alienation from school appear to increase significantly in the sixth grade. Programs that address the psychosocial developmental aspects of students may help to alleviate this alienation. These programs could help students avoid more severe alienation in adolescence.

This study was cross sectional and exploratory in nature and sought to identify variables associated with alienation from school in elementary and middle school students. Longitudinal panel studies which assess alienation in students and also follow students until they either complete school or drop out of school would be more useful in answering pertinent questions. Such an effort could enhance educators' understanding of the developmental aspects of alienation from school and the alienation/dropout paradigm.

Variables found in this study that predicted alienation from school need further examination. Specifically, characteristics and features of schools that influence student alienation are worthy of further study. Also, studies which examine factors associated with extreme levels of alienation from school could be useful. Much of the variability in these analyses was not accounted for by the predictors used. Subsequent studies should seek to find those omitted variables. Students' behavior at school, grade point averages, participation in school activities and organizations, and/or degree of underachievement or overachievement are possibilities. This study may have suffered from its lack of observable behavioral variables.

Further studies of alienation from school would be more effective if samples from more diverse populations were used. The findings from this study are limited in generalizability by the nonrandom selection of schools and by the fact that data from only one state were employed.

This study, however, may serve as the beginning of an empirically supported theoretical basis of alienation from school. From this theoretical basis researchers could conduct causal analyses which could provide insight into alienation and school dropout. This knowledge, in turn, may lead to effective strategies to reduce alienation from school and school dropout.

REFERENCES

Baker, J., & Sansone, J. (1990). Interventions with students at risk for dropping out of school: A high school responds. *Journal of Educational Research, 83,* 181-186.

Baker, R. A. (1991). Modeling the school dropout problem: School policies and prevention program strategies. *The High School Journal, 74,* 203-210.

Barrington, B. L., & Hendricks, B. H. (1989). Differentiating characteristics of high school graduates, dropouts, and nongraduates. *Journal of Educational Research, 82,* 309-319.

Besag, F. P. (1966). *Alienation and education.* Buffalo, NY: Hertillon Press.

Bryk, A. S., & Thum, Y. M. (1989). The effects of high school organization on dropping out: An exploratory investigation. *American Educational Research Journal, 26,* 353-383.

Borg, W. R., & Gall, M. D. (1989). *Educational research: An introduction* (5th ed.). New York: Longman.

Cairns, R. B., Cairns, B. D., & Neckerman, H. J. (1989). Early school dropout: Configurations and determinants. *Child Development, 60,* 1437-1452.

Calabrese, R. L. (1987). Adolescence: A growth period conducive to alienation. *Adolescence, 22,* 929-938.

Calabrese, R. L. (1988). Schooling, alienation, and minority dropouts. *The Clearing House, 61,* 325-328.

Calabrese, R. L., & Schumer, H. (1986). The effects of service activities on adolescent alienation. *Adolescence, 21,* 657-687.

Caliste, E. R. (1984). The effect of a twelve-week dropout intervention program. *Adolescence, 19,* 657-659.

Catterall, J. S. (1985). *On the social costs of dropping out of school.* (Report No. SEPI-86-3). Stanford Univ., CA: Stanford Education Policy Institute. (ERIC Document Reproduction Service No. ED 271 837).

Draper, N. R., & Smith, H. (1981). *Applied regression analysis* (2nd ed.). New York: John Wiley & Sons.

Elliot, D. S., & Voss, H. L. (1974). *Delinquency and dropout.* Lexington, MA: D. C. Heath.

Ellis, D. W., Gehman, W. S., & Katzenmeyer, W. G. (1980). The boundary organization of self-concept across the 13 through 18 year age span. *Educational and Psychological Measurement, 40,* 9-17.

Ekstrom, R. B., Goertz, M. E., Pollack, J. M., & Rock, D. A. (1986). Who drops out of school and why? Findings from a national study. *Teachers College Record, 87,* 356-372.

Evans, I. M., & DiBenedetto (1990). Pathways to school dropout: A conceptual model for early prevention. *Special Services in the Schools, 6,* 63-80.

Fetro, J. V. (1987). *Adolescent alienation: Verifying a web of causation through path analysis.* Dissertation Abstracts International, 49, 461A.

Fetro, J. V., & Vitello, E. M. (1988). Measuring feelings of alienation in adolescents. *Health Education, 19,* 36-41.

Finn, J. K. (1989). Withdrawing from school. *Review of Educational Research, 59,* 117-142.

Firestone, W. A., Rosenblum, S., & Webb, A. (1987). *Building commitment among students and teachers: An exploratory study of ten urban high schools.* Philadelphia, PA: Research for Better Schools. (ERIC Document Reproduction Service No. ED 303 535).

Fontes, C. O. (1988). *A qualitative study of middle school students' perceptions regarding school alienation: Causes and remedies for improved motivation.* Dissertation Abstracts International, 49, 418A.

Frase, J. D. (1989). *Dropout rates in the United States: 1988. Analysis report.* (Report No. NCES-89-6090). Washington, DC: National Center for Education Statistics. (ERIC Document Reproduction Service No. 313 947)

Gottlieb, D., & Tenhouten, W. D. (1965). Racial composition and the social systems of three high schools. *Journal of Marriage and the Family, 27,* 204-212.

Guterbock, T. M., & London, B. (1983). Race, political orientation, and participation: An empirical test of four competing theories. *American Sociological Review, 48,* 439-453.

Hartnagel, T. F., & Krahn, H. (1989). High school dropouts, labor market success, and criminal behavior. *Youth and Society, 20,* 416-444.

Hendrix, V. L., Sederberg, C. H., & Miller, V. L. (1990). Correlates of commitment/alienation among high school seniors. *Journal of Research and Development in Education, 23,* 129-135.

Howell, D. C. (1987). *Statistical methods for psychology.* Boston: PWS-KENT Publishing Company.

Howell, F. M., & Frese, W. (1982). Early transition into adult roles: Some antecedents and outcomes. *American Educational Research Journal, 19,* 51-73.

Kanungo, R. N. (1979). The concepts of alienation and involvement revisited. *Psychological Bulletin, 86,* 119-138.

Kelly, F. J., Beggs, D. L., & McNeil, K. A. (1969). *Research design in the behavioral sciences: Multiple regression approach.* London: Feffer & Simons.

Laosa, L. M. (1982). School, occupation, culture, and family: The impact of parental schooling on the parent-child relationship. *Journal of Educational Psychology, 74,* 791-827.

Lloyd, D. N. (1976). Concurrent prediction of dropout and grade of withdrawal. *Educational and Psychological Measurement, 36,* 983-991.

Lloyd, D. N. (1978). Prediction of school failure from third grade data. *Educational and Psychological Measurement, 38,* 1193-1200.

Longshore, D. (1982a). A research note on the problem of racial composition and white hostility: The problem of control in desegregated schools. *Social Forces, 61,* 73-78.

Longshore, D. (1982b). School racial composition and blacks' attitudes toward desegregation: The problem of control in desegregated schools. *Social Science Quarterly, 63,* 674-687.

Mann, D. (1986). Can we help dropouts: Thinking about the undoable. *Teachers College Record, 87,* 307-322.

McCaul, E. J., Donaldson, G. A., Jr., Coladarci, T., & Davis, W. E. (1992). Consequences of dropping out of school: Findings from high school and beyond. *Journal of Educational Research, 85,* 198-207.

McMillan, J. H., & Schumacher, S. (1989). *Research in education: A conceptual introduction* (2nd ed.). Glenview, IL: Scott, Foresman.

Mensch, B. S., & Kandel, D. B. (1988). Dropping out of high school and drug involvement. *Sociology of Education, 61,* 95-113.

Moyer, T. R., & Motta, R. W. (1982). Alienation and school adjustment among black and white adolescents. *The Journal of Psychology, 112,* 21-28.

Natriello, G., Pallas, A. M., & McDill, E. L. (1986). Taking stock: Renewing our research agenda on the causes and consequences of dropping out. *Teachers College Record, 87,* 431-440.

Newmann, F. M. (1981). Reducing student alienation in high schools: Implications of theory. *Harvard Educational Review, 51,* 546-564.

Patchen, M. (1982). *Black-white contact in schools: Its social and academic effects.* West Lafayette, IN: Purdue University Press.

Pittman, R. B. (1986). Importance of personal, social factors as potential means for reducing high school dropout rate. *The High School Journal, 70,* 7-13.

Psychological Corporation. (1989). *Stanford achievement test series: Technical data report (8th ed.).* Harcourt Brace Jovanovich.

Reitzammer, A. F. (1990). Reading success: a cornerstone of dropout prevention. *Reading Improvement, 27,* 287-288.

Rumberger, R. W. (1983). Dropping out of high school: The influence of race, sex, and family background. *American Educational Research Journal, 20,* 199-220.

Rumberger, R. W. (1987). High school dropouts: A review of issues and evidence. *Review of Educational Research, 57,* 101-121.

Rumberger, R. W., Ghatak, R., Poulos, G., Ritter, P. L., & Dornbusch, S. M. (1990). Family influences on dropout behavior in one California high school. *Sociology of Education, 63,* 283-299.

Seldin, C. A. (1989). Reducing adolescent alienation: Strategies for the high school. *National Association of Secondary School Principals Bulletin, 73,* 77-84.

Stenner, A. J., & Katzenmeyer, W. G. (1979). *Technical manual of the Self Observational Scales.* Durham, NC: National Testing Service, Inc.

Stevens, J. S. (1975). *Developmental changes in self-concept over the elementary school years.* Dissertation Abstracts International, 36, 3535A-3536A.

Stevens, R. & Pihl, R. O. (1982). The identification of the student at-risk for failure. *Journal of Clinical Psychology, 38,* 540-545.

Stroup, A. L., & Robins, L. N. (1972). Elementary school predictors of high school dropout among black males. *Sociology of Education, 45,* 212-222.

Tidwell, R. (1988). Dropouts speak out: Qualitative data on early school departures. *Adolescence, 23,* 939-954.

Vacca, R. T., & Padak, N. D. (1990). Who's at risk in reading? *Journal of Reading, 33,* 486-488.

Walters, H. E., & Kranzler, G. D. (1970). Early identification of the school dropout. *The School Counselor, 18,* 97-104.

Weber, J. M. (1988). *An evaluation of selected procedures for identifying potential high school dropouts.* Columbus, OH: Ohio State University, National Center for Research in Vocational Education. (ERIC Document Reproduction Service No. ED 311 348)

Wehlage, G. G., & Rutter, R. A. (1986). Dropping out: How much do schools contribute to the problem? *Teachers College Record, 87,* 374-392.

Wehlage, G. G., Rutter, R. A., Smith, G. A., Lesko, N., & Fernandez, R. R. (1989). *Reducing the risk: Schools as Communities of support.* New York: The Falmer Press.

Weitzman, M., Klerman, L. V., Lamb, G. A., Kane, K., Geromini, K. R., Kayne, R., Rose, L., & Alpert, J. J. (1985). Demographic and educational characteristics of inner city middle school problem absence students. *American Journal of Orthopsychiatry, 55,* 378-383.

Wynne, E. A. (1989). Youth alienation: Implications for administrators. *National Association of Secondary School Principals Bulletin, 73,* 86-90.

Evaluation Criteria

1. Is the general purpose of the study clear? Will the study provide a significant contribution?

The general research problem is stated at the beginning of the second paragraph before the Related Literature section. This statement is clear and helps you understand that there are two major purposes, one to identify predictors of alienation and one to investigate differences in alienation depending on grade level. The specific questions are stated in the next paragraph and are also clearly written and complete. It would also be common for these more specific questions to be found at the end of the review of literature. The introduction makes a very compelling case about the significance of the study. It effectively summarizes other literature that relates alienation to dropping out.

2. Does the review of literature establish the relationship between previous studies and the current one? Is the review well organized and up to date?

For the most part, this extensive review effectively summarizes other studies and shows how they relate to one another, but there is very little criticism of these studies. The findings are accepted without question or any analysis of quality. The review is up to date and well organized by topic rather than by date or article.

3. Is the specific research hypothesis or question clearly and concisely stated?

Specific questions are stated just before the Related Literature section. The first question clearly indicates the focus of the study. The second question could be more clear by indicating that the predictions will be analyzed separately for different grades.

Discussion Questions

1. How could the introduction be shortened and still make a convincing case for the significance of the study?

2. How could the authors be more explicit about the relationship of these studies to their research questions?

3. How could the second question be rewritten to more accurately indicate the purpose of the study and be more consistent with what is presented in the Results section?

4. Is the method of sampling clearly presented? Could the way the sample was obtained influence the results?

There is a large sample used in this study, and the random selection procedure from 19 different schools suggests a sample that would probably not be biased. However, we need to know how many students were selected from each grade. It would also be good to report other descriptive statistics on the sample. The range is a crude index of variability and can be affected by what are called "outliers" to give a biased perspective.

5. Is there anything in the procedures for collecting information, or in the instruments themselves, that could bias the results or weaken the study?

Much more information about the procedures for collecting information is needed. Without this detail we have no way of knowing whether something in what students were told or in the setting in which they answered the questions could have affected their responses. The "test-retest" reliability is reported to be .85, which is very strong (though one week is a short time frame between testing). The reference to "factor analysis" is a way of establishing validity, as is the discussion of how the School Affiliation scale measures values that are consistent with the work of other researchers.

6. Is the magnitude of the correlation or difference between groups large enough to suggest practical significance or importance?

The correlations reported, while "statistically significant," are small, and the failure to find consistency between grades makes it difficult to identify practically important results. Differences between the grade levels appears to show greater practical importance, though means and standard deviations need to be reported in conjunction with Table 2.

4. What additional information would be helpful in describing the sample? Why do the authors suggest that their cross-sectional sample may be biased?

5. How could the Instruments section be written to emphasize that the scores from the instruments, not the instruments themselves, are reliable and valid? What should be included by way of procedures for administration of the instrument?

6. Why would some independent variables contribute to a prediction of alienation in some grades and not others? Specifically, why would there only be one significant predictor for grade 7?

7. Do the conclusions and interpretations follow logically from the results presented? Are unwarranted causal conclusions made from correlational or comparison data? Are limitations indicated?

The Discussion section is extensive and relates the findings to other studies. Explanations are given for most of the contradictory results, but overall it is puzzling why, given the strong expectations from previous research, the results did not provide for greater prediction with more variables. Limitations of the cross-sectional nature of the study are mentioned, and there are good suggestions for future research.

7. What limitations related to the methodology, such as sampling or instrumentation, could have contributed to the results showing that few variables predict alienation?

The Extended School Year: Implications for Student Achievement

Robert Pittman Roy Cox Guy Burchfiel

Western Carolina University

∽

ABSTRACT

Public policy makers have focused some attention upon extending the length of the school year. The current study investigated the following question: How does the number of days of school attended influence the level of student achievement on standardized tests? The achievement scores of students from two different school systems were analyzed. These students had experienced an interrupted school year of approximately 1 month due to severe weather in 1976-77. Yearly comparisons between the achievement scores of 1976-77 and other school years were made within and across groups. The results of the various comparisons suggested that simply increasing the length of the school year would not likely produce marked changes in test score performance.

Several states are considering extending the length of the school year and/or the school day in response to public pressure. The proposals vary from state to state but all share the common theme of addressing noted problems in the current structure of public education. The foremost of these stated deficiencies is a low level of performance on standardized tests. According to proponents of the extended year, one of the benefits derived from its adoption would be increased test scores (Increased Class Time, 1983). The aim of the current study was to investigate the validity of the claim that lengthening the school year would produce corresponding changes in standardized test performance. The specific question considered was, How does the number of days of school attended contribute to the achievement level of students on standardized tests?

The rationale for extending the school year appears to be rooted in a position that emphasizes the amount of time allowed for learning. The most referenced statement that presents the importance of the time dimension in school performance is that of Carroll (1963). In it the level of learning was described as being a function of the time allowed for learning, student perseverance, special aptitudes, general ability to understand instruction, and the quality of instruction. These five factors were further reduced in the model to two temporal dimensions, the amount of time on task and the amount of time needed to learn the task. The validity of this conceptualization of school learning has been supported indirectly through research on mastery learning for which it provides a theoretical base (Bloom, Madaus, & Hastings, 1981).

Some studies have expanded the concept of learning time presented in Carroll's model to the more global concept of available school time for learning. Wiley and Harnischfeger (1974) compared achievement and quantity of class time across a sample of schools. Results indicated that those schools exhibiting the higher mean achievement also had the greater average time spent in class. Similar results were obtained by Richmond (1977), who surveyed administrators of extended school year projects. A majority of the respondents indicated they felt a positive effect on achievement resulted.

In contrast to these findings, other investigations do not support the notion that higher

Pittman, Robert, Cox, Roy, and Burchfiel, Guy. (1992). The extended school year: Implications for student achievement. *Journal of Experimental Education, 54*(4), 211-215. Reprinted with permission of the Helen Dwight Reid Education Foundation. Published by Heldref Publications, 1319 Eighteenth St., N.W., Washington, D.C. 20036-1802. Copyright © 1992.

levels of achievement can be expected from increasing the length of the school year. Efforts by Karweit to replicate Wiley and Harnischfeger's study produced less impressive results (Karweit, 1976, 1985). Similar conclusions were reached by Husen (Wiley & Harnischfeger, 1974) and by Price (Young & Berger, 1983). In each of these referenced works, the finding was that extending the school year did not result in a proportionate increase in academic achievement.

The area in which the extended school year appears to have the most consistent effect is in the retention of skills among special student populations. Bahling (1980) and McMahon (1983) reported the effects of attending a summer session upon skill retention in handicapped students. The common conclusion was that attendance in an extra school session arrested a regression in skills observed in the summer months for such populations. Overall, it seems that increasing the length of the school year might enhance retention of skills more than improve performance on standardized tests. The study reported here sought to determine the changes in achievement that can be expected from extending the school year. Based on the research evidence reviewed, particularly that of Karweit, it was hypothesized that the number of days of school attended, as defined in the study, would not affect the level of student achievement on standardized tests.

METHOD

The method employed to investigate the question was ex post facto using test scores obtained in the 1970s. During the 1976–77 school year, students in several western North Carolina counties missed the month of January and a portion of February due to bad weather. All but 5 of these school days were made up eventually, so that the 1976–77 school year was 175 days for some systems. At the time standardized tests were given in the spring of 1977, pupils had attended 10–20 fewer days of school than usual. Since students' attendance was approximately 20 days less that year than in previous years, it was felt that if the length of

the school year was the most critical factor, then test scores for that year would be lower than in years when more days of school were attended.

In order to investigate this, the results from standardized tests from two school systems in western North Carolina were analyzed. Both systems had employed the appropriate level of the Iowa Test of Basic Skills for the grades tested. System level grade equivalent scores for school years 1972–79 were available from one school system, while grade level percentile distributions for 1972–77 were obtained from the other. These data were obtained from public records, and the manner in which they were reported (i.e., grade level composites) prevented the generation of within-year measures of score variability or other descriptive statistics. They did contain sufficient information for making year to year within-grade comparisons as well as grade to grade comparisons in two instances. The data comparisons were made visually rather than statistically since Cook and Campbell (1979) indicated that approximately 50 observations were recommended for an adequate statistical analysis of a time series. In the current study, five to seven data points were available. The analyses were performed separately for each school system as the method of reporting summary data differed.

A related issue in the design of the study was whether lack of a comparison group would render any results regarding the length of the school year meaningless. A suitable control group would have been a school system that had used the Iowa Test of Basic Skills for the designated school years but that missed no or few days of school during the 1976–77 academic year. The addition of such an extra group in the study would have provided a means to eliminate "history" as a possible explanation for any differences in test scores from 1976–77 to any other school year. There were no school systems in the western part of the state that had few days of school missed during 1976–77. Using student populations from other parts of the state or from other states would have created the problem of the comparability of the groups.

This lack of availability of an adequate control group resulted in the study being restricted to the two previously identified school systems. This was not seen as an obstacle that would compromise the results. The study compared different groups from year to year; therefore, each separate class served as a partial control for all others tested at that grade level. Likewise, by restricting the analysis to grade level comparisons within a school system, each grade level and school system served as a control over "history" for the other grade levels and school system. The only event of "history" that could not be controlled was of such magnitude that it affected both school systems, and it occurred only during the 1976-77 school year. It was felt that any event of such significance was associated with the bad weather and hence simply magnified the effect of missing the days of school rather than being an unknown confound to the results.

RESULTS AND DISCUSSION

The data from the school system reporting grade equivalent scores will be presented first. These are displayed in Table 1. The numbers in the body of the table represent a composite score for all students in the school system at the given grade levels for the respective years. The presence of a year effect can be determined from such data by making year to year within-grade comparisons. Applying this approach to the data in Table 1 indicates that at practically each grade level there were year to year variations with few instances in which the scores remained the same. The score changes involving the 1976-77 school year were no greater than other year to year changes and reflected no uniform trend from one grade level to the next.

In order to reduce the "noise" attributed to yearly variations, the grade equivalent scores were examined in another format. This was accomplished by summarizing the pre- and post-1976-77 data using median grade equivalents. This approach simulated pre-treatment assessment, intervention, and post-treatment follow-up (where length of the school year represented treatment). The results are presented in Table 2. As in the first analysis, there was no uniform pre- to post-pattern at the different grade levels. Only at grade 7 was the trend consistent with what would have been anticipated from a school year effect. At grades 4, 5, and 8, the assumed school year effect was another data point in an overall upward or downward trend in the scores.

TABLE 1. System Level Grade Equivalent Scores by Year and Grade Level

Grade Level	School Year						
	72–73	73–74	74–75	75–76	76–77	77–78	78–79
4	4.6	—	4.7	4.5 (311)[a]	4.5 (298)	4.4 (277)	4.5 (316)
5	5.7	5.4	5.2	5.3 (300)	5.4 (313)	5.7 (307)	5.6 (282)
6	6.6	—	6.4	6.0 (331)	6.0 (296)	—	—
7	7.5	7.4	7.1	7.2 (354)	7.0 (329)	7.2 (309)	7.3 (335)
8	8.5	—	8.0	8.1 (325)	8.1 (356)	7.9 (350)	8.2 (317)

Note: Students had attended school 136 days in the 1975–76 school year at the time standardized tests were given, 120 days in 1976–77, 127 days in 1977–78, and 132 days in 1978–79. For school years 1972–75, the number of days varied from 130 to 139 at schools within the system because there was no uniform testing schedule.
[a]The number in parentheses represents the number of students on whom the composite score was based.

TABLE 2. Pre- and Post-1976-77 School Year Data by Grade Level Using Median Grade Equivalents

Grade Level	School Year		
	Pre-76	76-77	Post-76
4	4.6 (3)[a]	4.5	4.45 (2)
5	5.35 (4)	5.4	5.65 (2)
6	6.4 (3)	6.0	—
7	7.25 (4)	7.0	7.25 (2)
8	8.1 (3)	8.1	7.95 (2)

[a]Numbers in parentheses indicate the number of yearly data elements upon which the presented median was based.

The proponents of the longer school year could argue, justifiably, that a loss of 15 days should have produced about .1 change in a system level grade equivalent score. Such a small change could be expected to get "lost in the wash" and not show up in year to year comparisons. The data from the second school system provided a means for addressing this issue. These scores were in the form of grade level percentile distributions. As such, any changes in achievement caused by the loss of school days would be detected more easily than with system level grade equivalents. A school year effect would result in larger percentages of students scoring within the lower percentile ranges.

The percentages of students, at specified grade levels, scoring within given percentile ranges are presented in Table 3. Data from grades 4-6 were used because there was incomplete information at the other grade levels. The score distributions at each grade level showed yearly variations. Those associated with the 1976-77 school year were no greater than expected based on the scores from the other years, and only at grade 6 was the direction of the change suggestive of a school year effect when compared with the previous year.

In recognition of the fact that the analyses presented so far have involved comparing different groups, and, as such, group differences could be misinterpreted as year effects, the data from two student cohorts were examined. Student Cohort A was in grade 6 during the shortened school year and Cohort B in grade 5. By looking at the available data for these two groups only, it was possible to investigate a length of school year effect without comparing different sets of students. These data are presented in Table 4. The logic of the comparisons in this case was the same as that used with the data in Table 3. If attending school 10-12 days less in 1976-77 had an impact on test scores, then there would be a reduction in the percentages of the two cohorts at the upper percentile ranges. There was no uniform trend present with Cohort A; with Cohort B, the trend was in the opposite direction from what would have been hypothesized from a length of school year effect.

The limitation associated with this last analysis was that the basis for determining the percentile ranges changed for these student groups. The norms at the three grade levels were established using different samples. This shortcoming was not felt to limit the results in any way since the percentile norms on the ITBS from one grade level to the next can be assumed to be based on similar student populations. Therefore, the standards against which the percentile scores were determined were roughly comparable. Further evidence that the problem was a minor one, if it existed at all, was supplied by the congruence of these findings with those associated with Table 3. In the data in Table 3, there were no across norm group comparisons.

In summarizing the analyses presented, there were no uniform trends from year to year within grade levels or within groups. This would lead one to accept the hypothesis that increasing the length of the school year would have no influence on standardized test scores. However, given the ex post facto nature of this study, other explanations to this conclusion must be considered. Three alternatives for why

TABLE 3. Percentage of Student Population by Grade Level and Year Scoring within Given Percentile Ranges

School Year	N	Percentile Ranges				
		1–10	11–25	26–50	51–75	76–99
Grade 4						
72–73	716	8.4	10.5	22.9	30.2	27.9
73–74	737	8.9	11.8	24.7	28.8	25.6
74–75	751	8.8	11.9	24.8	28.9	25.4
75–76	614	9.3	11.9	24.8	29.8	24.2
76–77	725	6.8	9.3	24.8	28.2	30.8
Grade 5						
72–73	763	7.4	11.0	24.3	27.2	29.9
73–74	691	8.1	10.4	22.5	29.5	29.5
74–75	746	6.6	11.8	26.8	28.2	26.5
75–76	745	6.5	11.4	25.9	28.4	27.8
76–77	638	6.5	10.0	26.4	31.3	25.7
Grade 6						
72–73	749	8.3	10.6	25.4	28.1	27.8
73–74	766	10.7	11.1	26.4	27.5	24.3
74–75	682	8.8	15.2	22.3	26.8	26.9
75–76	750	7.4	10.1	28.4	29.4	24.7
76–77	746	8.0	11.5	27.6	29.1	23.8

Note: Students had attended school 155 days in the 1972-73 school year at the time standardized tests were given, 158 days in 1973-74, 153 days in 1974-75, 155 days in 1975-76, and 143 days in 1976-77.

TABLE 4. Percentage of Students Scoring within Given Percentile Ranges by School Year for Two Cohorts

School Year	Grade Level	Days in School[a]	Percentile Range				
			1–10	11–25	26–50	51–75	76–99
Cohort A							
74–75	4	153	8.8	11.9	24.8	28.9	25.4
75–76	5	155	6.5	11.4	25.9	28.4	27.8
76–77	6	143	8.0	11.5	27.6	29.1	23.8
Cohort B							
75–76	4	155	9.3	11.9	24.8	29.8	24.2
76–77	5	143	6.5	10.0	26.4	31.3	25.7

[a]Number of school days at the time standardized tests were given.

the longer time school was attended produced no differences seemed most probable. These were attendance patterns, independent work on studies outside school, and increased levels of student motivation.

The current study simulated a reduced school year using school time lost during the month of January for a single school year. It is possible that in a regular year, absences from school during January are normally much higher. This may be to such an extent that school being closed for that period of time would not radically alter the overall total days attended. This possibility was investigated by looking at the attendance rates for the 1983-84 school year for one of the school systems used in the study. For that year no days were missed during January due to inclement weather. If attendance during that school month was radically lower than the other months, then a differential attendance rate would be a likely explanation for why there were no well-defined patterns of test score differences associated with the 1976-77 school year. The observed attendance rate in the month of January for the 1983-84 school year was 93.7%. This compared to an overall average attendance rate (less the month of January) of 95.4%. Therefore, attendance during the month of January was 98% of what would be considered to be average attendance for the other school months. Generalizing this to other school years, it was felt that the slight difference in school attendance patterns for the month of January did not offer a valid alternative for why performance on standardized tests in 1976-77 was not systematically different than in the comparison years.

The other two alternatives were independent work outside school and increased motivation by students. If students had performed a large amount of school work at home while school was not in session, then the missed days and studies would have had a minimal impact on test scores. Likewise, if students were more motivated to study when school resumed, then the greater involvement and intensity in academics could have eliminated the possibility of any expected deficits due to school time missed. These two potential explanations were tested by surveying some of the teachers of one of the school systems used in the study. A brief questionnaire was distributed at each of the elementary schools in the system. It requested those teachers who were teaching in grades 4, 5, or 6 in that school system for the 1976-77 school year to respond. Of the approximately 70 teachers employed in the designated grades for the 1976-77 school year, 25 were still employed in the system and returned the questionnaire.

The responses to two questions on the survey form were most pertinent to this portion of the study. Ninety-one percent of the teachers felt that there was little evidence to indicate that students had done a significant quantity of school work at home. Assuming their recall was reasonably accurate, the lack of a difference in the test scores between 1976-77 and other school years could not be attributed to students doing work outside school. The response pattern was almost opposite on the question regarding student motivation. Seventy-six percent of the teachers indicated that a higher level of motivation existed after school resumed than was normally present. This suggested that greater student interest may have been at least a partial explanation for why test scores were not different in the target year. There could have been just as much active learning time for students in the shortened year as during a year in which time was not lost.

Based on the similarity in the results across the different types of analyses, the hypothesis that test scores would not be affected by length of the school year was accepted. This should not be construed as saying that the amount of learning time is unimportant, but that a simple extension of the school year may not increase learning time. The data that have been presented were not perfect for answering the question at hand, but they provided a good proxy. It can be argued that the impact of the loss of school days in 1976-77 should have been greater than just a simple reduction of the school year for an equivalent period. The manner in which the days were lost represented the disruption of 1½ months of school. The loss of days plus the added effect of the disruptive manner in which it occurred should have produced a larger difference than just missing school days.

The most viable reason for the minimized effect of these lost school days seems to be that when the school year did stabilize, there was a more concentrated effort to maximize the benefits of the school time available on the part of the students. Such an emphasis would have increased the proportion of learning time per unit of school time. At the time standardized tests were given in 1976-77, there was a difference in the number of school days attended when compared with other school years, but there may have been little if any difference in the actual amount of learning time. Individuals anticipating large changes in standardized achievement test scores solely as a result of increasing the length of the school year are likely to be disappointed. Further, if the implementation of a longer school year significantly impacted students' motivation to learn, then test scores could be expected to change accordingly. An alternative to extending the school year might be to concentrate on making more effective use of the currently available school time. This would increase the learning time to school time ratio and could be expected to produce higher student scores. An emphasis on this learning time to school time proportion has the added advantage of not being politically volatile as is extending the school year.

REFERENCES

Bahling, E. (1981, April). *Extended school year program, intermediate unit no. 5, June–August 1980.* Paper presented at the Annual International Convention of the Council for Exceptional Children, New York. (ERIC Document Reproduction Service No. ED 208609)

Bloom, B., Madaus, G., & Hastings, T. (1981). *Evaluation to improve learning.* New York: McGraw-Hill.

Carroll, J. (1963). A model of school learning. *Teachers College Record, 64,* 723–733.

Cook, T. D., & Campbell, D. T. (1979). *Quasi-experimentation: Design and analysis issues for field settings.* Chicago: Rand-McNally.

Increased class time gaining favor (1983, August 9). *The New York Times,* pp. 17, 20.

Karweit, N. (1976). A reanalysis of the effect of quantity of schooling on achievement. *Sociology of Education, 49,* 236–246.

Karweit, N. (1985). Should we lengthen the school term? *Educational Researcher, 14*(6), 9–15.

McMahon, J. (1983). Extended school year operations. *Exceptional Children, 49,* 457–460.

Richmond, M. (1977). Effects of extended school year operations. *Education, 97,* 392–398.

Wiley, D., & Harnischfeger, A. (1974). Explosion of a myth: Quantity of schooling and exposure to instruction, major educational vehicles. *Educational Researcher, 3*(4), 7–11.

Young, R., & Berger, D. (1983). Evaluation of a year-round junior high school operation. *NASSP Bulletin, 67,* 53–59.

Evaluation Criteria

1. Is the general purpose of the study clear? Will the study provide a significant contribution?

The research question for this study was repeated three times—once in the abstract and twice more in the first paragraph. All of these statements are clear and give you a general idea of the study. The specific question could have been more detailed, including grade level and subject areas tested. There are three independent variables in this study: school year, with either five, seven, or three levels; grade level, with either three or five levels; and cohort, with two levels. The dependent variable was standardized test scores. The responses of the teachers to the survey would not be considered a dependent variable. A case is made for significance, but it is not too compelling given the weak review of literature.

2. Does the review of literature establish the relationship between previous studies and the current one? Is the review well organized and up to date?

A review of previous studies on the same problem begins in the fourth paragraph. The review is very brief. The studies cited are only summarized, not analyzed or critiqued. While there is some support for the research hypothesis, there are conflicting predictions from previous studies.

3. Is the specific research hypothesis or question clearly and concisely stated?

The specific question is the last sentence of the first paragraph. It is concise and clear, but does not contain sufficient information about all the variables. Generally, it is more effective to state the specific question after the review of literature. It would have been helpful to analyze the literature to explain why the hypothesis was stated as it was. It is unusual to state a research hypothesis that expects no differences.

Discussion Questions

1. Would it have been helpful if the researchers used other dependent variables, such as grades? What would have been the advantages and disadvantages to this?

2. Why wouldn't the studies cited in the third paragraph be considered directly related to the problem? How could the review be organized differently to more effectively present previous findings?

3. How could the specific research question be rewritten to include more specific information about the sample and variables?

4. Is the method of sampling clearly presented? Could the way the sample was obtained influence the results?

The sample consists of two school systems in western North Carolina. There is no indication how these two were selected. As there is no mention of random selection, one can conclude that the systems were selected by convenience or availability. It is possible, though not likely, that the systems were selected because they showed little change in test scores over the years in question. Selecting more systems or using random selection would make for a much more convincing study.

5. Is there anything in the procedures for collecting information, or in the instruments themselves, that could bias the results or weaken the study?

Because standardized test scores were used, it is reasonable to assume that appropriate procedures were used. One factor that would contribute to changes in standardized test scores would be using a new form or norming group. Measures of what would have been taught would be more sensitive to change than the more broad measure of achievement in the Iowa tests.

6. Has the presumed treatment already occurred? Is the treatment well defined?

The treatment in this study is the number of school days. This has already occurred. The specific number of days missed each year by the selected systems needs to be indicated. Students missed from 10 to 20 days of school. This probably is not enough to affect such a general measure of achievement as a standardized test.

7. Are subjects in different groups similar except for the treatment?

Since systems were used as their own control, it is likely that the groups did not change significantly from one year to the next. That is,

4. What rationale do the authors use to decide not to include any "control" groups in the study? Is this rationale reasonable?

5. What further information about the standardized tests would be helpful in evaluating the study and understanding limitations of the results?

6. How "strong" do you think the treatment is for these students? Would the systems be likely to modify their curriculum following the missed school to make up for lost time?

7. What information could have been provided to make a better case for the constant composition of the students from year to year?

the composition of the student body would stay about the same each year. However, there are also group differences from one year to another, and if they selected a system close to Charlotte, there could be significant changes from a rural to a more suburban composition.

8. Do the conclusions and interpretations follow logically from the results presented? Are causal conclusions made with caution? Are limitations indicated?

The conclusions and interpretations are reasonable and are based on the results. Causal conclusions are made with caution, and there is good discussion of limitations. However, overall, studying two systems in one part of a state with standardized test scores is fairly limited in generalizability. Additional explanations for the results might include whether teachers increased time devoted to academics when students returned to "catch up," and whether there were any other internal events peculiar to the schools that could explain the lack of finding differences in achievement. It may well be the case that the measures used were simply not sensitive to the difference caused by missing so much school.

8. How could the authors integrate the review of literature into the discussion? What specific limitations exist concerning generalizability of the study to other school systems? Do you agree with the authors that history as a threat is controlled? Why or why not?

Chapter 3

Quantitative Experimental Designs

Experiments are what most people think of as "real science," probably because they create images of laboratories, white coats, and tightly controlled studies. Only part of this image holds for experiments in education. Broadly speaking, an experiment is used to investigate cause and effect relationships by determining whether a manipulated independent variable influences the dependent variable. The manipulated independent variable is controlled by the researcher who deliberately arranges conditions that the subjects will experience. It is these conditions that constitute the independent variable. Thus, the investigator has direct control over what the subjects experience and when they experience it. Usually groups are then compared that have different experiences. For example, a researcher interested in the effect of different types of homework assignments on student achievement may decide to do an experiment by giving some students one type of assignment and other students a different type of assignment and then seeing if the achievement of the two groups of students is different.

A **true experiment** is one in which there is *random assignment* of subjects to different treatments. Random assignment, or randomization, is what distinguishes true experiments from other types of experimental designs. The researcher begins with a group of subjects and then decides which subjects will receive which treatments on the basis of random chance. That is, each subject has the same probability of being in each group. Random assignment means that there is equivalence of the groups in terms of any subject characteristics such as ability, attitudes, and backgrounds.

A **quasi-experimental** study is an experiment in which there is no random assignment of subjects. Other aspects of the design, as well as the research questions, may be the same as found in true experiments. Typically, a quasi-experiment will have a pretest and a posttest. For example, a researcher may want to compare two methods of instruction, and has two intact classrooms that have volunteered to participate. Students were not randomly assigned to the classrooms. The researcher gives the students in each class a pretest, selects one class for each method, and then gives the students a posttest (dependent variable).

There are some other types of experimental designs that do not use random assignment of subjects. These are not always called quasi-experimental, but essentially they constitute investigations that have more potential weaknesses because there is no random assignment and, in some cases, no pretest or comparison group. Sometimes these designs are called **pre-experimental** or **pseudo-experimental** because they are even weaker in internal validity than quasi-experimental designs.

The simplest type of pre-experimental design involves a treatment and measurement of the dependent variable, without any comparison group. This type of study is weak because there is no basis of comparison, with either a pretest or a comparison group. If the researcher can be relatively sure of the status of the subjects prior to implementing the treatment, and if nothing else is likely to affect the subjects (extraneous events), then the study could be valid. If a pretest is added, then at least there is a basis for statistical comparison. Another type of pre-experimental design contains a comparison group but no random assignment or pretest.

Experimental designs can take many forms. Particularly common are designs that try to answer more than one question. For example, such a study might not only ask "Do two new science books produce different scores on a standardized achievement test?" but it might also ask "Does this achievement *also* depend upon the student's ability level?" Such experiments have more than one independent variable, and the design is called a **factorial design.** Factorial designs are useful because not only can they test the effect of the independent variables separately, they can also test whether the independent variables together have a unique effect on the dependent variable. This is called an **interaction,** in which the effect of one independent variable depends upon the value of another. In our example, the study would find an interaction if high-ability students achieved best with one textbook and low-ability students achieved best with the other. A good example of interaction is given in the Brown and Walberg article.

An important consideration in evaluating experimental designs is whether the procedures have been implemented such that accurate cause-and-effect conclusions can be made. Thus, in the procedures section you will want to look for characteristics of the study design that might lead to erroneous interpretations of the data. Researchers use the term **internal validity** to indicate the extent to which the study is free of so-called "extraneous" variables, or other factors that might account for the results. The apparent effectiveness of a new curriculum, for example, might be due primarily to the enthusiasm of the teacher, not to the curriculum itself. If the study is carefully conducted and it is clear that few extraneous variables could affect the results, then the study is strong in internal validity. If the study is conducted with the potential for extraneous variables to influence the results, then it is weak in internal validity. How do you know, then, that a study has established adequate internal validity? Depending on the design of the study, the following "threats" to internal validity should be considered:

Extraneous events (history)—Uncontrolled or unplanned events that occur during the study and affect the values reported for the dependent variable.

Selection—Inherent differences among comparison groups (such as ability, motivation, background) that influence results.

Maturation—Natural changes in subjects because they get older, stronger, tired, etc.

Subject attrition (mortality)—Systematic loss of subjects during the study.

Pretesting—Taking a pretest or responding to a questionnaire may affect the subjects.

Statistical regression—Groups of subjects who score very high or very low on a pretest will, because of measurement error, score closer to the mean on the posttest.

Diffusion of treatment—Changes in subjects because they learn about what is occurring with subjects in another group (the effect of the treatment is "diffused" to others).

Experimenter effects—Results that are affected by what the experimenter says or does, deliberately or unintentionally.

Treatment replications—If the number of times the treatment is implemented is smaller than the number of individuals in the study, factors confounded with the treatment may affect the results.

Treatment fidelity—The way the treatment is implemented is not the same each time.

Subject effects—Changes because someone is a "subject" in a study.

Instrumentation—Unreliability or changes in instruments or observers may affect the results.

By keeping these "threats" in mind, you will be able to make judgments about the internal validity of the study. Essentially you ask yourself whether it is likely that each threat could affect the results.

Criteria for Evaluating Experimental Studies

1. Is the general purpose of the study clear? Will the study provide a significant contribution?

2. Does the review of literature establish the relationship between previous studies and the current one? Is the review well organized and up to date?

3. Is the specific research hypothesis or question clearly and concisely stated?

4. Is the method of sampling clearly presented? Is there random assignment of subjects? If there was no random assignment, is there anything in the way the groups were formed that might influence the reaction of the group to the treatment?

5. What was manipulated as the independent variable or variables?

6. Are the procedures for collecting information described fully?

7. Are there any threats to internal validity that seem plausible?

8. Do the conclusions and interpretations follow logically from the results presented? Are limitations indicated?

9. Is the experiment so contrived and artificial that the findings have little generalizability?

Motivational Effects on Test Scores of Elementary Students

Steven M. Brown
Northeastern Illinois University

Herbert J. Walberg
Univeristy of Illinois at Chicago

ABSTRACT

A total of 406 heterogeneously grouped students in Grades 3, 4, 6, 7, and 8 in three K through 8 Chicago public schools were assigned randomly to two conditions, ordinary standardized-test instructions (control) and special instructions, to do as well as possible for themselves, their parents, and their teachers (experimental). On average, students given special instructions did significantly better (p < .01) than the control students did on the criterion measure, the mathematics section of the commonly used Iowa Test of Basic Skills. The three schools differed significantly in achievement (p < .05), but girls and boys and grade levels did not differ measurably. The motivational effect was constant across grade levels and boys and girls, but differed significantly (p < .05) across schools. The average effect was moderately large, .303 standard deviations, which implies that the special instructions raise the typical student's scores from the 50th to the 62nd percentile.

Parents, educators, business people, politicians, and the general public are greatly concerned about U.S. students' poor performance on international comparisons of achievement. Policy makers are planning additional international, state, district, and school comparisons to measure progress in solving the national crisis. Some members of those same groups have also grown concerned about the effects of students' high or low motivational states on how well they score on tests.

One commonly expressed apprehension is that some students worry unduly about tests and suffer debilitating anxiety (Hill, 1980). Another concern is that too much testing causes students to care little about how well they do, especially on standardized tests that have no bearing on their grades. Either case might lead to poorer scores than students would attain under ideal motivational states; such effects might explain, in part, the poor performance of U.S. students relative to those in other countries or in relation to what may be required for college and vocational success.

Experts and practicing educators have expressed a variety of conflicting opinions about motivational effects on learning and test scores (Association for Supervision and Curriculum Development, 1991, p. 7). Given the importance of testing policies, there is surprisingly little research on the topic. The purpose of the present study is to determine the effect of experimentally manipulated motivational conditions on elementary students' mathematical scores.

As conceived in this study, the term *motivation* refers to the commonsense meaning of the term, that is, students' propensity to engage in full, serious, and sustained effort on academic tests. As it has been measured in many previous studies, motivation refers to students' reported efforts to succeed or to excel on academic tasks. It is often associated with self-concept or self-regard in a successful student or test taker. A quantitative synthesis of the correlational studies of motivation and school learning showed that nearly all correlations were positive and averaged about .30 (Uguroglu & Walberg, 1979).

Brown, Steven M., and Walberg, Herbert J. (1993). Motivational effects on test scores of elementary students. *The Journal of Educational Research, 86,* 133–136. Reprinted with the permission of the Helen Dwight Reid Educational Foundation. Published by Heldref Publications, 1319 Eighteenth St., N.W., Washington, DC 20036-1802. Copyright © 1993.

Previous Research

The National Assessment Governing Board (NAGB, 1990) recently characterized the National Assessment of Educational Progress (NAEP) as follows:

> ...as a survey exam which by law cannot be reported for individual students and schools. NAEP may not be taken seriously enough by students to enlist their best efforts. Because it is given with no incentives for good performance and no opportunity for prior study, NAEP may understate achievement (NAGB, p. 17).

To investigate such questions, NAEP is adding items to ask students how hard they tried in responding to future achievement tests.

Motivation questions can be raised about nearly all standardized commercial tests, as well as state-constructed achievement tests. The content of those tests is often unrelated to specific topics that students have been recently studying; and their performance on such tests ordinarily does not affect their grades, college, or job prospects. Many students know they will not see how well they have done.

Some students admit deficient motivation, but surveys show reasonably favorable attitudes toward tests by most students. Paris, Lawton, and Turner (1991), for example, surveyed 250 students in Grades 4, 7, and 10 about the Michigan Educational Assessment Program. They found that most students reported that they tried hard, thought they did well, felt the test was not difficult or confusing, and saw little or no cheating. However, Karmos and Karmos's (1984) survey of 360 sixth- through ninth-grade student attitudes toward tests showed that 47% thought they were a waste of time, 22% saw no good reason to try to do well, and 21% did not try very hard.

Kellaghan, Madaus, and Arisian (1982) found various small fractions of a sixth-grade Irish sample disaffected by standardized tests, even though they are uncommon in Ireland. When asked about their experience with standardized tests, 29% reported feeling nervous, 19%, unconfident; 16%, bored; and 15% uninterested. Twenty-nine percent reported that they

did not care whether they took the tests, and 16% said they did not enjoy the experience.

Paris, Lawton, and Turner (1991) speculated that standardized tests may lead both bright and dull students to do poorly: Bright students may feel heightened parental, peer, or self-imposed expectations to do well on tests, which makes them anxious. Slower, disadvantaged students may do poorly, then rationalize that school and tests are unimportant and, consequently, expend less effort preparing for and completing tests. Either case might lead to a self-reinforcing spiral of decelerating achievement.

Surveys, however, cannot establish causality. Poor motivation may cause poor achievement, or vice versa, or both may be caused by other factors such as deficiencies in ability, parental support of academic work, or teaching. To show an independent effect of motivation on achievement requires an experiment, that is, a randomized assignment of students to conditions of eliciting different degrees of motivation. Such was the purpose of our study.

METHOD

Sample

The subjects for the study included students from three K through 8 public schools in Chicago. The student populations of the schools are generally lower-middle, working class, mostly Hispanic and African-American. Two normal heterogeneous classes within the schools were sampled from Grades 3, 4, 6, 7, and 8; because of exigencies, we did not sample Grade 5 classes.

Instrument

We chose Form 7 of the Mathematics Concepts subtest of the Iowa Test of Basic Skills (ITBS) 1978 edition, Levels 9–14, because it is a commonly used, highly reliable test. An earlier-than-contemporary edition was used so it would not interfere with current testing programs. In a review of the 1978 ITBS, Nitko (1985) judged that the reliability of its subtests is generally higher than .85 and that it contains content generally representative of school curriculum in Grades 3 through 9. "The ITBS," he concluded, "is an excellent basic skills battery measuring global skills that are likely to be highly related to the long-term goals of elementary schools" (p. 723).

Procedure

Pairs of classes at each grade level from each school were randomly chosen to participate. Classes were selected for experimental and control conditions by a flip of a coin.

The first author (Brown) met with all participating teachers in each school to explain the instructions from the ITBS test manual (see Appendix A). Then, the experimental teachers were retained for the following further instructions:

> We are conducting a research study to determine the effects of telling students that the test they are going to take is very important. It is extremely important that you read the brief script I have for you today EXACTLY as it is written to your students.

The following script was provided:

> It is really important that you do as WELL as you can on this test. The test score you receive will let others see just how well I am doing in teaching you math this year.
> Your scores will be compared to students in other grades here at this school, as well as to those in other schools in Chicago.
> That is why it is extremely important to do the VERY BEST that you can. Do it for YOURSELF, YOUR PARENTS, and ME.
> (Now read the instructions for the test.)

Following the administration of the test, teachers and the first author asked students for their reactions to the script that was read to them.

Analysis

An analysis of variance was run to test the effects of the experimental and normal conditions; the differences among the three schools and five grades; between boys and girls; and the interactions among the factors.

RESULTS

The analysis of variance showed a highly significant effect of experimental condition ($F = 10.59, p < .01$), a significant effect of school ($F = 3.35, p < .05$), and an interaction between condition and school ($F = 5.01, p < .05$). No other effects, including grade level, were significant. The means and standard deviations of selected factors are shown in Table 1.

The mean normal curve equivalent test score of the 214 students in the experimental group was 41.37 ($SD = 15.41$), and the mean of the control group was 36.25 ($SD = 16.89$). The motivational effect is moderately large, .303 standard deviations, which implies that the special instructions raised the typical student's scores from the 50th to the 62nd percentile. The special instructions are comparable to the effects of better (though not the best) instructional practices over conventional classroom instruction (Walberg, 1986). If American students' average achievement in mathematics and science could be raised that much, it would be more comparable to that of students in other economically advanced countries.

The motivational effect was the same for boys and girls and constant across grade levels, but it differed among schools. Figure 1 shows a very large effect at School A, a large effect at

TABLE 1. Normal Curve Equivalent Means and Standard Deviations

Grade	Condition	M	SD
3	Control	32.77	19.57
	Experimental	42.55*	16.59
4	Control	33.07	13.93
	Experimental	39.42*	13.12
6	Control	40.84	17.77
	Experimental	39.64	14.66
7	Control	43.21	16.07
	Experimental	41.21	16.48
8	Control	31.12	14.06
	Experimental	44.66**	15.94

$*p < .01; **p < .001.$

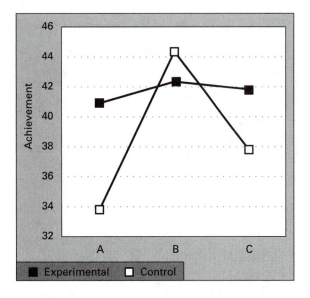

Figure 1. Means by condition and school

School C, and the control group somewhat higher than the experimental group at School B.

Only 62 students (15% of the total sample) were tested at School B, which may account for the lack of effect in this school. At any rate, although the overall effect is moderately large and constant across grade levels and for boys and girls, the size of the effect varies from school to school. Such differences may depend on test-taking attitudes of teachers and students in the schools, motivational and cultural differences in the student populations, variations in conditions of administration, and other factors.

Several comments made by students and teachers during debriefing sessions illuminate the statistical findings. Student Comments 1, 2, and 3 illustrate students' motivation to do well to please their parents and teachers. Teacher Comments 1 and 2 also confirm the reasons for the effect. The last student and teacher comment, however, illustrate motivational states and conditions that diminish or vitiate the effect. When students are unthoughtful or when teachers keep constant pressures on for testing, special instructions may have little effect.

CONCLUSION

The results show that motivation can make a substantial difference in test scores. Students asked to try especially hard did considerably better than those who were given the usual standardized test instructions. The special conditions raised the typical student's score .303 standard deviation units, corresponding to a 12 percentile-point gain from the 50th to the 62nd percentile. Although the effect was the same for boys and girls and for students in different grade levels, it varied in magnitude among the three schools.

The results suggest that standardized commercial and state-constructed tests that have no bearing on students' grades may be underestimating U.S. students' real knowledge, understanding, skills, and other aspects of achievement. To the extent that motivation varies from school to school, moreover, achievement levels of some schools are considerably more underestimated than in others. Such motivational differences would tend to diminish the validity of comparisons of schools and districts.

We would be heartened to conclude that U.S. students' poor performance on achievement relative to students in other countries is attributable to the test-motivation effect. That conclusion is overly optimistic, however, because the effect may also operate to a greater or lesser extent in other countries. Further research is obviously in order.

The motivation effect might be reduced in several ways. Highly motivating instructions could be given to all students. The content of school lessons and standardized tests could be brought into closer correspondence, making the tests more plausible to students, and perhaps justifying their use in grading. Some students, moreover, may be unmotivated because they never see the results. Providing timely, specific, and useful feedback to students, parents, and teachers on how well they have done might lead students to try harder.

APPENDIX A

DIRECTIONS FOR ADMINISTERING THE MATHEMATICS CONCEPTS SUBTEST OF THE IOWA TEST OF BASIC SKILLS (1979)

Now we are ready for the first mathematics test. Open your test booklets to page 73. (Pause) Find the section of your answer sheet for Test M-1: Mathematics Concepts. (Pause) Read the directions on page 73 silently while I read them aloud.

This is a test of how well you understand the number system and the terms and operations used in mathematics. Four answers are given for each exercise, but only one of the answers is right. You are to choose the one answer that you think is better than the others. Then, on the answer sheet, find the row of the answer numbered the same as the exercise. Fill in the answer space for the best answer.

Do not make any marks on the test booklet. Use your scratch paper for figuring. You will have 25 minutes for this test. If you finish early, recheck your work. Don't look at the other tests in the booklet. If you have questions, raise your hand, and I will help you after the others have begun. Now find your place to begin. (Pause)

Does everyone have the correct place? (Pause) Ready, BEGIN.

APPENDIX B

SELECTED ANECDOTAL COMMENTS

Students

1. Third-Grade Girl: My teacher always tells us to get good scores on tests. I wanted to make her happy and my parents happy.
2. Fourth-Grade Boy: I think I did well. My teacher works hard with us. I also want my school to be the best.
3. Eighth-Grade Boy: I wanted to do really well for my teacher. She does a great job, and I didn't want to let her down.

4. Seventh-Grade Girl: I just took the test, and really didn't think much about the instructions she gave.

Teachers

1. I don't know what the results will show but my gut feeling is that students in the experimental groups will do better. I think it's probably because of motivational reasons.
2. The script gives me a feeling of *family*. I think if we told students just how much we want them to do well, and that it will not only benefit themselves but the whole school, they will probably do better.
3. I think all the students (control and experimental) will probably do equally well, because we always stress how important the tests are.

REFERENCES

Association for Supervision and Curriculum Development (1991). *Update, 33*(1), 1–8.

Hill, K. T. (1980). Motivation, evaluation, and testing policy. In L. J. Fyans, Jr. (Ed.), *Achievement motivation: Recent trends in theory and research.* New York, NY: Plenum Press.

Iowa Test of Basic Skills normal curve equivalent norms (1978). Boston, MA: Houghton Mifflin.

Karmos, A. H., & Karmos, J. S. (1984, July). Attitudes toward standardized achievement tests and their relation to achievement test performance. *Measurement and Evaluation in Counseling and Development, 12,* 56–66.

Kelleghan, T., Madaus, G. F., & Arisian, P. M. (1982). *The effects of standardized testing.* Boston, MA: Kluwer-Nijhoff.

National Assessment Governing Board (1991). Issues for the 1994–1996 NAEP. Washington, DC: Author.

Nitco, A. J. (1985). Review of the Iowa Test of Basic Skills. In James V. Mitchell (Ed.), *The ninth mental measurements yearbook.* Lincoln, NE: Buros Institute.

Paris, S. G., Lawton, T. A., & Turner, J. C. (1991). Reforming achievement testing to promote students' learning. In C. Collins & Mangieri (Eds.),

Learning in and out of school. Hillsdale, NJ: Lawrence Erlbaum Associates.

Uguroglu, M. E., & Walberg, H. J. (1979). Motivation and achievement: A quantitative synthesis. *American Educational Research Journal, 16,* 375–390.

Walberg, H. J. (1986). Synthesis of research on teaching. In M. C. Wittrock (Ed.), *Handbook of research on teaching.* New York, NY: Macmillan.

Evaluation Criteria

1. Is the general purpose of the study clear? Will the study provide a significant contribution?

The purpose of the study is stated clearly at the end of the third paragraph. The authors' argument that we do not know nearly enough about how motivational conditions affect student performance on standardized tests is brief but persuasive. It is not immediately clear what the authors mean by "experimentally manipulated motivational conditions," however, particularly since they describe both *too much* concern and *too little* concern about test performance as possible problems of student motivation. We don't learn until later that they are only studying the latter condition here.

2. Does the review of literature establish the relationship between previous studies and the current one? Is the review well organized and up to date?

Under the heading "Previous Research," other literature is cited that underscores the importance of motivation and the attitudes of students toward testing. The authors point out that while some of these studies suggest that poor motivation might exist, none had established "causality," which their study purports to do. The review is fairly well organized by topic, but the studies that are summarized (no analysis) are not related directly to the purpose of the study, that is, whether students' motivation can be experimentally manipulated and whether different levels of motivation affect test scores. The references do appear to be up to date.

Discussion Questions

1. How congruent is the authors' purpose with the way they carried out the study? Now that you have read the study, would you phrase the statement of purpose differently? If so, how?

2. How well does the literature review support the assertion that this study will add significantly to our knowledge about the problem?

3. Is the specific research hypothesis or problem clearly and concisely stated?

Without any specific research questions or research hypotheses, we are not sure exactly how the authors are defining and manipulating "motivation," and we have to wait until we read the script given in the Procedure section before we can infer what the treatment is. We also don't know what all the independent variables are until we reach the Analysis section.

4. Is the method of sampling clearly presented? Is there random assignment of subjects? If there was no random assignment, is there anything in the way the groups were formed that might influence the reaction of the group to the treatment?

The convenience sample was selected by classroom, and assignment to treatment conditions was by classroom, not by student. Thus, while randomization did occur, it was not at the student level, and *treatment replication* becomes a significant problem (see also item 7). The authors do not indicate why they declined to sample from grade 5 classes, other than to cite unexplained "exigencies." Since intact groups were used, it is possible that factors unique to each of the groups could affect the results.

5. What was manipulated as the independent variable or variables?

The manipulated "treatment" variable is the directions given to students to influence motivation, which takes two values. The authors are also looking to see if performance varied according to schools (three), grades (five), and gender, for a total of four independent variables in all.

6. Are the procedures for collecting information described fully?

The instrument in this case is the standardized test, which would have uniform procedures in each class. Reliability was reported to be high.

3. Do you think that specific research hypotheses should have been given? If so, how would you phrase them and where would they go?

4. Could you make an argument that the random assignment of *classes* rather than *students* undermines the strength of this design as a "true experiment"?

5. Why do you suppose the authors chose not to display all of the independent effects and interactions?

6. Would another type of test be more likely to be influenced by motivation than a standardized test?

7. Are there any threats to internal validity that seem plausible?

A number of threats to internal validity exist in this design. *Extraneous events* could have accounted for the differences observed in the treatment effect across the three schools. Another potential threat is *selection*. Since the unit used for random assignment was intact classes, it is possible that, by chance, some of the experimental classes had higher-ability students in them. Because the unit of analysis is the classroom and the unit of interest is the student, *treatment replication* is a factor. Finally, *treatment fidelity* is potentially a major problem in this study. How do we know that the instructions delivered by the teachers are all done in the same way? Wouldn't differences in voice modulation and inflection play a role in the impact of the instructions? And wouldn't the effect of the plea for students to do their "VERY BEST . . . for ME" depend on students' prior attitudes toward their teachers?

8. Do the conclusions and interpretations follow logically from the results presented? Are limitations indicated?

The conclusions do follow from the results, but an observed interaction between the "motivation" condition and "school" complicates the interpretation: The effectiveness of the extra motivation depended upon the school where it was tried. The treatment "worked" in Schools A and C but not in School B. Because of this, the authors are hard pressed to claim effects of the treatment *overall.* They attempt to discount the lack of effect at School B by citing the low participation rate there, but other contextual factors may have been at work.

Virtually no limitations are noted by the authors. Those which could have been noted include the characteristics of students in the sampled schools (which limit external validity), treatment fidelity and replication issues, and the interaction problem. The comments that are included are not very helpful. We are

7. How could this study be redesigned to control for more of these threats? Would *other* threats now need to be considered?

8. If you were to derive your *own* conclusions from the data presented in this study, what would they be? Would they be different from the authors' conclusions?

not told how many comments were made, or how these particular ones were selected. We therefore have no way of knowing how representative they are. The comments are helpful in the sense that they illustrate how the treatment may have worked for some students.

9. Is the experiment so contrived and artificial that the findings have little generalizability?

While the study was done in real classrooms, with real tests, external validity is weak. This is because of the narrow demographics of the students sampled and divergent treatment effects in the schools where the study was done. This does not mean, however, that the study was not useful, or that its findings are not provocative. Lack of student motivation may well cause underestimation of student achievement, particularly in settings where standardized tests are viewed with suspicion. As the authors point out, the key may be to identify more long-term motivational strategies, none of which were investigated in this study.

9. Would the study have been more credible to you if the authors had listed and discussed design limitations?

Effects of a Children's Book and a Traditional Textbook on Fifth-Grade Students' Achievement and Attitudes toward Social Studies

C. Warren McKinney   H. Jon Jones
Oklahoma State University

❧

Three fifth-grade classes (N = 57 students) were randomly assigned to one of three groups and taught a 2-week unit on the American Revolution. One group received instruction based on a children's trade book. A second group received instruction based on the students' regular textbook. A third group received instruction based on their regular textbook and were encouraged to read the children's book at home. Students were pretested and posttested on their knowledge of the American Revolution and on their attitudes toward social studies. Results of analysis of variance indicated that groups did not differ significantly on the 25 items that covered content contained in both books. The two groups taught with the children's book differed significantly from the group taught with the textbook on the 15 items covered only in the children's book. The authors concluded that children who are taught with children's books may learn more because more content can be included in a book than in a unit within a textbook. Although attitudes improved for all groups, the group taught with the textbook only, showed the most dramatic improvement. However, this attitude change may have been related more to the instructional activities than the textbook itself.

Students usually rank social studies as one of their least favorite subjects (Naylor & Diem, 1987; Schug, Todd, & Beery, 1984). Students usually see it as boring and not relevant to their needs.

One reason for students' poor attitudes toward social studies may be textbooks (e.g., Levstik, 1990; Holmes & Ammon, 1985; Naylor & Diem, 1987), which have come under severe criticism during the last decade (Kretman & Parker, 1986; Larkins, Hawkins, & Gilmore, 1987). Naylor and Diem (1987) claimed that textbooks contain highly condensed information which leads to memorization of dates, names, and places. These authors write, "Textbooks are of value, but if they are not supplemented, social studies is often reduced to an overwhelming set of facts and an apparently sterile content, lacking both relevance and meaning" (p. 23).

It is not surprising that many writers have suggested that children's books which are usually written by professional writers be used to teach social studies (e.g., Holmes & Ammon, 1985). In fact, writers have suggested that children's books be used to teach nearly all aspects of social studies, and "how-to-do-it" articles are plentiful. Children's books are often suggested as alternatives to traditional textbooks in the teaching of history (e.g., Ahern & Moir, 1986; Common, 1986; Danielson, 1989; Freeman & Levstik, 1988; James & Zarrillo, 1989; Levstik, 1990; Odland, 1980; and Wright & Allen, 1976). They have been suggested as a means for correcting the inadequate treatment of minorities and women in regular textbooks (e.g., Anderson, 1987; Garcia, Hadaway, & Beal, 1988; Kazemek, 1990; Styer, 1984; Tauran, 1967;

McKinney, C. Warren, Jones, H. Jon. (1993). Effects of a children's book and a traditional textbook on fifth-grade students' achievement and attitudes toward social studies. *Journal of Research and Development in Education*, *27*(1), 56–62. Reprinted with permission.

Zarnowski, 1988). It has also been suggested that they can be used to develop critical thinking skills (see Holmes & Ammon, 1985; Brown, 1986; Lehman & Hayes, 1985; Mosher, 1986; Rieken & Miller, 1990).

McGowan and Sutton (1988) claimed that authors have recommended the use of children's books to teach social studies for over 6 decades, however, they were able to locate only six research studies that examined the claims of efficacy that many writers have suggested. Researchers have tended to focus on using children's literature to change students' attitudes. For example, the review for the present study found six studies that examined attitudinal change. Kimmel (1973) examined the role of children's books on fifth-grade students' attitude toward several countries. He reported that no attitudinal change occurred. Tauran (1967) reported that third-grade students' attitudes were positively affected when the students read positive accounts of Eskimos and negatively affected when the students read negative accounts. Fisher (1965) reported that fifth-grade students who read and discussed stories about American Indians displayed more positive attitudes toward Indians than students who only read stories with no discussion and those who did not read any stories about Indians. Also, students who read stories but did not discuss the stories possessed more positive attitudes than those students who did not read any stories. Brandhorst (1973) reported that 10th- and 11th-grade students' attitudes toward selected concepts were not affected by reading historical fiction. Kovalcik (1979) found that children's literature did not change fifth-grade students' attitudes toward social studies. He concluded that students taught with a regular textbook displayed more positive attitudes toward social studies than students taught with their regular textbook and collateral readings. Kemp (1989) reported that reading children's literature over a 10-week period did not significantly affect the moral development of fourth-, fifth-, and sixth-grade students.

Four studies were found that examined the effect of children's literature on content acquisi-

tion. Howe (1990) reported that fifth-grade students who read selections of historical fiction scored significantly higher on one measure of achievement than a control group. She also reported a small, but positive correlation between student attitudes and student achievement.

Kovalcik (1979) examined the use of collateral readings (14 trade books) and a regular textbook treatment of the American Revolution. He concluded that students (fifth grade) in the control group (i.e., regular textbook) scored significantly higher on an achievement test. Cunningham and Gall (1990) examined the effects of narrative (story) and expository (textbook style) materials on high school students' achievement. The two groups did not differ significantly on the achievement measure. In summary, the relationship between children's literature and textbooks on knowledge acquisition and attitudes towards content is equivocal.

The purpose of this study was to examine the role of a children's book and a regular textbook on fifth-grade students' knowledge acquisition and attitudes toward social studies and their textbook. First, we hypothesized that the students taught with a children's book or a combination of a children's book and their regular textbook would score significantly higher on an achievement test which measured content covered in both the children's book and the regular textbook than students taught with a regular textbook. Second, we hypothesized that the groups taught with the children's book would score significantly higher on a subtest of items which were taken from the children's book only than the students who were taught with the regular textbook only. Third, we also hypothesized that students taught with a children's book would have a more positive attitude toward that book than students taught with a regular textbook would have toward the textbook. Fourth, the two groups taught with a children's book would have more positive attitudes toward social studies than the students taught with the regular textbook. Fifth, students taught with the children's book would have ranked social studies more positively in comparison to other school subjects than students taught with the regular textbook. Sixth, the students in the two groups taught with the children's book would prefer reading the children's book to their regular textbook.

PROCEDURES

Sample

The sample consisted of 57 fifth-grade students enrolled in three social studies classes. There were 29 females and 28 males. Approximately 15% of the students were American Indian, while the remainder were Caucasian. There were no other minority students in the sample. Nearly all of the students, according to the three teachers, scored at or above the national mean on a standardized reading test.

Intact classrooms were randomly assigned to the treatments. Three days prior to the start of the study the students were administered a 25-item objective pretest to ascertain whether the groups differed on their prior knowledge of the American Revolution, the unit topic. This test was taken from the teacher's edition of the textbook used. The groups did not differ significantly on this test, $F(2,54) = .713$, $p = .49$. The means for the groups were 8.6 (s.d. = 4.2), 10.4 (s.d. = 4.8), and 9.3 (s.d. = 5.0) respectively.

The school that the students attended was located in a southwestern state. The small, rural town in which the school was located had a population of approximately 1,700 people. Most people worked in ranching, agriculture, or commuted to employment in a nearby small city.

One teacher taught all three classes. The teacher, certified to teach middle-school social studies, had 17 years of teaching experience.

Treatment and Lessons

The American Revolution was chosen as the topic of the lessons. This topic is typically taught in fifth-grade social studies classes. After reviewing several children's books, we decided to use *The American Revolution* by Bruce Bliven, Jr. (1958). This book was chosen because it is rich in content, would challenge these students, and is a children's classic. It is a part of the Landmark Books series. The children's regular textbook, published by Silver Burdett and Ginn (Helmus, Toppin, Pounds, & Arnsdorf, 1990), was used in two of the classes.

The class assigned to Treatment 1 ($n = 19$) read and discussed the children's book. The class assigned to Treatment 2 ($n = 18$) read and discussed the regular textbook in class and were encouraged to read the children's book at home. Only one student in this group completed the out-of-class assignment, however, nearly all of the students read approximately one-half of the book. The class assigned to Treatment 3 ($n = 20$) read and discussed the regular textbook only.

To maintain consistency across the groups, the same type activities were used in each class. The content of the activities differed according to the type of book. For example, when one class received a worksheet, the other classes also received worksheets that covered the appropriate content. The classes also played several games—the form of games was constant across classes with the specific content based on either the content of the textbook or children's book. Students played games that were adapted from those featured on television game shows, e.g., "Concentration," "Jeopardy," and "Wheel of Fortune." When one class was assigned homework, the other classes were also assigned homework. Again, the purpose was to control for teaching methodology.

The unit taught to the two groups that used the regular textbook lasted for 9 days with a test on the 10th day. The unit based on the children's book lasted 11 days with the test on 12th day. The second unit required more time because additional material was contained in the children's book.

Instrumentation

Two achievement tests were administered. Three days prior to the start of the study a 25-item objective test taken from the teacher's edition of the textbook was used to measure

TABLE 1. Results of One-way Analysis of Variance for the Subtest that Measured Content Common to Both Books

Source	D.F.	Sum of Squares	Mean Square	F Ratio	F Prob.
Between	2	12.4091	6.2045	1.0633	.35
Within	54	315.0997	5.8352		
Total	56	327.5088			

students' prior knowledge of the American Revolution. Following the completion of the units, a 40-item test was administered. Twenty-five items covered content discussed in both the children's book and the textbook. The reliability of this subtest, as estimated by Cronbach's alpha, was .77. Fifteen items of the test were selected from content taken from the children's book only. The reliability of this subtest, as estimated by Cronbach's alpha, was .88.

Three days prior to the start of the study a three-item attitude scale was administered. The three items were "I like reading my social studies book." "Social studies class is usually (a) exciting, (b) interesting, (c) boring." "Social studies is my (a) most favorite subject, (b) least favorite subject, (c) in-between favorite subject."

A similar attitude scale was administered with the posttest. The items were changed slightly to clarify to the students that the items referred only to the 2 weeks of data collection. A fourth item was administered to the two groups who read the children's book. This item asked the students to state which book they preferred reading. Students were asked to respond to the following statements. "I liked reading my social studies book on the American Revolution." "During the last 2 weeks social studies class was usually (a) exciting, (b) interesting, (c) boring." "Social studies is my (a) most favorite subject, (b) least favorite subject, (c) in-between favorite subject." "I prefer reading (a) my regular textbook, (b) paperback book, (c) both are about the same."

Analysis

One way analysis of variance was used to analyze the achievement data. Where significant differences were found, SNK tests were used to

TABLE 2. Means and Standard Deviations for Groups on Subtest of Common Content to Both Groups

Group	n	Mean	Standard Deviation
Children's Book	19	23.6842	2.1096
Children's & Textbook	18	23.5556	2.0926
Textbook Only	20	22.6500	2.4183

determine which means differed significantly. Responses to the attitude surveys were analyzed via frequencies.

FINDINGS

Achievement

Our first hypothesis stated that the groups taught with the children's book would score significantly higher on the items that measured content covered in both the children's book and the textbook. The results of one way analysis of variance did not support this hypothesis, $F(2, 54) = 1.06$, $p = .35$. The mean for the group taught with the children's book was 23.68 (s.d. = 2.11), while the mean for the group taught with the children's book and textbook was 23.56 (s.d. = 2.09). The mean for the group taught with the textbook only was 22.65 (s.d. = 2.42) (see Tables 1 and 2). Effect sizes were calculated and revealed that the difference between the group taught with the children's book and the group taught with the children's book and textbook was .06 standard deviations. The difference between the group taught with the children's book and the group taught with textbook only was .43 standard

TABLE 3.   Results of One-way Analysis of Variance for the Subtest that Measured Content Contained Only in Children's Book

Source	D.F.	Sum of Squares	Mean Square	F Ratio	F Prob
Between	2	253.3526	126.6763	10.2272	.0002
Within	54	668.8579	12.3863		
Total	56	922.2105			

deviations, while the difference between the group taught with both the children's book and textbook and the group taught with the textbook only was .38 standard deviations.

Our second hypothesis stated that the groups taught with the children's book would score significantly higher on the posttest than the group taught with the textbook only. These data supported the hypothesis, $F(2,54) = 10.23, p = .0002$. The mean and standard deviation for the group taught with the children's book were 8.79 and 4.66 respectively. The mean and standard deviation for the group taught with the textbook and children's book were 7.17 and 3.40 respectively. The mean and standard deviation for the group taught with the textbook only were 3.80 and 2.07 respectively. Follow-up tests (SNK) indicated that the two groups taught with the children's book differed significantly from the group taught with the textbook only. No other significant differences were found (see Tables 3 and 4). The difference between the group taught with the children's book and the group taught with the regular textbook was 2.41 standard deviations (effect size). The difference between the group taught with both the children's book and regular textbook and the group taught with the textbook only was 1.63 standard deviations, while the difference between the group taught with the children's book only and the group taught with both the children's book and textbook was .48.

Attitudes

The first attitude item attempted to measure the students' attitudes toward reading their textbook prior to the study and during data collection. Pretest frequencies indicated that

TABLE 4.   Means and Standard Deviations for Groups on Subtest of Content Contained Only in Children's Book

Group	n	Mean	Standard Deviation
Children's Book	19	8.7895	4.6617
Children's & Textbook	18	7.1667	3.3998
Textbook Only	20	3.8000	2.0673

TABLE 5.   I Like Reading My Social Studies Book

Response	Children's Book	Both	Textbook
	Pretest		
All of the Time	3	1	0
Some of the Time	3	6	8
Once In Awhile	9	3	5
Almost Never	4	8	6
	Posttest		
All of the Time	3	5	6
Some of the Time	8	4	5
Once in Awhile	7	6	5
Almost Never	1	3	4

more than one-half of the students almost never or only once in awhile liked reading their textbook. After the study more students reported that they liked reading the book assigned. Only four students on the pretest stated that they liked reading their textbook, while this number increased on the posttest to 14. Eighteen students stated that they almost never enjoyed reading their textbook on the pretest. This number decreased to only eight students on the pretest (see Table 5).

TABLE 6. Social Studies Class Is Usually:

Response	Children's Book	Both	Textbook
	Pretest		
Exciting	1	0	1
Interesting	12	9	11
Boring	6	8	7
	Posttest		
Exciting	4	5	11
Interesting	11	13	8
Boring	4	0	1

TABLE 7. Social Studies Is My:

Response	Children's Book	Both	Textbook
	Pretest		
Most Favorite	2	1	2
Least Favorite	4	8	7
In-Between Favorite	13	8	10
	Posttest		
Most Favorite	2	2	2
Least Favorite	6	2	3
In-Between Favorite	11	14	15

TABLE 8. I Prefer Reading:

| Response | Posttest Only | |
	Children's Book	Both
My Regular Textbook	0	6
The Paperback Book	9	7
Both Are About Same	10	5

The second attitude item asked the students to describe their social studies class. The choices were "exciting," "interesting," and "boring." Only two students described their classes as exciting on the pretest; 21 students described them as being boring. Following the teaching of the 2-week unit, students made a dramatic shift in their attitudes. On the posttest, 20 students stated their social studies had been exciting during the past 2 weeks. Only five students described social studies as boring.

The third attitude item required the students to compare their social studies class to their other classes. On the pretest, 19 students described social studies as their least favorite subject. Only five students described it as their favorite subject. Thirty-one students described it as their in-between favorite subject. On the posttest, 6 students stated that social studies was their most favorite subject while 11 students stated that it was their least favorite. Forty students described it as their in-between favorite subject on the posttest.

The final attitude item appeared on the posttest only and was administered to the two groups who read both books. It asked the students who were taught with the children's book and the textbook and children's book to state which they preferred to read. Nine of 19 students who were taught with the children's book only stated that they preferred reading the children's book to their regular textbook. Ten students in this group stated that the two

books were about the same. No one in this group stated that they preferred reading their regular textbook. Seven students who were taught with both books stated that they preferred reading the children's book while six stated that they preferred reading their regular textbook. Five students stated that the two books were about the same.

DISCUSSION

This study attempted to answer the question concerning whether students would learn more social studies content when taught with a children's book than with a traditional textbook. The answer appears to be an equivocal yes. This difference appears to be due to the fact that children's books include more content than regular textbooks. The children's book used in this study was 153 pages while the textbook's treatment was approximately 20 pages. The results of this study indicate that children did not learn content that was common to both books any better if they were taught with the children's book.

The statistically significant difference that was reported covered the content which was included only in the children's book.

Some writers have claimed that children's books are more interesting than regular textbooks. Findings from this study partially confirm this. On all of the attitude items, students showed a shift in their attitudes from the pretest to posttest. However, this shift was most dramatic for the group who received instruction from their regular textbook only. The teacher who regularly taught this class stated that she rarely used many of the activities that were used during the 2-week study because the students in this class tended to become rowdy. Consequently, she used low-key teaching methods. Therefore, we conclude that the dramatic shift in attitudes, especially for the textbook only group, was primarily due to the activities rather than the book used.

Although three groups participated in the study, only two of the groups were asked to read both the children's book and the regular textbook. Therefore, these two groups of students should be able to compare the two books. The group that read the regular textbook in class and the children's book outside of class split fairly evenly in their preferences. Six preferred their regular textbook, seven preferred the children's book, and five said both books were about the same. None of the students who were taught with the children's book stated that they preferred their regular textbook while nine stated that they preferred the children's book. Ten stated that they believed both books were about the same. Therefore, we concluded that children's books were preferred by only about one-third of the students.

Findings from this study provide evidence that children's books may be used effectively as a replacement for traditional textbooks. Also, children's books can be used to effectively supplement the regular textbook as out of class reading. Due to the costs of books, the out-of-class alternative may be more realistic. Finally, informal observation related to attitudes toward textbook usage indicates that teachers can more effectively utilize traditional textbooks by varying the types of activities used.

REFERENCES

Ahern, J. F., & Moir, H. (1986). Celebrating traditional holidays in public schools: Books for basic values. *The Social Studies, 77,* 234-239.

Anderson, N. (1987). Using children's literature to teach black American history. *The Social Studies, 78,* 88-89.

Bliven, Jr., B. (1958). *The American Revolution.* New York: Random House.

Brandhorst, A. R. (1973). *The effects of reading historical fiction on attitudes of high school students toward selected concepts.* Unpublished Doctoral dissertation, University of Missouri, Columbia.

Brown, L. (1986). Developing thinking and problem-solving skills with children's books. *Childhood Education, 63,* 102-107.

Common, D. L. (1986). Students, stories, and the social studies. *The Social Studies, 77,* 246-248.

Cunningham, L. J., & Gall, M. D. (1990). The effects of expository and narrative prose on student achievement and attitudes toward textbooks. *The Journal of Experimental Education, 58,* 165-175.

Danielson, K. E. (1989). Helping history come alive with literature. *The Social Studies, 80,* 65-68.

Fisher, F. L. (1965). The influences of reading and discussion on the attitudes of fifth graders toward American Indians. (Doctoral dissertation, University of California, Berkeley, 1965). *Dissertation Abstracts International, 26,* 6442.

Freeman, E. B., & Levstik, L. (1988). Recreating the past: Historical fiction in the social studies curriculum. *Elementary School Journal, 88,* 329-337.

Garcia, J., Hadaway, N. J., & Beal, G. (1988). Cultural pluralism in recent nonfiction tradebooks for children. *The Social Studies, 79,* 252-255.

Helmus, T. M., Toppin, E. A., Pounds, N. J. G., & Arnsdorf, V. E. (1990). *The United States yesterday and today.* Morristown, NJ: Silver Burdett & Ginn.

Holmes, B. C., & Ammon, R. I. (1985). Teaching content with trade books. *Childhood Education, 61,* 366-370.

Howe, K. (1990). Children's literature and its effects on cognitive and noncognitive behaviors in elementary social studies. (Doctoral dissertation, University of Minnesota, 1990). *Dissertation Abstracts International, 51/12A,* 4044.

James, M., & Zarrillo, J. (1989). Teaching history with children's literature. *The Social Studies, 80,* 153-158.

Kazemek, F. E. (1990). Human progress never rolls in on wheels of inevitability: Biographies of Martin Luther King, Jr., in the classroom. *The Social Studies, 81,* 65-69.

Kemp, M. R. (1989). A study of the influence of children's literature on the moral development of academically talented students. (Doctoral dissertation, Memphis State University, 1989). *Dissertation Abstracts International, 50/7A,* 1919.

Kimmel, E. A. (1973). Children's reading and attitude change. (Doctoral dissertation, University of Illinois at Urbana-Champaign, 1973). *Dissertation Abstracts International, 34/1,* 514A.

Kovalcik, A. L. (1979). The effect of using children's literature to change fifth grade students' attitudes toward social studies as an area of instruction. (Doctoral dissertation, University of Northern Colorado, 1979). *Dissertation Abstracts International, 40/5,* 2585A.

Kretman, K. P., & Parker, B. (1986). New U.S. history texts: Good news and bad. *Social Education, 50,* 61-63.

Larkins, A. G., Hawkins, M. L., & Gilmore, A. C. (1987). Trivial and noninformative content of elementary social studies: A review of primary texts in four series. *Theory and Research in Social Education, 15,* 299-311.

Lehman, B. A., & Hayes, D. (1985). Advancing critical reading through historical fiction and biography. *The Social Studies, 76,* 165-169.

Levstik, L. S. (1990). Research directions mediating content through literary texts. *Language Arts, 67,* 848-853.

McGowan, T. M., & Sutton, A. M. (1988). Exploring a persistent association: Trade books and social studies teaching. *Journal of Social Studies, 12,* 8-16.

Mosher, L. J. (1986). Using children's literature to develop thinking skills in young children. (Doctoral dissertation, University of Massachusetts, 1986). *Dissertation Abstracts International, 47,* 2439A.

Naylor, D. T., & Diem, R. A. (1987). *Elementary and middle school social studies.* New York: Random House.

Odland, N. (1980). American history in fact and fiction: Literature for young readers. *Social Education, 44,* 474-481.

Rieken, T. J., & Miller, M. R. (1990). Introduce children to problem solving and decision making by using children's literature. *The Social Studies, 81,* 59-64.

Schug, M. C., Todd, R. J., & Beery, R. (1984). Why kids don't like social studies. *Social Education, 48,* 382-387.

Styer, S. (1984). Women's biographies for the social studies. *Social Education, 48,* 554-564.

Tauran, R. H. (1967). The influences of reading on the attitudes of third graders toward Eskimos. (Doctoral dissertation, University of Maryland, 1967). *Dissertation Abstracts International.*

Wright, J. P., & Allen, E. G. (1976). Sixth-graders ride with Paul Revere. *Language Arts, 53,* 46-50.

Zarnowski, M. (1988). Learning about contemporary women. *The Social Studies, 79,* 61-63.

| **Evaluation Criteria** | **Discussion Questions** |

Evaluation Criteria

1. Is the general purpose of the study clear? Will the study provide a significant contribution?

The research problem statement is the first sentence of the seventh paragraph. The statement is fairly clear, indicating both levels of the independent variable (type of book—regular textbook or children's book) and the dependent variables. The use of the term *role* is vague; it makes the study seem more exploratory and less experimental. It would be better to state this problem earlier in the article. The significance of the study is well justified.

2. Does the review of literature establish the relationship between previous studies and the current one? Is the review well organized and up to date?

While the results of previous studies are summarized, there is no analysis or interpretation of the quality of the research. The review is well organized by topic, and the studies presented are directly related to the purpose of the research. The review is comprehensive and up to date.

3. Is the specific research hypothesis or question clearly and concisely stated?

The six hypotheses are clearly stated. There are six dependent variables: content common to both books, content only in children's books, attitudes toward social studies, attitude toward their book, ranking social studies textbooks, and reading preferences.

4. Is the method of sampling clearly presented? Is there random assignment of subjects? If there was no random assignment, is there anything in the way the groups were formed that might influence the reaction of the group to the treatment?

There is neither random sampling nor random assignment in this study. The first sentence of the abstract is misleading. Whole classes were

Discussion Questions

1. How could you rewrite the first two paragraphs to include a statement of the purpose of the study?

2. How could the review of literature be changed to be more effective? As it is, the conclusion is that the literature is "equivocal." If this is so, on what basis are the research hypotheses stated?

3. How could the hypotheses be presented more clearly?

4. How could a study like this be designed to avoid the sampling limitations?

randomly assigned, not individual students. If fifteen or twenty classes had been randomly assigned to each condition, then it would have been a true experiment. The lack of differences between the classes on the pretest helps to minimize the selection threat to internal validity, but other possible differences could be problematic.

5. What was manipulated as the independent variable or variables?

The independent variable was type of reading material, with three levels. One group used a children's trade book exclusively, one used a regular textbook exclusively, and the third used both books.

6. Are the procedures for collecting information described fully?

More information is needed about the instrumentation procedures. The reliability of the achievement tests is addressed by internal consistency (Cronbach's alpha) and is satisfactory if these correlations are from the group tested or a similar group. There are no reliability data for the attitude questions, nor is there any evidence of validity for either the achievement or attitude measures. The specific procedures for administering the attitude survey need to be stated, including, for example, what the students were told about the questions. Attitude questionnaires are especially prone to subject effects.

7. Are there any threats to internal validity that seem plausible?

There are several potential threats. *Selection* is a threat because this is a quasi-experiment. *Diffusion of treatment* could occur because the students were in the same school. *Experimenter bias* is possible if the teacher treated students differently, depending on which treatment the students had received (consistent with the hypotheses). *Treatment replications* is a threat because each of the three treatments was administered only once. With only one replication it is possible that other events or changes could be confounded

5. Do you think the treatment is strong enough to give the desired effects? How could the independent variable be changed so that it is stronger and more likely to affect the students?

6. What additional information should be provided in the Instrumentation section? Does the fact that the objective achievement test was taken from the teacher's edition enhance the quality of the instrument?

7. Does the fact that a single teacher taught all three classes strengthen or weaken internal validity? Do you suppose the teacher knew about the study? Would this knowledge affect the teacher's interactions with the students? Are there any other significant threats to the internal validity of the study? How would you design a study of these methods to control for treatment replications? Then would treatment fidelity be an issue? How would you control for it?

with the treatment. Given the weak test and attitude survey, *instrumentation* is a threat.

8. Do the conclusions and interpretations follow logically from the results presented? Are limitations indicated?

The tentative conclusions in the first paragraph of the Discussion section are reasonable and follow from the results. Conclusions in the last paragraph are unwarranted given the potential threats to internal validity. There was no indication of limitations in the Discussion section. Overall, the credibility of this study is not good. As a quasi-experiment there is not sufficient evidence to be confident that differences between the classes, as referred to by the authors in the Discussion section, could have accounted for the findings. Those aspects of the study that were significant were on attitude measures without evidence of reliability, and on content that one group would not be expected to know much about.

9. Is the experiment so contrived and artificial that the findings have little generalizability?

A strength of this study is that it is conducted in classrooms with what would seem to the students to be fairly typical reading materials. The generalizability is limited not so much by the artificiality of the situation as by the limited number and types of students.

8. What limitations would be appropriate for the authors to include in the Discussion section?

9. How would you design the study differently to obtain a more credible result?

Effects of Cooperative Learning among Hispanic Students in Elementary Social Studies

Judith R. Lampe
*Lubbock Independent
School District, Texas*

Gene E. Rooze
Texas Tech University

Mary Tallent-Runnels
Texas Tech University

ABSTRACT

Although research has indicated that cooperative learning enhances student achievement, promotes self-esteem, and improves interpersonal relations, few studies have focused on cooperative learning in elementary social studies. There is a close affinity between the goals of citizenship education and social skills promoted by cooperative learning. This investigation determined differences between achievement and self-esteem of Hispanic fourth graders who received instruction using cooperative learning or traditional instruction. Results indicated higher achievement with cooperative learning. Although self-esteem was apparently higher for boys than for girls, regardless of treatment, this result was inconclusive. Making connections between social studies goals and cooperative learning offers a valuable tool for improving social studies education.

During the past 15 years, research has indicated that cooperative-learning groups enhance student achievement (Johnson & Johnson, 1989; Slavin, 1990, 1991; Webb, 1989). Peer interaction is central to the success of cooperative learning as it relates to cognitive understanding. Cognitive developmental theories such as Vygotsky's (1978) emphasize that intellectual growth is a dynamic social-interactive process. Active verbalization, especially when it involves explanation, often leads to cognitive restructuring and an in-

crease in understanding. Comprehension is facilitated as learners, some of whom might normally "tune out" or refuse to speak out in a traditional setting, become actively involved in the learning process through group interaction. According to Stahl and VanSickle (1992), every cooperative-learning strategy, when used appropriately, can enable students to move beyond the text, memorization of basic facts, and learning lower level skills.

In addition to its academic benefits, cooperative learning has been found to promote self-esteem, interpersonal relations, and improved attitudes toward school and peers. In a competitively structured classroom, except for the few "winners" or students who succeed, self-esteem can suffer. Likewise, self-esteem and approval of classmates can be lower in individualistic learning situations than in cooperative ones (Johnson, Johnson, & Maruyama, 1984). When competition is promoted, students may learn to value winning at all costs, and cooperation may be discouraged (Conrad, 1988). Although advocates of cooperative learning are not opposed to all competition, they do oppose inappropriate competition (Johnson & Johnson, 1991). One cooperative learning model, Teams-Games-Tournament, builds a competitive phase into part of the instructional strategy (Stahl & VanSickle, 1992). Inappropriate competition, however, tends to widen the existing differences among students' academic knowledge and abilities, which, in turn, can widen negative perceptions

Lampe, Judith R., Rooze, Gene E., and Tallent-Runnels, Mary. (1996). Effects of cooperative learning among hispanic students in elementary social studies. *The Journal of Educational Research, 89,* 187–191. Reprinted with the permission of the Helen Dwight Reid Education Foundation. Published by Heldref Publications, 1319 Eighteenth St., N.W., Washington, DC 20036-1802. Copyright © 1996.

of others on the basis of gender, race, or ethnicity (Stahl, 1992).

Cooperative-learning groups have also been found to equalize the status and respect of all group members, regardless of gender (Glassman, 1989; Johnson, Johnson, & Stanne, 1986). Research by Klein (1985) revealed that competitively structured classrooms have the effect of favoring boys or reinforcing sex role stereotypes that may limit opportunities for girls. Studies in traditional classrooms have consistently shown that boys have more interactions with teachers than girls do (Brophy & Good, 1974; Cooper & Good, 1983) and that in our culture boys are often socialized to be assertive and demanding, whereas girls are to be responsible and compliant. In a comprehensive study (Martinez & Dukes, 1991) on self-esteem and ethnicity among students in Grades 7 through 12 ($N = 13, 489$), minorities and women generally reported lower levels of self-esteem than White males did. Within each race or ethnic category, satisfaction-with-self averages for girls were lower than those for boys. A particularly interesting finding regarding satisfaction-with-self was that male Hispanics reported the highest satisfaction of any ethnic group, including White males.

PURPOSE

There have been numerous empirical studies that confirm cooperative learning to be an effective way to structure learning activities (Johnson, Johnson, Holubec, & Roy, 1984; Montague & Tanner, 1987; Slavin, 1991). However, there is surprisingly little research that emphasizes social studies and even less that focuses on social studies at the elementary level. Furthermore, no studies of which we are aware have investigated the effects of cooperative learning and the interaction of gender on social studies and self-esteem at the fourth-grade level in a Hispanic, low-socioeconomic population. Thus, our purpose in the present study was to determine differences between the social studies achievement and self-esteem of Hispanic, economically disadvantaged,

fourth-grade male and female students who participated in cooperative-learning groups and those who received instruction using a traditional approach. Therefore, we addressed the following questions in this study:

1. Is there a difference in the social studies achievement self-esteem of fourth-grade students according to the treatments of cooperative learning or traditional instruction and according to gender across treatment groups?

2. Is there a difference in the social studies achievement of fourth-grade students according to the treatments of cooperative learning or traditional instruction and according to gender across treatment groups?

METHOD

Participants

This 12-week study was conducted in eight 4th-grade social studies classrooms ($N = 105$) in two elementary schools in the Southwest with low-socioeconomic, Hispanic populations. Percentages of the student populations receiving free or reduced lunches were 78% free and 10% reduced at School A and 88% free and 5% reduced at School B. Twenty-five boys and 26 girls received instruction based on cooperative learning; 24 boys and 30 girls received traditional, teacher-directed instruction. School district administrators assigned this research study to eight intact classrooms at two elementary schools; two classes of each treatment group were represented at each school. Teachers were randomly assigned by the researchers to the cooperative-learning treatment groups. They had received training in cooperative-learning group strategies through Johnson and Johnson "Brown Book" workshops, consultation with the researchers, sample lessons, and supplemental materials. Teachers using the traditional approach also had experience in cooperative-learning methodology but agreed to teach the content in a whole-class, textbook-centered, teacher-directed format. All of the female teachers (one Hispanic and the remaining Anglo) were deemed as performing effectively by their superiors. The most experienced teacher (approximately 20 years) and most inexperienced teacher (2 years) were assigned to the cooperative-learning treatment group. All of the remaining teachers were between 25 and 35 years of age and averaged 10 years of teaching experience.

Instruments

Because random assignment of treatment groups to students was not possible, we used pretest scores from researcher-constructed social studies unit tests and the Coopersmith Self-Esteem Inventory, School Form (Coopersmith, 1984), as covariates to determine equivalence of groups. Prior to the beginning of each of the two units, the social studies pretest was administered. Then at the end of each unit, the same social studies test was given as a posttest to measure achievement in social studies. In an effort to increase content validity, we developed these criterion-referenced objective tests by using the publisher's fourth-grade test data bank as a source. In constructing the 30-item multiple-choice tests, we included a variety of items that incorporated fact-recall, interpreting graphics (charts and maps), identifying cause and effect, drawing conclusions, sequencing, and inferencing. These social studies unit tests were piloted prior to the experiment with fifth-grade students in the same school system and yielded a .78 Pearson product-moment test-retest reliability coefficient and a .79 Kuder-Richardson Formula 20 reliability coefficient for interitem consistency. The interval for the test-retest analysis was 23 days.

To measure self-esteem, the Coopersmith Self-Esteem Inventory, School Form, was administered both as a pretest and posttest, before and after the 12-week treatment period. The school form consists of 50 items, resulting in a total self score and subscale scores of General Self, Social Self–Peers, Home–Parents, and School–Academic. Reliability coefficients (K–R 20s) for measuring internal consistency were reported by Kimball (1972) to be between .87 and .92 when administered to 7.600 public schoolchildren in Grades 4 through 8.

This sample included students of all socioeconomic ranges and Black and Hispanic students. The concurrent validity coefficient was reported to be .83 when the Coopersmith Self-Esteem Inventory was compared with the Hare Self-Esteem Scale (Mitchell, 1985).

Treatment Procedures

During the 12-week period, both treatment groups studied the same content material on Texas history drawn from two 4th-grade Scott, Foresman and Company (1988) social studies units titled "Settling Our State" and "A Changing Texas." During the treatment period, students in the cooperative-learning classrooms were instructed by teachers who followed the guidelines of Johnson, Johnson, and Holubec (1990), also known as "Brown Book Training" for structuring heterogeneous cooperative-learning groups. Teachers incorporated the basic elements of cooperative learning into the group experience: positive interdependence, face-to-face interaction, individual accountability, social skill development, and group processing. In addition, teachers specified both the academic and social skill objectives, explained the tasks and goal structures, assigned roles within the groups, and described the procedures for the learning activity. Group interaction was evidenced by much student–student talking; they often sat in groups on the floor as they worked on their mutual group goal. Students took turns reading the social studies content to each other and then discussed it by asking questions, summarizing, and clarifying each other's understandings.

Many different types of cooperative-learning group interactions were experienced. Jigsaw II groups and Group Investigation project groups were formed for some lessons as students worked together on their specified tasks. Examples of group activities included (a) writing letters from a historical character's perspective, (b) developing and using flash cards on Texas history, (c) discussing controversial issues (Civil War and slavery), and (d) becoming "experts" on a certain aspect of Texas history in a specialized group and then teaching the content to another base group (Jigsaw II strategy). Teachers in the cooperative-learning classrooms acted as facilitators of learning as they formed groups, made placement decisions, specified tasks, assigned roles, monitored, intervened only when necessary, evaluated, and performed group processing.

While the cooperative-learning groups studied social studies content using group interaction, the traditional groups learned the same content about Texas history from the same two 4th-grade textbook units, but did so during instruction in a whole-class, teacher-directed, textbook-centered approach. Instead of discussing the material, helping each other, or developing projects in groups, students read the assigned reading material silently, completed worksheets independently at their seats, did individual reports on Texas history, watched filmstrips, or engaged in discussions with the teacher in response to teacher questions. Traditional classrooms were characterized by a quiet, orderly atmosphere with the students seated at their desks, and teachers in these classrooms dispensed facts, served as resources, or provided information. Observations of both treatment conditions were documented by researcher field notes.

DATA ANALYSIS AND RESULTS

Data were analyzed using analysis of covariance (ANCOVA) to explore differences among groups. First, a two-way ANCOVA was performed with social studies achievement as the dependent variable and the social studies pretest as the covariate. Another two-way AN-COVA was then conducted with the Coopersmith Self-Esteem posttest as the dependent variable and the Coopersmith Self-Esteem pretest as the covariate. The independent variables for both analyses were treatment and gender. The two treatment conditions were cooperative learning and traditional, teacher-directed instruction.

The interaction of the covariate with treatment that was used to test for homogeneity of regression for the self-esteem test was not statistically significant, $F(1, 102) = 0, p = .95$. The homogeneity of regression tests for the interaction between the covariate and gender was also not statistically significant, $F(1, 102) = .79$, $p = .38$. This indicated that the assumption of parallelism of slopes was met and lends support for the use of ANCOVA in this study. For the social studies achievement test, the interaction of the covariate with gender used to test for homogeneity of regression was not statistically significant, $F(1, 95) = 0, p = 1$. For the interaction of the covariate with treatment, the test for homogeneity of regression was statistically significant, $F(1, 95) = 28.96, p = .0001$. This departure from linearity sometimes results in biased estimates of treatment (Kirk, 1982). Therefore, our next step was to plot the regression lines for the covariate by treatment interaction. When these lines were plotted, they were both positive, and the slopes were only slightly different. Therefore, we concluded that the use of this covariate was appropriate.

Means and standard deviations of raw scores for the social studies achievement pretests and posttests, as well as the adjusted means for the social studies achievement posttest, are shown in Table 1. Results of the ANCOVA revealed a statistically significant main effect for treatment. $F(1, 93) = 25.72, p < .001$, as shown in Table 2, favoring cooperative learning over traditional instruction; however, no statistically significant effects were found for gender or for an interaction between treatment and gender on social studies achievement. The correlation r between the pretest and the posttest was $.67, p = .001$.

The raw score means, standard deviations, and the adjusted means for self-esteem reflect similar scores for both treatment groups (Table 3). Results of the ANCOVA for self-esteem revealed no main effect for treatment and no statistically significant interaction between treatment and gender; however, a statistically significant main effect for gender was revealed, $F(1, 100) = 6.68, p < .011$, favoring boys over girls, regardless of treatment group (Table 4). The correlation between the pretest and the posttest was $.60, p = .001$. An effect size was

TABLE 1. Observed Means, Adjusted Means, and Standard Deviations for Achievement, by Treatment and Gender

Group	Cooperative Learning			Traditional		
	n	*M*	*SD*	*n*	*M*	*SD*
	Pretest					
Boys	22	24.77	6.43	23	21.04	5.13
Girls	23	23.44	4.07	29	21.17	5.02
Total	45	24.09	5.33	53	21.11	5.02
	Posttest					
Boys	22	48.73 (46.32)	8.32	24	33.33 (35.07)	9.81
Girls	23	44.87 (43.95)	9.63	29	37.00 (38.59)	10.34
Total						
obs. mean	45	46.98	8.83	53	35.34	10.17
adj. mean		(45.07)			(37.02)	

Note. Adjusted means are presented in parentheses.

TABLE 2. Analysis of Covariance of Social Studies Achievement

Source of Variation	SS	df	MS	F	p
Within cells	5,557.73	93	59.76		
Regression	3,142.57	1	3,142.57	52.59	.001
Treatment	1,537.13	1	1,537.13	25.72	.001
Gender	8.01	1	8.01	.13	.715
Treatment by gender	209.14	1	209.14	3.50	.065

TABLE 3. Observed Means, Adjusted Means, and Standard Deviations for Self-Esteem, by Treatment and Gender

Group	Cooperative Learning			Traditional		
	n	*M*	*SD*	*n*	*M*	*SD*
	Pretest					
Boys	25	54.88	11.86	24	59.67	13.00
Girls	26	61.58	16.13	30	61.23	13.31
Total	51	58.29	14.46	54	60.54	13.07
	Posttest					
Boys	25	62.40 (65.27)	13.47	24	66.67 (66.46)	14.73
Girls	26	61.31 (59.87)	19.37	30	59.67 (58.45)	14.63
Total						
obs. mean	51	61.84	16.58	54	62.78	14.95
adj. mean		(62.53)			(62.09)	

Note. Adjusted means are presented in parentheses.

TABLE 4. Analysis of Covariance of Self-Esteem

Source of Variation	SS	df	MS	F	p
Within cells	17,125.40	100	171.25		
Regression	7,808.14	1	7,808.14	45.59	.001
Treatment	.34	1	.34	.00	.001
Gender	1,143.84	1	1,143.84	6.68	.011
Treatment by gender	43.99	1	43.99	.26	.613

calculated for the main effect for the gender result because it appeared difficult to explain. (*eta* squared = .066) (Thompson, 1994).

CONCLUSIONS AND DISCUSSION

Achievement

The results of this study indicated that there was a difference in the social studies achievement of 4th-grade students according to the treatment of cooperative-learning or traditional instruction. The cooperative-learning group instructional approach was a more effective way than traditional instruction to structure learning in 4th-grade social studies. However, no difference in social studies achievement was found according to gender across treatment groups. Both boys and girls profited from participation in cooperative-learning groups. This points out the need for educators to provide opportunities for all students to engage in cooperative-learning groups in elementary social studies. It is not suggested that all social studies content be studied using cooperative-learning groups; however, social studies educators are encouraged to recognize the effectiveness and benefits of this alternative approach and structure more cooperative-learning-group lessons in their classrooms.

A possible explanation for the effectiveness of cooperative learning in this study involves the students' active involvement in the learning process through frequent verbalization in both an extensive and intensive way. Extensive interaction was apparent through the variety of exchanges—summarizing, explaining, clarifying, encouraging, probing, extending, and questioning. Intensive interaction was exhibited by the on-task behavior, the high level of motivation, and the "eye-to-eye," "knee-to-knee" communication posturing as the students interacted in cooperative-learning groups.

With little research having been conducted in social studies on cooperative learning in Hispanic, low-socioeconomic populations, a major contribution of this study is that the cooperative-learning instructional approach can be more effective than the traditional approach for producing achievement gains in such a population. In an effort to meet the needs of an increasingly diverse, multicultural student population, cooperative learning provides social studies educators with an effective instructional approach for enhancing the success of our youth.

Self-Esteem

No difference was found in the self-esteem of 4th-grade students according to the treatment of cooperative learning or traditional instruction. Although prior research indicated that cooperative-learning groups can equalize the status and respect of all group members regardless of gender, this study demonstrated no such equivalence. Although differences in self-esteem were not attributable to the type of instructional approach used, the results did indicate that gains in self-esteem were related to one's gender across treatment groups; boys outscored girls on the posttest regardless of whether we used cooperative learning or traditional, teacher-directed instruction.

However, because of the small effect size for this analysis, these results should be interpreted with caution. There appears to be an effect, however, considering the small size, we find the results to be inconclusive. Although the current findings of the discrepancy in gains between boys' and girls' self-esteem may be related to the ethnicity factor previously reported in the Martinez and Dukes study (1991), the small effect size and short length of the study (12 weeks) cannot be regarded as conclusive evidence. It is suggested that differences in self-esteem for boys and girls according to ethnicity be explored further in research studies of greater length across the curriculum, including the social studies.

In summary, cooperative learning provides a valuable instructional approach for social studies education. In addition, teachers working with Hispanic populations should consider cooperative learning in planning productive activities for their students. Making connections between social studies goals and cooperative-learning strategies may enhance the possibility of developing knowledgeable, responsible, and participating citizens for our pluralistic society.

REFERENCES

Brophy, J., & Good, T. (1974). *Teacher-student relationships: Causes and consequences.* New York: Holt, Rinehart & Winston.

Conrad, B. (1988). Cooperative learning and prejudice reduction. *Social Education, 52*(4), 283–286.

Cooper, H., & Good, T. (1983). *Pygmalion grows up: Studies in the expectation communication process.* New York: Longman.

Coopersmith, S. (1984). *Coopersmith self-esteem inventories.* (3rd printing). Palo Alto, CA: Consulting Psychologists Press.

Glassman, P. (1989). *A study of cooperative learning in mathematics, writing, and reading in the intermediate grades: A focus upon achievement, attitudes, and self-esteem by gender, race, and ability group.* Dissertation, Hofstra University, New York.

Johnson, D., & Johnson, R. (1989). *Cooperation and competition: Theory and research.* Edina, MN: Interaction Book Company.

Johnson, D., & Johnson, R. (1991). *Learning together and alone: Cooperative, competitive, and individualistic learning* (3rd ed.). Englewood Cliffs, NJ: Prentice-Hall.

Johnson, D., Johnson, R., & Holubec, E. (1990). *Cooperation in the classroom.* Edina, MN: Interaction Book Company.

Johnson, D., Johnson, R., Holubec, E., & Roy, P. (1984). *Circles of learning.* Alexandria, VA: Association for Supervision and Curriculum Development.

Johnson, D., Johnson, R., & Maruyama, G. (1984). Interdependence and interpersonal attraction among heterogeneous and homogeneous individuals: A theoretical formulation and a meta-analysis of the research. *Review of Educational Research, 53,* 5–54.

Johnson, R., Johnson, D., & Stanne, M. (1986). Comparison of computer-assisted cooperative, competitive, and individualistic learning. *American Educational Research Journal, 23,* 382–392.

Kimball, O. (1972). Development of norms for the Coopersmith Self-Esteem Inventory: Grades four through eight (Doctoral dissertation. Northern Illinois University, 1972). *Dissertation Abstracts International, 34,* 1131–1132.

Kirk, R. (1982). *Experimental design* (2nd ed.). Belmont, CA: Brooks/Cole.

Klein, S. (Ed.). (1985). *Handbook for achievement of sex equity through education.* Baltimore, MD: The Johns Hopkins University Press.

Martinez, R., & Dukes, R. (1991). Ethnic and gender differences in self-esteem. *Youth and Society, 22* (3), 318–338.

Mitchell, J. (Ed.). (1985). *The ninth mental measurements yearbook.* Lincoln, NE: The University of Nebraska.

Montague, M., & Tanner, M. (1987). Reading strategy groups for content area instruction. *Journal of Reading, 30,* 716–725.

Scott, Foresman and Company. (1988). *Texas: The study of our state.* Fourth-grade textbook. Scott, Foresman.

Slavin, R. (1990). *Cooperative learning: Theory, research, and practice.* Englewood Cliffs, NJ: Prentice-Hall.

Slavin, R. (1991). Synthesis of research on cooperative learning. *Educational Leadership, 48,* 71–82.

Stahl, R. (1992). From "academic strangers" to successful members of a cooperative learning group: An inside-the-learner perspective. In

Cooperative learning in the social studies classroom: An invitation to social study. Washington, DC: National Council for the Social Studies.

Stahl, R., & VanSickle, R. (1992). Cooperative learning as effective social study within the social studies classroom: Introduction and an invitation. In *Cooperative learning in the social studies classroom: An invitation to social study.* Bulletin No. 87. Washington, DC: National Council for the Social Studies.

Thompson, B. (1994). *The concept of statistical significance testing.* ERIC/AE Digest, Report No. (EDO-TM-94-1). Washington, DC: ERIC Clearinghouse on Assessment and Evaluation. (ERIC Document Reproduction Service No. ED 366 654).

Vygotsky, L. (1978). *Thought and Language.* Cambridge, MA: MIT Press.

Webb, N. (1989). Peer interaction and learning in small groups. *International Journal of Educational Research, 13,* 21–39.

Evaluation Criteria

1. Is the general purpose of the study clear? Will the study provide a significant contribution?

The research problem statement is first indicated in the middle of the Purpose section. It is clear, indicating both dependent variables, both levels of the independent variable, and the nature of the sample. It would have been helpful to state this purpose much earlier in the article. The questions are clear, except that there is a mistake. The first question does not make sense; probably the words "social studies achievement" should have been deleted. The significance of the study could be enhanced by making a better case for the need to study cooperative methods with this particular population, and by exploring how results may be different due to characteristics of the population (Hispanic fourth graders). Just because something has not been studied doesn't mean it should be studied.

2. Does the review of literature establish the relationship between previous studies and the current one? Is the review well organized and up to date?

The review, while short, appears to be fairly comprehensive, though this is an area of research for which there are hundreds of published studies. With a couple of exceptions,

Discussion Questions

1. How would you rewrite the first paragraph to include a general statement of the problem? There is a need for research hypotheses in this study—how would they be stated?

2. Is there any part of the review of literature that is unnecessary? How could the review be organized differently to be more effective and serve as a basis for research hypotheses?

most of the references are secondary sources. It would be nice to see more information on the "few" studies that have focused on social studies. The organization is fine. The review is a general overview of the cooperative learning literature and does not relate previously conducted studies to the present one.

3. Is the specific research hypothesis or question clearly and concisely stated?

There are no research hypotheses stated. The specific research questions are clear.

4. Is the method of sampling clearly presented? Is there random assignment of subjects? If there was no random assignment, is there anything in the way the groups were formed that might influence the reaction of the group to the treatment?

This is a nonprobability, convenience sample in which most teachers within each school were randomly assigned to treatments (the most and least experienced were assigned to the cooperative group). The nature of the sampling suggests bias on the part of the teachers who received the cooperative training. This would not be considered a true experimental study because the classes were intact and only four classes were randomly assigned to each condition. (With so few randomly assigned, systematic differences are likely to exist. This is illustrated by the different pretest means between the cooperative learning and traditional groups.)

5. What was manipulated as the independent variable or variables?

The manipulated independent variable was method of instruction, with two levels—cooperative and traditional. Gender would also be considered an independent variable, though it cannot be manipulated. Table 1 shows that the cooperative groups had higher pretest scores. This may mean that these groups are brighter or more able, which suggests a selection threat to internal validity.

3. The research literature points to certain expected results. How could the research questions be rewritten as research hypotheses that would be consistent with the literature?

4. Given that the schools mentioned comprised the entire sample of students, what other ways could classes and teachers be selected to strengthen internal validity?

5. What further detail could be provided about the treatments to document interventions as planned? There is mention of "researcher field notes," but what else could be provided?

6. Are the procedures for collecting information described fully?

The instruments are well described, though it would be helpful to have some examples of the items. It is not clear if exactly the same achievement test was used for both the pretest and the posttest. The evidence provided for reliability is adequate. It was good to indicate reliability coefficients as well as the type of reliability. Appropriate content-related evidence for validity is presented for the achievement test. It would be good to include construct-related evidence for the self-esteem measure. Overall, the instrumentation is a strength of the study.

7. Are there any threats to internal validity that seem plausible?

The nature of the design suggests *selection, treatment replication, diffusion of treatment, treatment fidelity, experimenter (teacher) bias,* and *subject effects* (e.g., those not in cooperative groups may be unhappy) as plausible threats to internal validity. We presume that all the treatments were given at the same time, though this could be more clearly stated. If the 12 weeks were in the very beginning of the school year the results may be different than if the unit was introduced after the class was well established (e.g., if the class was used to doing group work and then had to do it individually, they would not be very happy!).

8. Do the conclusions and interpretations follow logically from the results presented? Are limitations indicated?

The last sentence clearly goes far beyond the data collected. Only evidence for achievement was compelling, and certainly nothing about responsibility or citizenship was researched. Appropriate limitations are provided (e.g., small sample size), although more could be included about what aspect of cooperative learning appears to have been significant in raising achievement. You can't really know what part of the treatment package was responsible

6. What is the difference between the "test–retest" and "interitem" reliability in the Instruments section? What is another, more common label than "interitem?"

7. In what additional ways could the classes be different that may have affected the results of the study? What else could the researchers have done to lessen treatment fidelity as a possible threat to internal validity? What other kind of information could be gathered and presented to lessen the selection threat to internal validity?

8. How could the Conclusions and Discussion section be rewritten to be more consistent with the results and potential threats to internal validity? Why do you think no differences were found for self-esteem?

for the effect. This diminishes the external validity of the study.

9. Is the experiment so contrived and artificial that the findings have little generalizability?

What limits the generalizability of the results is the nature of the students, subject matter, and cooperative learning that is employed. This would include the teachers and the training the teachers received, as well as the time of year. In sum, while the study is done in a field setting, which usually enhances generalizability, these conditions actually limit generalizability considerably.

9. How could the study be designed to increase generalizability? (Hint: Is there a way to implement a "standard" type of cooperative learning that could easily be used in other settings?)

Chapter 4

Qualitative Ethnographic Designs

The term "ethnography" (or "naturalistic inquiry," as some authors call it) is a research perspective that shares most or all of the following characteristics:

Search for meaning—Ethnographic studies are designed to better understand the interpretations and meanings people give to events, objects, other people, and environmental contexts.

Constructed reality—Reality is not a set of objective "facts" to be discovered but rather is socially constructed and constantly changing.

Natural settings—Ethnographic studies emphasize the understanding of behavior as it occurs naturally, without artificial constraints or controls.

Rich narrative description—Data are collected as words and/or pictures rather than as numbers. Rich or "thick" descriptions are made to enhance understanding.

Direct data collection—Ethnographers collect data directly from persons or documents. They establish close, trusting, and empathetic relationships with the individuals being studied.

Concern with process—An important goal of ethnographic studies is to understand how and why behavior occurs, rather than to predict and control behavior, which is characteristic of quantitative research.

Inductive data analysis—No hypotheses are used in ethnographic research. Data are gathered first and synthesized inductively for understanding. Conclusions are "grounded" from the "bottom up."

Participant perspectives—Ethnographers take a phenomenological approach. They are interested in the sense people make of their lives, how people interpret experiences, define terms, and conceptualize their lives. The point of view of the individuals studied is critical to this understanding.

Emergent research design—The research procedures are flexible, evolving and change during the study.

Results as cases or stories—The results of ethnographic studies are reported in narrative form and, in essence, tell a story about the phenomenon under study.

As the above characteristics indicate, a good ethnographic study is a lot more than just collecting qualitative data about a topic through interviews or focus groups. A study of parental attitudes toward school choice, for example, which relies on data collected through telephone interviews, would not qualify as an ethnographic study unless the researchers spent considerable time with the parents or schools in question, collected a lot of other data, and reported their findings as in-depth narratives.

Research Problem

Ethnographers begin with what is called a foreshadowed problem. A **foreshadowed problem** is a general statement or question that communicates the broad purpose of the study. It provides a framework and a focus for beginning the study, and is refined during the study. By stating such general problems, rather than a specific research question or hypothesis, the researcher stays open to all possible interpretations and meanings.

Methodology

Qualitative researchers use several **purposeful** (not random) **sampling** techniques to select "participants" (not "subjects"), documents, or settings. Purposeful sampling is done to select individuals, sites, or documents that will be most informative.

Data collection is done by interviewing or observation. Interviews may be very open ended, with few predetermined questions, or the interview may have a more structured format, like a focus group.

Observations vary in the extent to which the researcher is involved in the natural events of the setting. At one extreme is the **complete observer**, who does not participate at all in the setting. At the other extreme is the **participant observer**, who is an actual participant, along with others, in the setting. A complete observer would view the events in a classroom from the back of the class, whereas a participant observer would be a student or teacher.

Observers write extensive, highly detailed **field notes** to record their observations. These field notes are analyzed by constructing codes that can be used to categorize the observations. The notes are coded and reorganized to illustrate important patterns or relationships that lead to generalizations and conclusions. Interviews that are taped are transcribed and analyzed in a similar fashion.

Like quantitative researchers, ethnographic researchers consider the internal and external validity of a study, but the meaning of these terms is somewhat different for judging ethnographic studies.

Typically, ethnographic research is strong in internal validity and weak in external validity. This is because the primary purpose of the research is to obtain an understanding of the phenomenon under study, and because the methodology, which is labor and time intensive, uses a limited number of persons, situations, or events (often only one in a case study).

The internal validity of ethnographic research typically revolves around the issue of credibility. **Credibility** is the extent to which the data, data analysis, and results are accurate and trustworthy. Threats especially troublesome to the credibility of an ethnographic study are instrumentation and researcher bias.

Recall that the principal characteristics of a good data collection tool in quantitative studies are reliability and validity. **Reliability** in an ethnographic study is the extent to which what is recorded is what actually occurred in the setting. Two ethnographic researchers working in the same setting might well come up with different data, as they may have observed different things; the question is whether the data are accurate. Reliability is enhanced by: using detailed field notes, audio and video recording, and teams of researchers; searching for negative cases or discrepant data; and having interview and observation notes reviewed by participants for accuracy. **Validity** is strong in these studies if there is a good fit between the intent of the research (foreshadowed questions) and what was actually studied. Validity is enhanced by establishing rapport with interviewees, unobtrusive observation (so that the participant is unaware of being observed), appropriate selection of participants, repeated patterns illustrated by the data, and sufficient detail in the data and depth of the analysis.

One of the most common techniques used to reduce researcher bias, and thus enhance credibility, is triangulation. **Triangulation** refers to the use of different data sources, time periods, and data collection methods that result in similar findings. In other words, if the results of several different approaches to gathering data are similar, there is triangulation of the data. For example, if what is found in interviews coincides with what is observed and what is found in documents, then these three data sources triangulate. A second important way to increase credibility is **member checking,** submitting notes to informants to ensure that their perspectives have been recorded accurately. A third common technique (actually set of techniques) is **cross-examination** of the evidence, wherein a researcher submits preliminary findings to a disinterested third party, who analyzes the logic behind any inferences drawn, much like an attorney who is cross-examining a witness in court.

External validity takes on a completely different meaning in ethnographic research. Since there is no intent in this kind of research to generalize from a sample to a larger population, but rather to understand the phenomenon itself, external validity is usually discussed using such terms as **transferability** or **comparability.** The key issue is the extent to which the results provide insights useful in other comparable settings. The heart of the external validity question for an ethnographic study is what the study can teach us—about our students, our organizations, or our lives. The best studies, therefore, are complete enough and rich enough that readers are able to engage in what Stake (1978) called a "vicarious experience": They identify sufficiently with the case that they are able to discern what might be most applicable to their own settings.

Criteria for Evaluating Ethnographic Research

1. What is the foreshadowed problem and how clearly is it stated? Is it reformulated later on, after some initial data have been collected?

2. Is the conceptual and theoretical framework for the study clear? How well does the literature review argue for the importance of the current research?

3. What are the biases and preconceived ideas of the researcher? How are these dealt with in the study? Is the researcher well prepared to complete the study?

4. Is the method of selecting participants clear and appropriate to the foreshadowed problem? How well are the participants and sites described?

5. How involved is the researcher in the setting being observed? Would this involvement affect the behavior of the participants?

6. If appropriate, are multiple methods of data collection utilized? What was the duration and intensity of data collection?

7. Are issues of credibility directly addressed by the researchers? How, and how effectively?

8. Are the findings presented clearly? Are the data sufficiently detailed to allow a rich description? Are results accompanied by illustrative quotes and specific instances?

9. Do conclusions and interpretations follow logically from the results presented?

10. Is sufficient detail provided to discern which parts of the study might be applicable to other settings? To which contexts is the study transferable?

Influencing Engagement through Accommodation: An Ethnographic Study of At-Risk Students

Sandra E. Miller   Gaea Leinhardt   Naomi Zigmond
University of Pittsburgh

This study used ethnographic methodology to explore the academic world of regular and learning disabled high school students to determine what aspects of that world might relate to potential dropout behavior. It was conducted in a high school that was discovered to have a lower dropout rate than anticipated in view of national or local trends.

We describe the accommodating nature of this high school that may enhance the ability of students to become and remain academically engaged and hence accounts for the comparatively low dropout rate. This accommodation is described in terms of institutional, classroom, and interpersonal processes that reflect the school's responsiveness to the needs of students as those needs are perceived by various institutional actors. The effect of these accommodation processes results in a modification of demands made of students and the provision of support for students to enhance their ability to meet those demands.

This research is concerned with documenting the high school experience of a small number of learning disabled (LD) and non-learning disabled (non-LD) adolescents in order to understand what features of that experience may influence them to stay in school until graduation or to drop out of high school.

Two assumptions have guided the design of the present study. The first is that LD students are an important group of marginal students to study. LD students represent a sizeable popula-tion (3 to 8% of school populations) and ac-count for more than 40% of students served in special education. A greater percentage of LD students drop out of high school than non-LD students (Levin, Zigmond, & Birch, 1983; Zigmond & Thornton, 1985). Like other at-risk students, LD students' academic performance is often poor, they often experience difficulties in social interactions with peers (Dudlay-Marling & Edmiaston, 1985; Garrett & Crump, 1980), and they tend to exhibit low self-esteem, external locus of control (Rogers & Saklofske, 1985), and the phenomenon of learned helplessness (Thomas, 1979). It also appears that the conse-quences of dropping out are particularly serious for LD students (Zigmond & Thornton, 1985).

The second assumption is that school fac-tors are important elements that interact with personal attributes of students to affect student stay-in or dropout behaviors. Many factors, in-cluding background characteristics and school-related attributes, affect whether a high school student stays in school or leaves before gradua-tion. One set of factors that has been given a great deal of attention in the research literature involves the personal attributes of students that are correlated with dropout behavior such as coming from low socioeconomic families, sin-gle parent families, and families in which one or both parents did not finish high school (Ekstrom, Goertz, Pollack, & Rock, 1986; Rumberger, 1983); low self-esteem (Sewell, Palmo, & Manni, 1981); a sense of helplessness (Hill, 1979); and an external locus of control

This work was supported by funds from the Handicapped Research and Demonstration Branch of Special Education Programs, Education Department, through Grant #G008530042, Secondary Education Transitional Services for Handicapped Youth. An early version of this paper was presented at AERA, Washington, D. C., April, 1987.

(Ekstrom et al., 1986). Other factors involve school-related attributes such as poor academic performance (Ekstrom et al., 1986; Wehlage & Rutter, 1986), a general lack of interest in school, poor attendance, and disciplinary problems (Peng, 1983).

Relatively little research, however, has examined school conditions that may contribute to, or ameliorate the problem of student dropout. There does exist a small body of retrospective studies in which students who have dropped out of school have been asked to relate their reasons for having done so. These studies suggest that students' perceptions of the school (too dangerous, unfair in its disciplinary policy, without caring teachers) are important factors in the decision to either stay or leave (Wehlage & Rutter, 1986). Except for these few retrospective reports of high school dropouts, very little is known about the school experiences of "high risk" students (Goodlad, 1984) or about their perceptions of that experience.

In developing the current research plan, we have made use of the concepts of integration and alienation (Newmann, 1981; Wehlage, 1983). We believe that a sense of integration with the school must be developed in order for students to be willing to stay in high school until graduation, especially for students whose family backgrounds, low intellectual functioning, or other personal attributes leave them at risk for school dropout. We see integration into the fabric of school life as describable on a continuum, the end points of which are engagement and disengagement. Students who are highly integrated into school would be expected to be highly engaged in many aspects of school life. Such students would not typically be viewed as at risk for dropping out, partially because disappointment or failure in one part of the system can be counterbalanced by success or positive connection in other parts of the system. Conversely, students who are less integrated into many aspects of school life would be expected to be disengaged and (other things being equal) at greater risk for dropping out. Like Natriello (1984), we see inattentiveness in class as one indicator of mild disengagement, and excessive truancy as one indicator of higher disengagement. It is a continual increase in disengagement that results in alienation and ultimately in school dropout.

Alienation occurs in varying degrees and it occurs for many students, even those who are not otherwise at risk for dropping out and who indeed graduate from high school. For example, Wehlage and Rutter (1986) found that students who graduated did not differ from dropouts in their perceptions of teachers (as uncaring) or of the disciplinary system (as unfair and ineffective). All students may experience some degree of alienation, but for some students this alienation is more acute and more dangerous than for others.

Within our framework then, many of the school-related characteristics traditionally viewed as correlates or causes of dropout behavior, such as poor grades, truancy, and disciplinary problems, are characterized as indicators of a high degree of disengagement. Such a conceptualization takes the focus of investigation off the student and places it on an entire system of environmental factors that may affect integration. It also forces a view of dropping out not as a single event in the life of a high school student, but as the culmination of a process of increasing disengagement from school. Using this framework leads to a focus on the day-to-day nuances of the school experience that might make a difference in student engagement.

If we agree that integration is crucial to holding the at-risk student in school, what elements of school life facilitate this integration? A number of authors suggest that both academic and social features of the school must be understood to explain how students become integrated into the institution. Elliott, Voss, and Wendling (1966) describe the format (academic) and informal (social) aspects of school that can affect students at risk for dropping out. A similar dual view of integration has served as a framework for a study of student withdrawal from college (Tinto, 1975). Both academic and social reasons for dropping out can also be found in retrospective studies of dropouts. Lack of academic success is the school-related reason most often cited by dropouts for having left school (Peng, 1983). Yet almost half of the general reasons given relate to some aspect of the student's personal relationships within the school (Pittman, 1986).

Our own conceptualization of student integration in school is composed of these same two subcomponents. The first is the student's level of social engagement in the school. This is the degree to which the student has developed comfortable, cooperative relationships with others (peers, teachers, counselors, administrators). The second is the student's level of academic engagement in the school. This relates to the ways in which the student responds to the academic demands and learning tasks that are confronted in school. Like Tinto (1975) and Elliott et al. (1966), we believe that student engagement in at least one subcomponent, either academic or social, is necessary (and may be sufficient) for keeping at-risk students in school.

Thus, our framework for examining the experiences of LD adolescents in high school has two major foci: (a) student experiences related to the social (socialization) aspects of schooling, and (b) student experiences related to the academic (cognitive) aspects of schooling. Within each of these two foci there are subcomponents that will be explored as the entire data set is analyzed. This paper focuses on the structural aspects of academic engagement. Other papers will deal with the cognitive subject matter aspects of academic engagement, the personal aspects of social engagement, and the unique experience of one student who is in the process of disengaging from school.

THE RESEARCH SITE

The data for this study were collected at a small junior-senior high school, which we will call Wilson Township Junior-Senior High School. It is located in a blue-collar community of 24,000. About half of the labor force (54%) works in the community's growing business district; the median annual income per family is $17,000. Approximately 13% of the population is listed in the 1980 census as below the poverty level.

Approximately 63% of Wilson Township's population is white. In addition to a considerable migration into the township of younger black families in the last 10 years, there has been a shift in the age of the population. For blacks, the median age is 26; for whites it is 41. Thus, the school population is expected to have a lower percentage of white students over time.

Main Street in Wilson Township is bordered by shops and fast food restaurants and is generally bustling with activity. Thanks to federal urban renewal funds, the town's streets and public buildings are in good repair, giving it an air of prosperity.

Wilson Township Junior-Senior High School (WT) is located on a brick street one block north of Main Street, next to the former junior high school, which is now empty and boarded up. The senior high school building was opened in 1911, with an annex built in 1927. WT serves a total student population of 997 in grades 7–12; approximately 85% of the student body is black. There are 80 classroom teachers in the school, approximately 4% are black males, 14% black females, 44% white males, and 38% white females. The principal estimates that 25–28% of graduating students enroll in some form of post-secondary education.

The school system underwent a significant transformation in the 1983–84 academic year. Due to declining enrollments and budgetary constraints, the junior high school was closed and its students were moved into the high school building. The seventh-, eighth-, and ninth-grade students are now housed on the third floor of the 76-year-old structure; the 10th- through 12th-grade students are on the bottom two floors. There is some scheduling of the younger and older students together in study halls and nonacademic subjects such as gym or art. The combination of the two schools has caused some space problems; study halls, for example, are sometimes scheduled in the auditorium or the gymnasium.

Special education services are provided by the district, with the exception of services for emotionally disturbed students (which are provided by the local Intermediate Unit).

Approximately 7% of the student population is labeled as learning disabled. The learning disabilities program consists of three self-contained LD classrooms in the junior high school and three resource rooms in the high school (one for math, science, and health; one for English; and one for social studies).

SUBJECTS

Six students—three LD and three non-LD—were chosen as target students for this study. Target students were selected from six pools of 10th- and 11th-grade students in regular and vocational education tracks: 10th-grade LD, 10th-grade regular education, 11th-grade LD normal track, 11th-grade LD vocational track, 11th-grade regular education normal track, and 11th-grade regular education vocational track. The design included 10th-grade rather than 9th-grade because 9th-grade is considered part of the junior high school. Only boys were included in the student pools because factors associated with dropout for girls appear to be different from those associated with boys (Peng, 1983), and because boys are dominant in the LD population (Hallahan & Kauffman, 1986).

In any study of dropping out, researchers are confronted with a dilemma: include poor attenders in the pools, who, if selected, would be difficult to observe and interview, or exclude them from the student pools so that all subjects would be present for data collection on a regular basis. We chose the second course; by selecting LD students who were present regularly, we would still be able to visit classrooms of at-risk students.

Figure 1 summarizes the numbers of eligible students in each of the six pools from which subjects for this study were randomly selected. There were only two subjects in the 11th-grade LD vocational education cell who had reasonable attendance records, and both declined to participate in the study. Thus we were forced to select a low attender to represent this cell.

Table 1 shows achievement data for the three LD students selected for the study at time of placement and Table 2 shows achievement

| | Grade 10 | Grade 11 | |
	General	General	Vocational
LD	6	6	(3) 2 + 1
Regular Ed	64	39	17

Figure 1. Student pools for subject selection

data for the three regular education students at the most recent testing. Data were unavailable for one regular education student.

RESEARCH METHODS

In the spring of 1986, a pilot study was conducted in one learning disabilities classroom to develop a full field note data gathering procedure and to collect preliminary data. At that time, 15 classes were observed, and three students were interviewed. High-achieving high school students were also interviewed to get a sense of contrast, that is, how their experience might differ from regular and LD subjects. Based on the results of the pilot study, the observation protocol and interview guide for use during the subsequent school year were designed.

Data were collected from November, 1986 to May, 1987. Each of the six target students was observed in three classes (English, math, and social studies) for three consecutive days each month, using the full field note method (Olson, 1976). Observers took extensive field notes during classroom observations, attempting to keep an ethnographic record of the class as a whole, the activities of the teacher, and the behaviors of the target student at least every 2 minutes. These notes were then elaborated through dictations into a tape recorder and transcribed to form a rich data base of the classroom life experiences of LD and regular students.

A second component of the data base was provided through formal, semi-structured interviews of target students, conducted once each month. Students were asked to describe the events of their day and their feelings about those events. The opportunity was also taken to ask

TABLE 1. Target Students' Achievement Data for Special Education Students

	IQ	Year of Placement	Grade When Placed in LD	Grade Equivalents at Time of Placement		Source
				Math	Reading	
George	85	1982	6.8	4.5	3.5	Stanford
Rahvid	83	1982	6.8	4.9	5.9	Stanford
Marvin	108	1980	5.1	4.5	2.1	WRAT

Note: WRAT = Wide Range Achievement Test.

TABLE 2. Target Students' Achievement Data for Regular Education Students

	Year When Tested	Grade When Tested	Grade Equivalents		Source
			Math	Reading	
Tod	1985	8.7	9.0	8.0	CAT
Elliott	1985	9.6	8.0	8.9	CTBS
Neil	—	—	—	—	—

Note: CAT = California Achievement Test; CTBS = Comprehensive Test of Basic Skills.

students to reflect on the classes that had been observed and to elaborate their impressions of classroom events. Formal interviews were tape recorded and transcribed for analysis. These data bases were supplemented by less formal field notes based on observations outside of classrooms and informal interviews with teachers, administrators, and nontarget students.

Finally, in order to document the nature of the cognitive demands made of students in both the special education and mainstream settings and the general school climate, archival materials such as teacher plans, student assignments, and school policies were also collected and carefully analyzed.

The greatest threat to validity of this methodology is what Smith and Geoffrey (1968) refer to as the "two realities" problem. Because field notes cannot include everything that occurs in the classroom, there exists a potential bias in the selection of events to record. An attempt was made to overcome this and other possible sources of bias through several triangulation techniques. First, to counteract possible biases in data collection, multiple observers were employed (Denzin,

1978; Patton, 1980). Observations and interviews were conducted by the first author and three graduate student assistants. Second, multiple data sources were used to compare the consistency of emerging trends (Patton, 1980). As often as possible, a trend that was identified in one data source was corroborated by at least one other data source. Third, two analysts independently reviewed the data set and compared their findings. Finally, the data were thoroughly searched for disconfirming evidence (Erickson, 1986; Wolf, 1975).

For the period of November through May, the data base consists of field notes on 211 English, math, and social studies classes (59 special education and 152 regular education) and 29 formal interviews.

FINDINGS

Our overriding impression of WT was that the skill levels of students were quite low and the setting demands of mainstream, as well as special education classes, also seemed to be at a low level. It was also clear, early on in the data collection, that the common displays of institutional alienation, such as perceptions of unfair discipline or uncaring teachers, were not present. The overall dropout rate for learning disabled students at WT appeared to be about 25%, approximately 10% lower than that of the large urban district adjacent to WT (Morrow, Thornton, & Zigmond, 1987).

During data collection and analysis, our initial impressions of a lower standard of expectation at WT grew into the perception of a larger, more complex process of support and institutionalized responsiveness which we refer to as *accommodation*. Accommodation is defined as an environmental responsiveness to the needs and/or desires of students, as those needs or desires are perceived by various institutional actors. It represents an effort to adjust the demands of school life to bring them more into correspondence with the realities of adolescent life, a willingness to compromise on the part of the school in order to reconcile student needs and school demands. Accommodation functions in a variety of ways: to modify the demands made of students, to provide support for students in meeting those demands, or to provide alternate means by which students may meet the demands of schooling. It also operates at various levels: *institutional* accommodation is reflected in schoolwide rules and policies and their waiver, *classroom* accommodation is reflected in the adjustments that teachers make to tasks and setting demands, and *personal* accommodation is reflected in the responsiveness of teachers to the personal needs of individual students.

These accommodations appear to facilitate the academic engagement of students who are at risk and may serve to retard a gradual process of academic disengagement that might normally affect this group of students. Since programs which offer responsive environments for students have often been recommended for potential dropouts (Natriello, McDill, & Pallas, 1985), we might even speculate that there is some relationship between the high levels of accommodation to students that we observed and the comparatively lower dropout rate found in this high school.

Evidence for each of the three types of accommodation is presented in the next section. This is followed by a discussion of how accommodation may relate to the larger issue of academic integration of at-risk students, and the possible unintended negative side effects of such accommodation.

Accommodation at the Institutional Level

Accommodation at the institutional level is defined as a concern for student needs that is reflected in the administrative processes that govern the school. At the institutional level, accommodation was noted in several respects. First, school policies reflected a concern for maximizing students' chances of successfully meeting the demands of schooling. Second, such policies embedded a degree of flexibility that enabled administrators, counselors, and teachers to adjust conditions to individual circumstances.

One of the best examples of accommodation at the institutional level was reflected in the school response to a fairly strict attendance and promotion policy. The attendance policy stipulated that:

> any student who is absent from school and/or class for a period of eleven (11) days or more during the total school year for reasons other than verified medical (doctor's note), or administratively approved absences will not receive credit for the year, or the class. (Wilson Township, Board Policy and Procedures)

This policy has serious implications for at-risk students because it would make it virtually impossible for students with poor attendance records to pass any of their classes and would ensure retention.

Institutional level accommodation was reflected in a supplemental policy that gave students a second (or third or fourth) chance to pass the year. By attending an afterschool program, students were allowed to "buy back" their unexcused absences and clear their records. Attendance at three afterschool sessions (of 1 ½ hours each) bought back one unexcused absence. Thus, it was theoretically possible for a student to miss up to 45 days of school in the beginning of the school year, and still have enough school days left to make up the time in the afterschool program.

Approximately 20 students per day attended the afterschool program. During the afterschool period, students were required to be working on school work, although there were no stipulations about what work that should be. One of our target students, Marvin, took advantage of the afterschool program in the year prior to this study, and despite a month's worth of absences was able to pass 10th grade.

Accommodation at the Classroom Level

Classroom level accommodation reflects the ways in which teachers modify the setting demands of their classrooms in response to students who may have trouble in meeting higher levels of demand. Setting demands (Schumaker & Deshler, 1984) are conceptualized as the teacher's expectations for students and the skills students must develop in order to meet those expectations. Mainstreaming literature suggests that in order to maximize the possibility of special education students' success in the mainstream, mainstream teachers might make modifications in the materials they use, in their teaching procedures, and in the tasks that they require of these students (Laurie, Buchwach, Silverman, & Zigmond, 1978; Lewis & Doorlag, 1983). A review of field notes in these areas revealed accommodations in: (a) the selection of curricular materials, (b) the selection of instructional delivery methods, (c) the selection of academic tasks required of students, and (d) the selection of assessment procedures.

Selection of Curricular Materials. One trend noted in classroom observations and corroborated through interviews is that most teachers in WT believed it necessary to modify curricula and simplify tasks that they required of *all* their students, not just the mainstreamed special education students.

Four of the mainstream teachers involved in this study commented independently that they had simplified the content of their courses because their students would otherwise have difficulty. Mr. E., for example, confided that each math class in WT was actually taught at an academic level below that suggested by its title. Thus, a class that is listed as "academic" was actually taught as a "general level class" and a "general" class was actually taught as a "remedial" one.

Reflecting a similar view, Mr. C. expressed concern with finding suitable curriculum materials for a mainstream literature class:

> A student in the class asks Mr. C. whether or not he is going to use the 'academic book'. The student is referring to a book that is on Mr. C.'s desk called *Adventures in Appreciation.* Mr. C. explains that he wants to start using the book with this class, and they will probably start using it in January. A student asks, "Is it only this class you're going to try it with?", and the teacher says, "yes." After class, Mr. C. explained to me that he wants to use the literature book, but thinks it might be too difficult for these students. In any case, he'll give it a try. (field notes, December 12, 1986)

In February, Mr. C. explained that he preferred the *Adventures in Appreciation* book because it contained works by Poe, Chekhov, and other prominent literary figures, but that he had aborted his attempt to use it because it was too difficult. Instead, he was assigning stories from the Delta level of the *Journeys* series, which is actually a 10th-grade book for this 11th-grade class. His 10th-grade class would continue using the Banner level of *Journeys,* which is actually an eighth-grade book.

Instructional Delivery. Accommodation was also evident in the way teachers delivered instruction; teachers chose a means of instructional delivery that minimized the skills required of students to acquire information.

For example, social studies students are typically required to extract important information from reading text materials (Deshler, Putnam, & Bulgren, 1985). Students in Mr. G.'s mainstream American History class, however, were almost never required to exercise such skill because Mr. G. (in 80% of the classes observed) read the text aloud. As students followed along in their books, Mr. G. stopped intermittently to define terms or give examples. He also paraphrased the main ideas from each passage after he read it.

In special education, the instructional delivery model obviated *any* need for students to read text material. Mrs. J. outlined each textbook chapter on the blackboard, then asked questions that could be answered by referring to the blackboard outline. Questions on the material were assigned as seatwork, but students relied on their outlines to answer these questions, without ever having to refer to the text material itself.

Two additional forms of instructional delivery were observed that helped students who had poor notetaking skills to record information that was important. One was a notetaking guide. It consisted of a ditto outline of information that the teacher reviewed in a lecture presentation. In various places on the notetaking guide, important information was left blank and students were required to fill in the missing information. In a variation of this technique, the teacher wrote on the blackboard or on an overhead projector an outline of the important points of the lecture that students copied into their notebooks. These notetaking guides (along with "review sheets") not only presented the material to the students in such a way that independent thought was unnecessary, but also played an important role in two additional forms of accommodation, the nature of student assessment and the simplification of cognitive tasks that students were asked to perform.

Assessment. Evaluation of student performance reflected accommodation of students in several ways. First, student grades were determined not only by their test scores but also by the number of homework assignments students completed. Second, even during times of academic accountability, such as during test-

ing, teachers often gave students "a break" to enhance their performance. Finally, there was an extremely high degree of overlap between tests and instruction. Each of these examples of accommodation is described below.

Students' final grades for each nine-week grading period were derived from quizzes, tests, and homework assignments. Invariably, teachers did not grade homework assignments for accuracy, but rather assigned students points for having completed their homework assignments. Students who had trouble with the course material could improve their grade by completing homework, even though they did not complete it accurately, because in many cases homework completions were weighted equally with test scores to determine the final grade.

Neil, one of the target students, explained how homework grading worked in several of his classes:

[He's checking] if we have our homework and how it is done. We might miss a few problems. We have a check and a check minus. Zero is when we don't do it at all, check minus is when half of it is like incomplete, and check is when it is all complete, and a check is worth 15 points, check minus is worth 10 points, and zero is worth nothing. At the end of the nine weeks, he (Mr. N.) adds them all up, and they'll be like 105 points and a certain number out of 105 is an A, B, and all the way down to F. However many points you got, that is your grade....

[In geometry] we give him our paper, and we get a check if it's done or at least tried, and if you don't, you get a zero. I get all the checks for every homework so I get 100%.

Interviewer: So, if you have 10 problems and you have 5 of them correct? See I don't know about that, but if you have like 8, he'll still give you a check for the problems that you tried.

[In geometry] how well I do on the test [is most important] cause that is where I do low at. My homework is good, I get 100% on my homework, but I study for the test and I don't get them right.

In English ... he just marks down how many we got done for the whole year. We go over it like a few times in class like when we're in the English book ... He don't really touch it, he just looks at the notebook, and he turns the pages all the way to, if we like have 10 for the 9 weeks, we turn it to the 10 pages and he marks in the book 10 homework assignments ... That's one thing, he'll never know if we got them wrong ... I like that a lot cause I don't care. (interview with Neil, February 3, 1987)

A second form of accommodation that affects the process of evaluation of student performance is teacher flexibility. George described this flexibility when we asked him what happens in his LD class if he falls behind in his work:

I could just, once I get done with first, um, work I did, I can go to the day that I missed, I mean the day that I missed the work ... I do that work and then just go on, go on like that. And he'll give me enough time to, um, finish it. He'll give me, if I don't finish it, the, um, period I suppose to finish it, then don't worry about; um, 'I'll give it to you next period when you get done with your English.' ... And he'll let you off the hook. If you [don't] do your homework, he'll say 'Okay, you do, do it now and turn it in and if you get a 'F' on a paper, he'll give the paper back to you, say, 'Do it over' and he'll grade it over again. (interview with George, June 11, 1986)

Another way of "letting students off the hook" is by modifying procedures for testing to maximize the student's ability to perform well. In regular education, it was Mr. G.'s policy to allow students to use their notes and textbooks during the last 5 minutes of the test. In special education, Mrs. J. postponed a test for two students when she discovered that the students hadn't learned the material. In some instances, tests no longer functioned as occasions in which students independently demonstrated the level to which they had mastered the material. This was particularly true in LD classrooms where students received considerable assistance from the teacher during "tests." As can be seen from the following excerpt, even when the teacher verbalized that students were expected to perform independently, they actually did not. On this day, George was one of two students who was taking a test on map reading skills using a road map of Pennsylvania:

[Ms. J.] explains that she will give the test to the two people who are ready and the others will have to work on their make up work ... [Later], she is with George ... who is asking for help on one of the items on the test. The question reads . . . "What state runs along Pennsylvania's northern border?" Ms. J. tells him, "Let me say that on Friday there was a short question which asked you to name the states that border Pennsylvania." She asks him if that sounds familiar, and he says, "yeah" and points to an area on the map. She says, "Northern" and asks him to show her which direction is north. George points up towards the top left corner of the map in a northwesterly direction. Ms. J. indicates he should think about it for a while, then she goes to Paul who's asking a question about ... the worksheet. ...
At 12:48 Ms. J. is [again] with George asking [him], "Did you figure which way north is?" [While she asks this] she holds up the corner of the map that has a compass indicator, showing north, south, east, and west ... At 12:50 the teacher is with George explaining that his answer is right, "except you left off the first word" ... [Later, when] Anthony finishes his worksheet ... Ms. J. asks him if he feels confident enough to take the test and explains, as she had to George earlier: "I can help you with the reading and understanding the questions, but not with the answers."
At 12:59 George asks a question about State College, referring to a question on the test which requires him to locate the town. He seems puzzled by this. Ms. J. says to him, "Well, it wouldn't be here," pointing to the list of recreation areas where George had been looking, "It's a city." Once she tells him this, he seems to understand. At 1:07 George turns in his test paper and asks Ms. J. if she's going to check it now. She sits down at her desk and pulls out the map ... [when she] finishes, [she] tells George that he got them all right. (field notes, October 14, 1986)

A third form of accommodation in student assessment was evident in the nature of tests themselves, specifically their overlap with content. Overlap is the degree to which material on a specific test has been covered by instruction (Leinhardt & Seewald, 1981). A high degree of overlap is accommodating to students because it does not require students to bring knowledge gained outside of the class to the test situation in order to pass the test. It is also a form of accommodation because if students are told explicitly where and how the overlap will occur, they not only know what material they should study for the test, they also do not have to engage in the metacognitive task of "knowing what to know."

In WT, we noted that the review sheet or notetaking guide played a critical accommodating role in student evaluation by defining the overlap of course content and test. Mr. G. reminded his class often that the smart person will pay close attention to the reviews because some of those questions "might show up again."

The more that teachers accommodated to students' low metacognitive functioning, the more comfortable students felt about their classes. Tod described how difficult he found a class at his former high school where he had to take notes independently and did not know what would be on the test. He then compared the former teacher's method with Mr. T.'s, his current World Cultures teacher:

> He'd show us movies on the solar system and all that and we would take notes on it, and from our notes, we would have to study for a test. He wouldn't give us any notes. We would have to take notes for ourselves. We wouldn't know what was on the test or if our notes was correct or not, so you could be writing down certain things and they wouldn't even be on the test. You could be writing down facts and studying, and they ain't going to be on the test, and you'll be all messed up . . . .
> Like you know, like Mr. [T.], he knows what's going to be on the test and he writes on the overhead and he tells you to write that down and study that. The other teacher didn't do that, and we didn't know what was going to be on the test. He gives us, you could say it's notes because he gives us a ditto, right, and it has like completion questions, and the answers are in the book, and like if you read the whole chapter and there are certain sentences that he wants you to know, like the facts, they are already written down on the ditto sheet, and then you just fill in the answers from the book. That's like your notes. You know for sure that the other notes are going to

be on the test. You study from that, you'll pass the test with ease . . . You could say it's all in the dittos though. The whole test is on the dittos. (interview with Tod, December 18, 1986)

Student perceptions of classroom activities were greatly affected by their expectations for explicit overlap between classroom presentations and tests. The content of the test defined for students the content matter of the course, thus considerably narrowing the scope of the information students attended to (LeMahieu & Leinhardt, 1985). Elliott, for example, found much of social studies class irrelevant because he knew that the elaborations and embellishments to the text being presented by the teacher were not going to be on the test. As a result he often fell asleep in class:

> [On the tests] all you got to do is write down what he said and he gives you credit for it. He is kind of, I wouldn't say boring, yeah, he is kind of boring . . . cause um, in my other classes, they give a lesson, I'm wide awake . . . I'm awake and I listen to the teacher . . . [but he] puts me to sleep cause he confuses me, sometimes cause he'll relate something that went on like in American History like in the Revolution with today's problems . . . It don't really mean nothing cause he ain't really talking about the book . . . That's what's confusing. They ain't on the test. (interview with Elliott, December 12, 1986)

A final example of accommodation in assessment was evident in relatively low levels of cognitive demand of the tests themselves, a natural outcome of the high degree of overlap between study guide or review sheets and the test. For example, in one social studies test, 18 out of 22 test items (81%) were items that had been included on the review sheet that the teacher read aloud just before the students took the test. Of those 18 items, 13 required a verbatim answer, that is, an answer that required students to use the same language in answering the test item as was used in instruction, or to provide the same examples that were provided in instruction (Anderson, 1972). The cognitive task required for studying for a verbatim item exam is quite different from that required for a test composed of paraphrase items or items in which students must draw inferences. Verbatim items require a kind of memorization that may even interfere with comprehension of the material being learned (Doyle, 1983). We viewed the predominance of memorization tasks over comprehension items on tests as a cognitive accommodation that demands little complex thinking on the part of students.

Personal Accommodation

The final level of accommodation, termed *personal accommodation,* relates to the personal relationship between individual students and teachers in WT. Personal accommodation refers to the general level of teacher involvement with students, their expressions of interest, acceptance, and support. Personal accommodation manifests itself in teacher responsiveness to individual student needs, either academic or nonacademic.

Personal accommodation was much more evident in special education than in regular education classes. It was clear that LD teachers at Wilson have a great deal of knowledge about and concern for the students in their charge. This was noticeable in their faculty room conversation: "Was Marvin absent again?; George is really having difficulty in his mainstream health class, maybe we should move him back into the resource room; Rahvid forgot the job application you gave him."

It was also noticeable in the nurturing atmosphere of the LD classroom:

I'm seated in the classroom . . . when Billy, a student not in this class, and another boy come in and walk over to Mrs. A., who is sitting at her desk. He says, "We're coming up to your house tonight to get back that tape." Mrs. A. laughs and exclaims that it's not her fault that they weren't here yesterday to pick up the tape, and pulls a videotape from her drawer and hands it to Billy. Another boy comes into the classroom frowning. Mrs. A. says to him, "It's such a beautiful day, what's the matter with you?" He says he has a headache. At this moment, Mike enters the room carrying a wine rack that he has made in wood shop. The teacher's aide, Mrs. D.,

and Mrs. A. both compliment him profusely on the rack and he beams. The bell rings and Rahvid enters the classroom with Lionel. Mrs. D. asks Rahvid about a speech that he is planning to read during announcements for black history week. She is inquiring how long it is, and Rahvid comments that he's afraid that it will take about five minutes. Mrs. A. reassures him that if Mrs. Q. helped him to write it, it will be alright. The aide asks about another student who is not present. She saw him driving his grandfather's car on Sunday and wonders because she thought he wasn't allowed to drive anymore . . . [Later], Mrs. A. comments sympathetically to Kevin, who's been sitting with his head down on his desk, "Your head's really hurting pretty bad, huh?" He tells her yes, that he had been to the nurse's office and they didn't do anything, but that it hurts behind his eyes and his eye is blurry. Mrs. A. sounds concerned, "You mean you can't see out of your eye?" . . . She then asks the aide to please walk with Kevin down to the office and tell them that his head hurts badly, and he can't see out of one eye, so Mrs. D. and Kevin leave the room. (field notes, February 11, 1987)

It was also apparent that students found their LD teachers to be a major resource when they needed some form of assistance. LD teachers, because they had a personal involvement with and concern for their students, coached them in preparation for tests in other classes, helped them write speeches to read over the P.A. system, helped them fill out job applications, offered advice, listened sympathetically to complaints, and very often, simply chatted with their students:

Interviewer: What will you do in math class tomorrow?
Well, probably talk about this school, Lincoln, and get some information [from Mrs. Q.]. I talked to her about it, you know. I talked, but see, she went to this school, Chelsey University. We're going over all the information I have, but she knew about the school cause she went to Chelsey. She talked about PHEAA, it's like financial aid . . . I was just asking her what would be the best financial aid for me even though I get this scholarship. (interview with Rahvid, November 7, 1986)

Accommodation in LD and Regular Education Settings

Because a large part of the data set for this study was gathered in classrooms, classroom level accommodation and personal accommodation that occurred in the classroom setting can be examined more fully than institutional level accommodation. In order to more closely examine this phenomenon and to ascertain the degree to which it was present differentially in mainstream and LD classrooms, field notes were coded for instances of classroom and personal accommodation. These instances were then used to derive accommodation scores for each setting.

Accommodation scores represent the degree to which teachers take advantage of accommodation opportunities. A score greater than 1 indicates that more than one accommodation was made per opportunity to accommodate. (A teacher might engage in personal interactions with students on several occasions during one class, for example.) A score of less than 1 indicates that accommodation occurred in a proportion of the opportunities. (A teacher might engage in personal interactions once out of every two observations, for example, yielding a score of .5.) Table 3 shows a comparison of the accommodation scores in both regular education and LD classrooms in the three subject areas that were observed. The scores suggest some interesting trends.

Accommodation occurred to some degree in all subject matters in both the regular education classrooms and the LD classrooms, although the type of accommodation preferred by teachers seems to differ from the resource room to the mainstream.

Instructional Accommodation Scores. Unexpectedly, instructional accommodation appears to be more prevalent in regular education than in special education. This may be due to the nature of instruction in the mainstream as compared to special education. Mainstream teachers teach large group lessons, including lecture and recitation formats where accommodations such as note taking guides and copying teacher notes are more likely. In contrast, special education instructors generally deliver instruction through monitored seatwork activities. The comparatively small difference in accommodation scores between regular education social studies and special education social studies (where both settings used whole group instruction) bears this out.

It is possible that the type of instructional accommodation prevalent in special education is more likely to be reflected in a high degree of curricular accommodation which is, by definition, endemic to special education but not demonstrable in this data set.

Assessment Accommodation Scores. The level of assessment accommodation appears to be equivalent in regular and LD settings, except in math, where the LD setting is much more accommodating. A closer examination of the subcategories of assessment accommodation in

TABLE 3.   Accommodation Scores in LD and Regular Education

	English		Math		Social Studies	
	LD	NLD	LD	NLD	LD	NLD
Instructional						
Accommodation	.06	.19	0.0	.34	.43	.59
Assessment						
Accommodation	.53	.64	2.36	1.05	.76	.63
Personal						
Accommodation	1.04	.02	.60	.08	.37	.15

Note. LD = learning disabled; NLD = not learning disabled.

LD math reveals two things. Most of the accommodation was in the form of the teacher's providing assistance on tests. Further, only one test was observed in this setting (out of a total of 10 observations). That tests are relatively low frequency events was borne out by interview data where students report few tests in LD math.

By contrast, the regular education math setting shows most assessment accommodation to occur through grading. The grading accommodation score (.95) indicates that the mainstream math teacher made some alteration in grading almost every time that grading was observed.

Personal Accommodation Scores. The most consistent trend noted in the accommodation scores is that personal accommodation was much more prevalent in the LD setting than in the mainstream. It is difficult to determine the extent to which this phenomenon may relate to class size. The average size of the LD classroom was 6 students as compared to the average size of 20 students in the regular education class. One might expect teachers to become more personally involved with students when they have fewer students to interact with and get to know.

Yet even subcategories of personal accommodation that might be unaffected by class size (allowing students to work on other activities and helping them with such activities, for example) show larger scores in LD classrooms. Accommodation scores for these two subcategories are zero for all regular classes except one (in which the score was only .02).

Effects of Accommodation

Observations and interviews in Wilson Township Junior-Senior High School over five months have confirmed our contention that schools can play an important role in affecting students' academic engagement and overall integration into school life. We found numerous examples by which school policy and staff were able to facilitate this academic engagement through institutional, classroom, and personal accommodation. We found that administrators and teachers consciously tried to limit the demands made on students or to provide alternate means by which students could meet those demands. And we found that students were aware of the accommodating aspects of their environment and even came to anticipate accommodation. We believe that the kinds of accommodations outlined in this paper may play a key role in keeping students academically engaged enough to be able to complete their high school careers. Although accommodation may be helpful in reducing the most extreme levels of disengagement and alienation, and may impact positively on the school's holding power, it does not necessarily promote active engagement in school and it may have some unintended negative side effects that actually limit what students get out of school.

One side effect has to do with student expectations that accommodations will always be made. These expectations are evident at the institutional level as well as at the personal level. For example, Marvin was unconcerned that he was not meeting school attendance requirements because he expected that some "arrangement" would be made to help him pass the year, as had been done before. When asked what he thought was going to happen as a result of his large number of unexcused absences, he explained:

> [Last year] I had to go to afterschool for a month . . . like after school . . . like in the spring. [This year, I'm doing] bad . . . F's; All F's. So that means I got to get straight A's [to pass]. I have to talk to Mr. R. [the counselor] . . . to see how many days I got to make up . . . I won't flunk though . . . I'll probably go to summer school. (interview with Marvin, February 17, 1987)

A second side effect is that school learning did not require even moderate levels of active student engagement with the content of instruction. Our six target students spent a great deal of classtime "shuffling" information from one external form to another, without ever truly learning it: They copied information from the blackboard into their notebooks, read information from their notebooks aloud to the class, and copied information from their notebooks onto their homework papers. But interviews revealed that students could perform these information shuffling tasks without paying very much attention to the information itself or even understanding the ideas that were conveyed in the notes they were copying or in the answers they were reading. Tod explained: "I never pay attention to what he says in World Cultures, I just write down the notes . . . I can't even remember what he said today" (interview with Tod, November 24, 1986).

Or students like George participated in class discussions and did well in homework assignments as long as study guides or outlines were in front of them, but ran into difficulty every time they were required to use the information they were supposed to be learning without the guide. We saw students commit information that they did not understand to memory and be relatively unconcerned about making sense out of the information. In an interview after a social studies class, Rahvid explained how he was going to go about working on his first term paper: "Well, first you read the book, and then you see if there's any bibliographies, that's lost, lost articles . . . lost articles that have to be found like in the encyclopedia" (interview with Rahvid, December 4, 1986).

A review of Rahvid's assignment sheet revealed a typographical error on the note-taking guide ("Bibliography: a lost [sic] of articles"). Rahvid appeared unconcerned about this definition. When questioned about it, he looked puzzled and seemed to realize that it did not make sense, but he proceeded with the assignment anyway.

A third side effect of accommodation was student boredom and apathy: "It's just boring. Class is boring. Seem like the class is never goin' end. We just take notes and read all the time. That ain't no fun all the time" (interview with Tod, January 28, 1987). Some students felt they had been exposed to the same material too often (and they probably had been). Elliott, who did not pass an end-of-year test for Introductory Algebra I, was placed in basic math class instead of Algebra II. He felt that it was too easy for him

and that he shouldn't be in that class because it was: "old stuff. Stuff I did. Some of it, I think second grade could do the work" (interview with Elliott, November 20, 1986).

Students like Elliott hungered for a challenge in their educational experience: "I like [this new unit on the metric system]. I like it cause it's hard, it's a challenge. The other chapters wasn't a challenge" (interview with Elliott, December 12, 1986).

Paradoxically, the same students who complain of the lack of challenge did not necessarily perform well in their "easy" classes. They often assumed that they knew the material and didn't need to study for tests, although this perception was often inaccurate:

> Interviewer: How did you do on your report card?
> S: I got a B in it. I'm gonna get an A but I messed up one test on multiplying decimals or just plain multiplying with like three-digit numbers. I thought I knew it, but I'll get an A. Most definitely. (interview with Elliott, November 20, 1987)

CONCLUSIONS

It appears that accommodation, as described in this paper, may serve to keep at-risk students from total alienation and increase the holding power of a high school. Yet our research also suggests that accommodation may unintentionally limit students' levels of academic engagement and, because of its unintended negative side effects, ultimately limit the usefulness of students' school experiences.

Such a conclusion demands further investigation into accommodation. At present, for example, we know very little about what types of accommodation most influence students' level of engagement with school or are most valued by students. For example, do classroom level instructional accommodations impact students more positively than accommodations in student assessments? Do personal accommodations differ in importance from accommodations related to academic demands? Does the impact of each accommodation differ from one student to another? And, perhaps most crucially, does accommodation necessitate the lowering of academic standards, as appears to have happened at WT?; are lower academic standards necessary in order to keep students in school (see Natriello, McDill, & Pallas, 1985)?

Further research into accommodation may lead us toward answers to these questions. A promising possibility is that personal accommodation may be quite potent in and of itself. A separate analysis of our data suggests that personal accommodation of LD students provides a mechanism by which teachers can influence students' social integration into the school community (Miller, Zigmond, & Leinhardt, 1988). The sense of belonging and attachment that results may be the strongest positive influence that holds at-risk students in school (see Fine, 1985; Wehlage, 1983).

If further research into accommodation yields fruitful results, the next step will be to examine school factors that facilitate or impede it. In this context, McPartland's (1987) work supports our impression of a trade-off between academic excellence and a responsive school environment. His data demonstrate that goals of higher achievement are often met at the expense of positive teacher-student relations, and vice versa. Continued research on school organization may lead to creative solutions to the dilemmas facing schools and teachers in meeting both goals of academic excellence and positive, responsive student-teacher relations.

Our sense is that accommodation, although it may keep students in school, may not only limit adolescents' acquisition of formal knowledge, but may also be a poor model for preparing adolescents for the world beyond school. Believing that there will always be a second chance, learning that you can get through school without challenge and hard work, and being bored may teach students to look for second chances, to not seek challenges or hard work, and to not persist. Examining these unintended negative side effects of accommodation, and understanding how different types of accommodation affect students sets an important research agenda for under-

standing why students choose to leave school. For, to paraphrase Wehlage and Rutter (1986), the challenge at Wilson Township Junior-Senior High School and other secondary schools is not simply to keep students in school until graduation, but to provide them with educationally worthwhile experiences while they are there.

REFERENCES

Anderson, R. C. (1972). How to construct achievement tests to assess comprehension. *Review of Educational Research, 42*, 145-170.

Denzin, N. K. (1978). *The research act.* New York: McGraw-Hill.

Deshler, D. D., Putnam, M. L., & Bulgren, J. A. (1985). Academic accommodations for adolescents with behavior and learning problems. In S. Braaden, R. B. Rutherford, & W. Evans (Eds.), *Programming for adolescents with behavioral disorders* (pp. 21-31). Reston, VA: Council for Children with Behavioral Disorders.

Doyle, W. (1983). Academic work. *Review of Educational Research, 53*, 159-199.

Dudlay-Marling, C. C., & Edmiaston, R. (1985). Social status of learning disabled children and adolescents: A review. *Learning Disability Quarterly, 8*, 189-209.

Ekstrom, R. B., Goertz, M. E., Pollack, J. M., & Rock, D. A. (1986). Who drops out of high school and why? Findings from a national study. *Teachers College Record, 87*, 356-373.

Elliott, D. S., Voss, H. L., & Wendling, A. (1966). Capable dropouts and the social milieu of the high school. *Journal of Educational Research, 60*, 180-186.

Erickson, F. (1986). Qualitative methods in research on teaching. In M. Wittrock (Ed.). *Handbook of research on teaching.* New York: Macmillan.

Fine, M. (1985). Dropping out of high school: An inside look. *Social Policy, 16*, 43-50.

Garret, M. K., & Crump, D. W. (1980). Peer acceptance, teacher preference, and self-appraisal of social status among learning disabled students. *Learning Disability Quarterly, 3*, 42-48.

Goodlad, J. I. (1984). *A place called school.* New York: McGraw-Hill.

Hallahan, D. P., & Kauffman, J. M. (1986). *Exceptional children: Introduction to special education.* Englewood Cliffs, NJ: Prentice Hall.

Hill, C. R. (1979). Capacities, opportunities, and educational investments: The case of the high school dropout. *The Review of Economics and Statistics, 61,* 9-20.

Laurie, T. E., Buchwach, L., Silverman, R., & Zigmond, N. (1978). Teaching secondary learning disabled students in the mainstream. *Learning Disability Quarterly, 1,* 62-72.

Leinhardt, G., & Seewald, A. M. (1981). Overlap: What's tested, what's taught? *Journal of Educational Measurement, 18*(2), 85-95.

LeMahieu, P., & Leinhardt, G. (1985). Overlap: Influencing what's taught: A process model of teacher's content selection. *Journal of Classroom Interaction, 21*(1), 2-11.

Levin, E., Zigmond, N., & Birch, J. (1985). A follow-up study of 52 learning disabled adolescents. *Journal of Learning Disabilities, 18,* 2-7.

Lewis, R. B., & Doorlag, D. H. (1983). *Teaching special students in the mainstream.* Columbus, OH: Merrill.

McPartland, J. M. (1987). *Balancing high quality subject-matter instruction with positive teacher-student relations in the middle grades: Effects of departmentalization, tracking and block scheduling on learning environments* (Report No. 15). Baltimore, MD: Johns Hopkins University, Center for Research on Elementary & Middle Schools.

Miller, S. E., Zigmond, N., & Leinhardt, G. (1988, April). *Experiential features of high school for students at risk for dropout: An ethnography of social integration.* Paper presented at the annual meeting of the American Educational Research Association, New Orleans.

Morrow, D., Thornton, H., & Zigmond, N. (1987). *Graduating and dropping out of high school.* Unpublished manuscript, University of Pittsburgh, Institute for Practice and Research in Education.

Natriello, G. (1984). Problems in the evaluation of students and student disengagement from secondary schools. *Journal of Research and Development in Education, 17*(4), 14-23.

Natriello, G., McDill, E. L., & Pallas, A. M. (1985). School reform and potential dropouts. *Educational Leadership, 43,* 10-14.

Newmann, F. M. (1981). Reducing student alienation in high schools: Implications of theory. *Harvard Educational Review, 51,* 546-564.

Olson, S. (1976). *Ideas and data: Process and practice of social research.* Homewood, IL: Dorsey.

Patton, M. Q. (1980). *Qualitative evaluation methods.* Beverly Hills, CA: Sage.

Peng, S. (1983). *High school dropouts: Descriptive information from high school and beyond.* Washington, DC: National Center for Education Statistics.

Pittman, R. B. (1986). Importance of personal, social factors as potential means for reducing high school dropout rate. *The High School Journal, 70*(1), 7-13.

Rogers, H., & Saklofske, D. H. (1985). Self-concepts, locus of control, and performance expectations of learning disabled children. *Journal of Learning Disabilities, 18,* 273-278.

Rumberger, R. W. (1983). Dropping out of high school: The influence of race, sex, and family background. *American Educational Research Journal, 20,* 199-220.

Schumaker, J. B., & Deshler, D. D. (1984). Setting demand variables: A major factor in program planning for the LD adolescent. *Topics in Language Disorders, 4*(2), 22-40.

Sewell, T. E., Palmo, A. J., & Manni, J. L. (1981). High school dropout: Psychological, academic, and vocational factors. *Urban Education, 16*(1), 65-76.

Smith, L. M., & Geoffrey, W. (1968). *The complexities of an urban classroom.* New York: Holt, Rinehart and Winston.

Thomas, A. (1979). Learned helplessness and expectancy factors: Implications for research in learning disabilities. *Review of Educational Research, 49,* 208-221.

Tinto, V. (1975). Dropout from higher education: A theoretical synthesis of recent research. *Review of Educational Research, 45,* 89-125.

Wehlage, G. G. (1983). The marginal high school student: Defining the problem and searching for policy. *Children and Youth Services Review, 5,* 321-342.

Wehlage, G. G., & Rutter, R. A. (1986). Dropping out: How much do schools contribute to the problem? *Teachers College Record, 87,* 374-392.

Wolf, R. L. (1975). Trial by jury: A new evaluation method. *Phi Delta Kappan, 57,* 185-187.

Zigmond, N., & Thornton, H. (1985). Follow-up of post-secondary age LD graduates and dropouts. *LD Research, 1*(1), 50-55.

Evaluation Criteria

1. What is the foreshadowed problem and how clearly is it stated? Is it reformulated later on, after some initial data have been collected?

The foreshadowed question for this research is stated in the first sentence. Once we have read the whole study, however, it appears as if the focus of the study has shifted somewhat, or at least become sharper. The study moves from "documenting the high school experience of LD adolescents in order to understand what features of that experience may influence them to stay in school" to an emphasis on the direct and side effects of "accommodation."

2. Is the conceptual and theoretical framework for the study clear? How well does the literature review argue for the importance of the current research?

A strong theoretical framework is developed around issues of integration and alienation. The authors point out that most of what is known about the effects of these factors on school dropout has come from "retrospective" studies; the implication is that by studying *current* students considered to be at high risk, more useful and powerful inferences will be possible. The literature review, while relatively short, manages to compile an impressive array of evidence to support the argument that the degree of student engagement is predictable based upon certain social and academic influences, and that a study such as this should be able to identify these influences and assess their potential strength.

3. What are the biases and preconceived ideas of the researcher? How are these dealt with in the study? Is the researcher well prepared to complete the study?

The presence of bias is difficult to assess in this study, as the authors do not address the

Discussion Questions

1. Is the problem statement too general? If so, how would you rephrase it?

2. Based on the framework presented, how, if at all, is the actual study different from what you might have expected it to be?

3. If you had reviewed the same body of literature, would you have asked different research questions? What might they be?

issue directly. However, previous work by the authors that is cited, on such subjects as "classroom accommodation" (Zigmond) and "overlap" (Leinhardt), suggest that these concepts did not originate with the current study but were imported from previous research. The investigators seem well prepared; this is clearly no "fishing expedition."

4. Is the method of selecting participants clear and appropriate to the foreshadowed problem? How well are the participants and sites described?

The context of the study is well described, although one might wonder about the value of knowing that the town's Main Street is "bordered by shops and fast food restaurants." Inclusion of information regarding the demographic makeup of the school is absolutely necessary, as is the description of physical arrangements of the school and the nature of special education services. In their choice of student participants, the authors delimit their study to male students who attend school regularly. The researchers appear to have had a difficult time gaining participation of the LD students, and were forced to accept at least one student who didn't meet their initial criteria. Given that the LD sample was limited to three, this is a potentially serious problem.

5. How involved is the researcher in the setting being observed? Would this involvement affect the behavior of the participants?

Except for the regular interviews with students, researcher involvement is largely passive, limited to classroom observation and analysis of archival data.

6. If appropriate, are multiple methods of data collection utilized? What was the duration and intensity of data collection?

As noted above, three major data collection methods were used: systematic observation, regularly scheduled and structured interviews,

4. The researchers have clearly done work on this topic before; in what ways is this experience useful for the current study? Not useful?

5. Does the sample size seem small, especially since only three LD students participated? Do you think it would have been better to study a larger group of students less intensively? Why did the authors choose their participants at random, when the general rule for ethnographic studies is to use purposeful sampling?

6. How much do you think the presence of the researchers affected classroom dynamics, especially those involving the target students? How much do you think the interviews affected the target students' later behavior? Can you think of a potentially important source of data that was *not* used in the study?

and an assortment of "archival materials." Observation and recording were extensive: Each of the six target students was observed in class for a total of 211 classes over a seven-month period. The "full note method" resulted in a voluminous data base. The length of the monthly interviews is not given.

7. Are issues of credibility directly addressed by the researchers? How, and how effectively?

The authors refer to the problem of "two realities," acknowledging the potential of bias in the selection of events to record during a classroom observation. They deal with this by employing triangulation, using multiple observers and multiple sources of data. They also engage in cross-examination of the data through independent analyses and a search for "disconfirming evidence," although the procedures for doing the latter are not disclosed.

7. How persuasive do you find these procedures as ways of overcoming bias? Do you think it would be important to know something about whether the "independent analysts" had different perspectives going into the analysis?

8. Are the findings presented clearly? Are the data sufficiently detailed to allow a rich description? Are results accompanied by illustrative quotes and specific instances?

The results contain a generous dose of quotes, and in general these are helpful in understanding the authors' conclusions. Notice, however, how no distinction in the quotes is made between the LD and non-LD students: Often what *appears* to be a statement made by an LD student is instead a quote from a non-LD student in the target group. As a result, the reader is confused about whether "accommodation" pertains just to the LD students or to the entire student body. This point is addressed later in the article, but not very effectively: The accommodation "scores" are inconsistent, and may not even measure accommodation very well, anyway.

8. Is the number and length of direct quotes about right? (Trust your intuition here—there are no hard and fast rules about how much to include.)

9. Do conclusions and interpretations follow logically from the results presented?

The authors present their conclusions and interpretations first, then the evidence

9. Does the order of presentation—overriding concepts first, supporting documentation second—make you suspicious of bias? Or is this just a good and understandable way of presenting complex results?

supporting these conclusions. As noted above, this approach works with only mixed results. Potentially the most intriguing and powerful findings were the "side effects" of accommodation in the form of lowered academic engagement. It is precisely these kinds of unexpected results that make ethnographic studies, with their flexibility to new developments and insights, so useful.

10. Is sufficient detail provided to discern which parts of the study might be applicable to other settings? To which contexts is the study transferable?

Material provided in the quotes, in particular, presents much with which school personnel might identify. The study leaves the reader with a provocative question: How can one "accommodate" LD students—as well as those with other disabilities—and engage them academically at the same time? In this case the implications of the study are highly transferable, well beyond the limited context of the research setting.

10. In ethnographic studies, transferability is up to the reader. What about this study transfers to your own context or experience? What doesn't?

Rites of Passage among Women Reentering Higher Education

Nancy P. Redding
Lima, Ohio

William D. Dowling
Ohio State University

ABSTRACT

The purpose of this article is to review the rites of passage concept; to describe the rites developing among reentry women in both university and home environments; and, finally, to discuss the purposes of and necessity for such rites. Nineteen adult women students were interviewed in depth on the campus of a major midwestern university. Analysis of the data indicates that reentry women and their families are fashioning rites of passage peculiar to their return to higher education in quest of a degree. These rituals facilitate the transition, offer approval, and mark progress during the passage from non-degreed to degreed status. Spontaneous development of ceremonies suggests there are some needs specific to women who are simultaneously student, wife, and mother that are not being met by traditional university rituals and familial practices.

Rites of passage peculiar to the returning higher education female student in an intact marriage with children are demonstrably present in her passage from non-degreed to degreed status. The study reported here confirms that the modern woman student, her husband, and her children, individually and collectively, are developing rituals which facilitate the transition, offer approval, and mark progress on the way to her degree. Simultaneously, institutions of higher learning are redesigning their procedures to accommodate this new, non-traditional student.

The general purpose of this study was to examine the cultural phenomena that surround a spouse and mother who is assuming the additional role of student in order to get a degree. We believed that an identification and analysis of the patterns of adjustment that these women, their families, and colleges find necessary would be useful to educators and to students. Hypothesizing that rites of passage theories under development by anthropologists since the beginning of the century might afford an appropriate guide for conducting the investigation, our specific goal was to determine if indeed there are any passage rites operant among reentry female students and, if so, what was the nature of these rites.

Our purpose in this article is to review the rites of passage concept; to describe the rites we found to be developing among reentry women in both university and home environments; and finally, to discuss the possible purposes and the degree of necessity for such rites. It may help to point out at the outset the difference between a passage and a rite of passage. While it is quite clear that reentry women are making a significant transition in status from non-degreed person to student to degreed person, it might be questioned whether there are associated rites.

REVIEW OF THE LITERATURE

The French/Flemish anthropologist, Arnold van Gennep, coined the term "rites of passage" in 1908 (1960, p. 10) to refer to those rituals that mark and organize the passage of an individual through various stages in the life cycle. Van Gennep identified the stages as "birth, social puberty, marriage, fatherhood, advancement to a higher class, occupational specialization, and death" (1960, p. 3). "Such changes of

Redding, Nancy P., and Dowling, William D. (1992). Rites of passage among women reentering higher education. *Adult Education Quarterly, 42*(4), 221–236. Reprinted with permission of Adult Education Quarterly and Nancy P. Redding.

condition do not occur without disturbing the life of society and the individual, and it is the function of the rites of passage to reduce their harmful effects" (1960, p. 3). For example, elevation in rank results in the loss of a laborer in the community, or the selection of one family for a task may be perceived as a slighting of another family. Van Gennep held that entry into and exit from these passages were always marked by ritual not only in primitive and ancient civilizations but in modern civilizations as well. The purpose of these rites was and is to "develop an emotional state which facilitates bridging the gap between the old and the new" (Winnick, 1977, p. 461). The passage rites follow a more or less standard pattern. Van Gennep recognized among the rites three general classifications: rites of separation, rites of transition or liminality, and rites of regeneration or incorporation. Rites of separation remove the subjects from their environment or current status, rites of transition take place while they are waiting on the threshold between two states, and rites of regeneration confer a new status. Much overlapping occurs in the rites; while one type usually dominates, it is common to find elements of one or both of the others in the rites under consideration. Subsequently, countless anthropologists, psychologists and adult educators have built upon van Gennep's concept so that "rites of passage" has become a popular term in contemporary society.

Where van Gennep (1960) focused primarily on life stages and social relationships, Fortes (1962) approached rites of passage from the perspective of the conferring of office and the dialectical connection between the actor and the role in an office. Fortes saw that the recipients must appropriate part of the office to themselves because it is in a sense outside of the self. Recognition of this dialectic, Fortes believed, is the clue to understanding why there is a need for ceremony in office-giving. Status, in Fortes' opinion, is an elementary form of office. It is represented in a profession such as medicine or the law and "even in an occupation as low in our scale of class esteem as that of janitor or dustman" (Fortes, 1962, p. 61).

We anticipated that Fortes' (1962) observations about rites of passage would extend to rituals associated with gaining a degree in higher education. Rites confer status or office, legitimate it by the declaration of authority, and present it as belonging to society. Rites remind the public of the sacred trust which thus imposes obligation on both the recipient and society to preserve the office. Rites extinguish the existing statuses to be abandoned and define the new domains of action. Rites help maintain and exercise an office by determining how it is to appear to the holder. They impose functions to be performed and accountability; they symbolize the utilitarian reason for the statuses. While van Gennep (1960) investigated the mechanics of the rites of passage and Fortes (1962) looked at the conferring of office and the effect on the recipient of the rites, Max Gluckman (1962) weighted the societal aspects. Pondering the relatively large number of rituals in tribal societies as compared to western civilization, Gluckman developed several correlations. Where there is less technological development, there is more reliance on mystery and magic to explain and control events. Where there is closer interdependency in a group for care of its biological and physical well-being, there is more need for rites to ease anxiety. Where fewer persons share a multiplicity of roles, there is greater need of ceremony to differentiate these roles.

In a small-scale, less fragmented society, every conflict may be at once a domestic, economic, and political crisis requiring special etiquette to manage the multifaceted conflict. In a larger, more fragmented social structure, on the other hand, the fragmentation itself dissipates the area of friction. Gluckman (1962) noted that it is necessary to isolate multiple roles for analysis but that individuals carry all of their roles even when one role is contextually dominant. One purpose of rites of passage, then, consistent with Gluckman's view, would be to explain and control social relationships and conflicts in terms of the history and tradition of a culture, a type of ritual Gluckman termed "substantive or constitutive" (p. 23) which frequently carried a moral component. A second purpose would be to increase the well-being of a community which Gluckman termed "factitive" ritual (p. 23). A third purpose would be to separate undifferentiated and overlapping roles. A final purpose would be to manage role conflicts without necessarily resolving them.

Gluckman's (1962) analysis would lead one to expect no or few rituals in modern western civilization. Van Gennep (1960), however, held that rites of passage are pervasive throughout all societies—primitive, ancient and modern. We believe we have found evidence that reentry women and their families indeed are developing rites of passage peculiar to their situation. Moreover, higher education also is making changes in its routines, symbolizing support for the new multiroled adult student.

Coping and Accommodation Strategies

Linda H. Lewis (1988a) edited an important sourcebook, *Addressing the Needs of Returning Women.* In the opening chapter she identified the balancing of multiple roles as characteristic of reentry women. "Many returning women are pulled in several (and often conflicting) directions by a seemingly endless stream of demands from work, family, friends and community" (p. 7). She observes that it is not unusual for friends, spouses, family members, and employers to oppose a woman's educational pursuits. The returning student's lack of time forces her to develop a wide range of coping behavior in order to maintain existing relationships and avoid conflict. Reentry is a "transitional time, when the absence of institutional and personal support can make the difference between continuing participation and dropping out" (p. 8). Lewis enumerates the typical personal concerns of reentry women and the institutional barriers they most commonly meet.

Lewis (1988a) concludes with thirty ways to facilitate reentry, but warns, "Regardless of a program's potential it will be perceived as marginal if it is not somehow incorporated into a

visible sub-structure" (p. 15). In the sourcebook's final article, "Extending an Invitation to Returning Women," she cites the need for attitudinal, emotional and functional support both on the institutional and personal levels. Attitudinal support reflects others' perspectives on appropriate roles for women. Emotional support involves approval of a woman's educational goals, while functional support is a division of labor and household responsibilities. Lewis (1988b, p. 100) subcategorizes supporters of reentry women as "rooters" who encourage learners in their efforts, "resources" who assist learners by providing services and information, and "challengers" who serve as critical evaluators, role models, and mentors. Sadly, there are also countersupporters, subdivided into "constants" who prefer learners to stay as they are, and "toxics" who put learners down and inhibit their efforts. An article by Tarule (1988) examines needs from the perspective of learning theory for adult women. Safman (1988) explores the special needs of various socioeconomic subgroups. Howell and Schwartz (1988) look at support systems developed by community-based organizations and industry.

The disturbances in social relationships van Gennep mentioned are emphasized in Rice and Meyers' (1989) review of research on continuing education for women in the 1980's. Their chapter in the *Handbook of Adult and Continuing Education* (1989) has a wealth of information on the impact reentry women and their families' experience from the women's degree-seeking activities. The barriers faced, both at the institution of higher education and within their families, are documented. Recommendations for institutional responses are suggested in several of the works cited by Rice and Meyers.

Ekstrom (1972) cited three categories of barriers women encounter as they enter or reenter postsecondary education. They are institutional, situational, and dispositional. The barriers found within the institutions where women would learn include sex and age quotas in admission practices, financial aid practices, regulations, deficiencies in curriculum planning, insufficient student personnel services, and faculty/staff attitudes. For example, part-time students, many of whom are adult women, are most often excluded from consideration for student loans or scholarships. Eriksen (1990) found that academic counselors perceived adult students differently based on their age alone and consequently gave different advice because of the assumptions they held about them.

Ekstrom's (1972) situational barriers include sociological, familial, financial, residential, and personal factors. Examples of these are: socioeconomic restraints, traditional spousal attitudes toward women's roles, lack of qualifications for desired curricula, not knowing about existing opportunities for study, and attitudes of peers and other significant persons that do not encourage participation in higher education.

Her third category, dispositional barriers, includes attitudes, motivation and personality—factors within women themselves that deter their participation or create problems for them once they are enrolled in a postsecondary institution. Their own views of what is appropriate for women to do can influence whether they engage in intellectual activity within an institution. Also, their preparatory education may have been unsuited for their present objectives.

The work of Mezirow (1978) is of importance in understanding the challenges mature women students face. In his 1978 article, "Perspective Transformation," he explains that such a transformation is a crucial dimension of adult development and, therefore, of adult education. We all acquire from our culture a "meaning perspective" (p. 108), an integrated psychological structure with dimensions of thought, feeling and will. "What one wants to learn, his readiness to learn, the problems he chooses to act upon, . . . his conception of what is bad and good . . . all depend upon his meaning perspective" (p. 108). Adults have the potential of becoming critically aware of their perspectives and of changing them. In doing so they move from what Mezirow termed "an uncritical organic relationship to a self-consciously contractual relationship with individuals, institutions and ideologies" (p. 108). Perspective transformation is precipitated by life's dilemmas and crises. It can only happen through taking the perspective of others who have a more critical awareness of the psychocultural assumptions which shape our history and experience. Adult education can be used to precipitate, facilitate, and reinforce perspective transformation as well as to implement resulting action plans. Mezirow believes there is no higher priority for adult educators than to develop its potential for perspective transformation.

From his research on reentry women, Mezirow (1981) further concluded that the dynamics of perspective transformation appeared to include the following elements: (1) a disorienting dilemma; (2) self examination; (3) a critical assessment of personally internalized role assumptions and a sense of alienation from traditional social expectations; (4) relating one's discontent to similar experiences of others or to public issues—recognizing that one's problem is shared and not exclusively a private matter; (5) exploring options for new ways of acting; (6) building competence and self-confidence in new roles; (7) planning a course of action; (8) acquiring knowledge and skills for implementing one's plans; (9) provisional efforts to try new roles and to assess feedback; and (10) a reintegration into society on the basis of conditions dictated by the new perspective (p. 7). The new dimension explored by our research was a rite of passage. Are the family members and educators making use of ritual to help women juggle their conflicting roles, find meaningful support, and make the all-important perspective transformation? Can rites be added to the list of strategies for helping reentry wives and mothers cope?

METHODOLOGY

Women in intact marriages with children, pursuing a baccalaureate degree, five or more years beyond typical high school graduation, were selected for interviewing. The researchers solicited voluntary participation at three required student orientation sessions, through an article in a campus newsletter for non-traditional students, and by use of flyers describing the research distributed in student lounges. The participants were interviewed in keeping with the principles of naturalistic inquiry as presented by Bogdan and Biklen (1982), and Lincoln and Guba (1985). Open-ended questions were employed, avoiding the technical language of rites of passage theory, and spontaneous responses were invited. The semi-structured interviews conducted over a twelve-week period were taped and transcribed. Sessions ranged in length from one hour to an hour and a half. For the purpose of masking, each person was invited to assume a name other than her own; most chose not to do so; during transcription all names were replaced with code numbers.

Along with recorded interviews and transcripts, three other sources provided data: field notes, the researcher's reflective journal, and participant observation grounded in the respondents' milieux, that is, campus and environs, their homes and neighborhood locales, and their work places. As soon as possible after the interview, field notes were prepared using thick description. "As soon as possible" requires clarification. For example, one respondent followed the interviewer and continued the interview for an hour. On other occasions the interviewer and respondent crossed paths days or weeks later, yielding more data. Once the tapes were handed over to the transcriber, the researcher had to rely on field notes for determining refinements of the questions for successive interviews. Usually seven to ten days elapsed before the observer had both the recorded tape and transcript in hand.

"Field notes using thick description" also needs amplification. While respondents accepted the opportunity to be interviewed, civility required easement into the mechanics. Some respondents seemed to delay the process. One subject decided that she and the interviewer should bring bagels and coffee from a bakery next door into the subject's workplace for the session. Another disliked a classroom with a window in the door and insisted on a move to a restroom lounge. All data of this nature along with facial expressions, gestures, display of emotion, and clothing were duly recorded in the field notes and weighed in the analysis. Also considered noteworthy were introductions to spouses, children, friends, and employers whom the subjects wanted the interviewer to meet, although all sessions were conducted in private.

Bogdan and Biklen (1982) state that a personal log "helps the researchers to keep track of the development of the project . . . and to remain self-conscious of how he or she has been influenced by the data" (p. 74). The principal researcher indicated "Observer Comments" (OC) in the field notes. A separate reflective journal was also maintained. In it were recorded the highs, lows, and plateaus of the interviewer during the research. The journal was further used to question the guidelines of the experts' methodology when the real situation did not seem to conform to textbook descriptions. Lastly, the researcher would note questions or feelings to discuss with the peer debriefer. Responses of the debriefer were written down and mulled over in the reflective journal.

In several ways the principal researcher functioned as an observer/participant, at least in the sense that she had within the year completed a transition in status, although at a higher educational level than the respondents. She, too, was a reentry woman with children in an intact marriage, having lived on campus in a dormitory and off campus in an apartment, while at the same time holding employment to defray educational expenses, a situation common to many of the participants. She was totally familiar with the university procedures and traditions, as well as the campus and its surroundings. These circumstances were revealed to the interviewees at the outset; hence she did not appear to them as an outsider but as a participant herself. Her observations and reflections from this perspective found expression in the field note, and reflective journal. The recorded interviews, transcripts, field notes and reflective journal comprised the data of this research.

DATA ANALYSIS

Data analysis began with the completion of the first interview and field notes. Points raised by each respondent out of her experience were tested in interviews with subsequent respondents. Transcripts, field notes, and the reflective journal were examined for patterns, trends, gaps, or contradictions. Eventually categories for organizing the transcribed information took shape. Files were set up according to the categories with quotations from subjects, transcript page numbers, citations from field notes, and journal entries. The results of the research presented here are drawn from the responses to questions about recognizable milestones, turning points, or routines whereby the students were supported or deterred by family or friends, about episodes which had deep meaning, recognitions and confirmations, and occasions of celebration or commiseration.

Lincoln and Guba (1985) maintain that in qualitative research there are four major criteria for assessing the trustworthiness of data: credibility, transferability, dependability, and confirmability. The credibility of the data that follow was established by prolonged engagement in the field. Over a three-month period the researchers worked solely on this project, not only interviewing the 19 women whose experiences are reported here but also, previously, another 11 in a pilot study on a satellite campus. The transferability of the findings was assured by detailed description in the field notes about the environment which enables sound judgments to be made about "fittingness" with other contexts. The absence of random sampling and the reliance solely on volunteers may limit transferability in that possibly the responses of target group members who were not disposed to volunteer would be missing in the resultant data. Dependability was guaranteed by the careful laying of an audit trail through the preservation

of all documents used at every stage in preparing the research. An experienced auditor performed an audit, finding that, "the research was conducted in a professional manner in conformity with generally accepted qualitative research principles" (Beck, 1990, p. 97).

In order to provide confirmability and to guard against investigator bias, a professor of social psychology and later a professor of sociology, in the role of peer debriefer, on six occasions during the course of the study, tested the interpretation of the data with the researchers. Experiences reported by the respondents which could be considered as rites of passage or elements thereof were found almost exclusively in two environments, the university and the family.

FINDINGS

Rites Of Passage—University

In the college setting there are traditional prescribed formalities that fall readily within van Gennep's (1960) description of rites of passage. In our judgment, the entire curriculum forms a single rite of passage with component parts which "facilitate bridging the gap between the old and the new" (Winnick, 1977, p. 461). Two questions facing the researchers at the outset were 1) whether the time-honored formalities actually speak to reentry spouses/mothers who are trying to take on an additional status as college graduates; and 2) are the leaders of higher education attempting to accommodate the conventional rites or to develop fresh ones for their emerging non-traditional student body?

The answer to the first question was affirmative. All traditional rites apply and collectively achieve their intended effects. The respondents commonly described the harrying routines of application, acceptance, registration, and opening day in terms reminiscent of van Gennep's (1960) description of rites of separation. "It was a nightmare," remembered one. Two felt like "idiots." One had "ten feet." "They do not accept my credits," lamented one interviewee. Another complained: "A lot of them transferred, something like 104 credits, but I had to do two and a half years work here anyway." The orientation course required of all new students, a rather obvious rite of separation in our opinion, was criticized by the majority of the respondents. As one expressed it: "I had to take (a ten week orientation course). I don't think it is something that should be forced on somebody. It is a waste of time." The observer commented in her reflective journal: "This lady was 'forced' but she submitted; she had been 'separated' from her former status. The 'separation,' judging from the complaints of the women, never completely stopped. A husband: 'That's a flunk-out course.' A sociology professor: 'Tough, we all have problems.' An advisor: 'That's a priority for you; you had better get your priorities straight.' "This separation function, however, tends to be concentrated at the beginning of the rite of passage, although van Gennep advises us to look for it through the entire process.

The transition rites appear mostly in the long middle period of the university formalities. One participant's recitation of the courses she would be required to take sounded like a litany: "My plan is to keep taking math, the Basic Education requirements (BERs), humanities, science, social science, then electives." Receiving grades was also a significant ritual for returning females. Said one interviewee: "I like to get A's, B's are okay, C's I don't like." Another, fully in transition, remarked: "It makes me feel good when I get good grades. It's definite feedback that I'm accomplishing something." The participants, too, marked passage through quarters, cumulative grade averages and increasing credits. "I have junior hours, five quarters out of twelve completed. I'm going straight through," announced one subject confidently. Another reflected: "When you see the hours on the bottom of the grade sheet, you know you are a little closer." A third reentry woman speculated: "Maybe at some point I will have what it takes to get a 4 point rather than a 3.5." Acceptance into their colleges after completing basic requirements carries great meaning for our subjects: "I found my niche in the College of Home Economics."

Regeneration, incorporation, new status, of course, come towards the end of the long transition. To the observer, one of the subjects was describing the ultimate function of a rite of passage when she summarized: "It was just a matter of discipline and goals. Set the goals, make plans. Then you know the steps, and follow through with it. I don't know where it all came from, but it is all there now." Outside the publicly legitimated regimen of higher education, she had no way to achieve that goal. The degree is the symbol of the regeneration, the reincorporation into society at a new level. The women described it in their own words as: "a tool for my future," "the ground work so I can progress," "people don't listen to common sense without a degree," "self-satisfaction," "something I would be able to do the rest of my life . . . just for me," "achievement," and "my real dream."

Only one of the participants referenced the culminating regeneration rite of the university, the graduation ceremony itself. "I want both of the kids to come . . . .They've seen this so far that I want them to come." The principal observer, however, noted the assembled college officials, representatives of the community-at-large, families and friends at her own commencement. The candidates were called forth and saluted with Elgar's "Pomp and Circumstance," along with lofty oratory. The coveted "sheepskin" was bestowed upon them, pronouncing them elevated to the status of the degreed. There may be some who would not allow that the entire process from application onwards is a rite of passage, but there is no doubt that the graduation ceremony rivals medieval pageantry. It remains to address the second question, whether the leaders of higher education are attempting to accommodate the conventional rites or are they attempting to develop new ones for reentry women with children in intact marriages? From the sample of this research, only tentative first steps at the university's administrative level can be reported. One woman was admitted without having to meet the high school essentials required of traditional students. Three were grateful for the "forgiveness rule" which allowed their previous college grades below C to be disregarded. A licensed practical nurse in the College of Nursing was able to "proficiency," that is, to test after a year of study to the rank of a senior student, thus omitting her junior year. Two benefited from refresher mathematics courses designed for reentry students. The women experienced more sensitivity and flexibility than indifference and rigidity from individual college employees. Examples were: encouragement by a librarian to apply for a scholarship, two hours spent by an instructor charting quarter by quarter class schedules, an explanation by a department chair of time slots for higher-level classes, shifting test times by two professors, public declarations by two other professors that the age and experience of the more mature students would add depth to the class.

Katz (1976) found similarly that the beginning or reentry to higher education was facilitated for the women of his study by counselors and other personnel who were perceived as being especially supportive. The women prized counseling they believed was provided in a personal manner. They appreciated such personal touches as some contact with the top echelon administrators of the school. We believe, that the entire degree-granting process is a rite of passage; not one of the accommodations reported revealed enough regularity and prominence to be termed a "rite" in itself.

Rites of Passage—Family

The university has been developing its liturgies for a thousand years. The family of the female reentrant, however, has only had since the 1960s to begin ritualizing its modes of support when more mature women began returning to college in large numbers (Wallis, 1989).

Visits to Campus with Husbands and Children. The ceremonials emerging in the respondents' families appear to cluster around special places and times, perhaps corresponding to van Gennep's rites of separation. The special place of studenthood is the campus, which is generally perceived as large and frightening at the beginning—"scary," "a maze," "crazy," "a battle ground," "a robber," "a brick wall,"—as our women students characterized it. A formal visit to the campus in an effort to allay fear and impart ease was initiated by the degreed husbands of two respondents. A third brought her non-degreed and merely tolerant mate to campus.

> He doesn't have any college. He's kind of reluctant about my classes. He's not real happy about them. He's tolerating them ... I took him over to the library ... I think it helped a lot. He got some idea of part of the hassle that you have to go through while you're there. It was his first time to really be in any of the buildings. . . . I've not been trying to force him to have anything to do with it, but I was going over. It was a Sunday afternoon and I thought he was not real happy about me leaving. I said, "Why don't you go with me? Mom and Dad will watch the kids." He said that he would like to do that.

Eight women reported introducing their children to the campus. One, for example, brought her eighteen-year-old to a couple of classes so he could see what college life was like. She brought her daughter to the library. Later she brought her four-year-old son to purchase football tickets and walk around campus with her. Two others let their children play on campus in summer while they attended class, as one explained, "so the children will know in winter where I am."

Inviolable Time and Place for Study. Time set aside for undisturbed study is essential for the respondents as it ritualizes the separation of roles. The functions of wife and mother are so powerfully entrenched in Western culture that without extraordinary effort the newer role of student would simply be subsumed.

In some cases the women carved out the sacred periods for themselves. One studied during the long ride from her home to campus; another used her two days a week off from work. A third reserved every afternoon from 2:00 to 3:30 p.m. when the children had to sit quietly and color or play with puzzles. A fourth waited until her three-year-old had been put to bed, while a fifth waited until the entire family, including her husband, was bedded down.

In other cases the husband helped create the time. When one wife had studying to do, her partner would take the children to the mall. Another spouse would announce, "I can do [laundry and supper]. You take your books and go do what you need to do." Another mate entertained the children on Saturday. Sometimes the inviolable time for study was not understood by very young family members. One respondent reported, "I found myself screaming at my child, 'I've got to study.' I was depending on that hour and a half that he takes a nap." The inviolable place also may have been found by trial and error.

> I tried keeping the book open and I would be reading, cooking, and talking to the kids . . . that didn't work at all. . . . It was no good for the kids and the family. They felt like I was ignoring them. . . . I wasn't getting anything from the studying . . . the way for me to study. . . . concentrate . . . is to get those kids in bed and just devote myself to it.

Employers, too, cooperated: one gave a participant an office key for use after hours; another accommodated work time to class schedules. We believe these behaviors demonstrate that husband and wife and occasionally employers are participating in rituals intended to bridge the gap between the old and the new behavior.

Efforts to Preserve Spousal Role

Unlike the traditional female student with only the student role, these more mature students need to dedicate time to preserving their other roles as wives and mothers. One said, "I made a promise to myself that they (my family) should not suffer because of this." Another attested, "I have created responsibilities in my life and I will not shirk them. They are more important to me than school." Balancing and integrating these three responsibilities is an uncharted course and requires sensitive and intelligent cooperation of all family members. Where normally the traditional student is forging her independence and preparing to separate from her family of orientation, these reentry non-traditional students in intact marriages are struggling to build interdependence and have no intention of leaving. Rituals of this type seem to belong to the transition period and anticipate the reincorporation into society with the new status. One respondent indicated, "He (her husband) is at work when I get home from campus. We make a point of talking daily on the telephone." Another said, "There isn't a day goes by that we don't discuss what went on in my day and class and papers." One wife fed the children early in order to allow a quiet supper with her husband every night at 10:00. Another wife made Friday night special. "I would buy wine, get a VCR tape and make a nice meal." A reentrant had made a sacred place of study out of the conjugal bed, reverting to her college days when she spread her books out on the covers and prepared for classes. One night her husband came up and put on the record, "You Are My Hero," explaining, "I don't get to say this very often." He had two glasses of wine. She put the books away. "It had been a long while since we sat down and talked."

Efforts to Preserve Parental Role

The children also receive their precious moments. One student and her husband set aside Friday night for their children and kept Saturday night for themselves. Another kissed her children every night when she came home from class, even if they were asleep. A respondent had her oldest daughter leave the little one sleeping downstairs so she could carry the child up to her bed after class. Yet another woman's sacred family time was the early Sunday afternoon dinner when married children and families gathered. Even the most mundane activity can take on special meaning. A respondent said, "We're all home pretty much on Sundays. It sounds funny; we all do the grocery shopping together."

Reentry women in intact marriages with children bring their entire family along through the rites of passage. One respondent expressed it graphically. When the interviewer asked, "How does your husband introduce you?" she replied:

> Sometimes he will tease me with my friends and call me a coed. I think he is really proud of the effort I do. [He and the children] take credit for part of my grades because all pitch in and help. I've gotten grades now so many times in the mail that the kids know what the envelope looks like. . . . The driveway is pretty far back from the house. They will get the mail, run up the driveway and say, 'Our grades are here, our grades are here!' . . . I peel my grades back. . . . They are real proud of how it turns out.

DISCUSSION

Who needs rites of passage? Van Gennep (1960) said that persons passing from one status to another need rites to mark and organize their passage both for themselves and their community. Thus we note that the conventional signs of progress used in academia have meaning not only for the reentry woman but also have at least as much for her husband and children. Van Gennep stated that the rituals attempt to reduce the disturbance on the group caused by the alterations of social relationships. Examples of this purpose observed in our study were the student's introducing family members to campus, daily phone calls or conversations about work, college, home life, and sharing "our" grades. Fortes (1962) studied the function of ritual in office-giving (which, as explained above, we believe extends to degree conferment). He held that there is a dialectical connection between the actor and the role because the status is outside the self and is presented by society. In the interviews, women were heard complaining about their struggle in overcoming their present limitations and taking on the new status. They resented the mandatory student orientation course, the rejection of formerly earned credits from other institutions, the sacrifice of time and money, but they submitted nevertheless to the academic regimen as the only route to achieve the cov-

eted degree status. Fortes declared that the ceremonials legitimate the new office and impose on the social group the responsibility of assisting the initiand. We heard of husbands cooking, doing laundry, taking the children to the mall so that the wife/mother could perform in her student mode. Also the rites, according to Fortes, teach recipients what their new status is going to entail. We heard the students recite the course work ahead; one declared that she had found her niche. One woman, a quarter away from graduation, expressed it thus: "You know the steps and follow through with it. I don't know where it all came from, but it's all there now."

Gluckman (1962) related the need for rites to situations where there is close member interdependency for biological and physical well-being. It is no surprise, then, that the majority of emerging ceremonials were found to be in the family setting rather than the academic. Gluckman further linked the need for ritual to small-scale societies where members assume multiple roles. The subjects of this study were conscious of themselves as struggling to reconcile three roles: wife, mother, student, and often a fourth, employee. The rites help them to clarify the often conflicting duties and to manage, if not resolve, the turmoil. For our subjects, this differentiation, balancing and juggling of responsibilities, was accomplished mostly through setting aside special times and places for the various functions; Friday night for the children and Saturday night for the couples. In one case, between two and three p.m., the children had to sit quietly and color or play with puzzles while the mother/student studied. Another respondent arranged to have her youngest child sleep on the couch downstairs while she attended evening class so that when she came home she could resume her mother role by carrying the child upstairs and tucking the child into bed.

Gluckman (1962) also believed that an important element in rites of passage is mystery, which was one reason that he did not expect to find many rites of passage in a technologically developed culture. "Substantive rituals"

(p. 23), as he termed them, express altered social relationships by reference to mystical or ancestral lore, which among other things give insight into the meaning of the passage and tie the participants to their history. The researchers explicitly asked the subjects if religion or God played any role in their decision to go back to college. Their responses indicated that the participants had experienced no special divine guidance beyond that which they encountered in all areas of life. We were thinking particularly of the importance of the person, the freedom to develop, the right to equal treatment, and opportunity unhampered by prejudicial discrimination. Emancipation gained by civil rights and women's movements doubtlessly has played a significant role in heightening family members' awareness of the rights of wives and mothers. We believe we caught strong expressions of those principles in the testimony of our subjects. The degree was seen by many as self-fulfilling, "something for me." One husband was reported to be "happy because he knows it is something I have wanted to do for so long." One mother said, "I don't think it is good for you to live your whole life for your children—not for you, not for them." As though in response a second mother's children urged, "We don't care . . . go back, do it!" By way of supportive ceremony an entire family rearranged their morning schedule for the new student, "even taking showers together, leaving a little earlier." The sense of equal treatment and particularly the idea that, after having helped husband and children further their education, it was now her due occurred repeatedly in the dialogues. "Look, I'm here, too. We need to do something for me, too," demanded one interviewee. Another reported, "My husband is very supportive, he says, 'Now it's your turn.' (My family) seems real happy to give me back some of what I gave them for thirteen years." As the observer-participant noted in her journal, the familial rites of passage among reentry women discovered by this research say to the student/wife/mother: "It's your turn, Mom, you too are important; you must make your own

personal development primary; don't live your life in us, your spouse and children; you best serve us when you serve yourself."

One swallow does not a summer make nor do 19 women allow wide generalization. The authors would like to see this research replicated in other academic settings, for example,—two-year colleges, rural campuses, private institutions,—and with other populations, such as, the husband and children of the female reentrant, male reentry students, and reentry women without children or spouses. We believe that a working knowledge of the passage rites currently developing among returning married women would greatly enhance the efforts of adult educators in higher education settings to serve this important and burgeoning sector of student enrollment. Pitman (1986) deplored the lack of rites of passage in continuing education. She theorized that women had taken a tentative step towards role transition by coming to the university, but unfortunately were not assisted to make the passage by appropriate ceremonies or symbols of success.

> This study suggests that the continuing education programs were designed by a previous generation with the purpose of assisting women by creating more role options. More important, it may suggest that the social institutions, especially the educational institutions of complex urban societies, should provide the ceremonial processes that facilitate role and status passage. By eliminating all elements of ceremony, the Center became static . . . Rigorous entrance requirements and specified course requirements, common only to a group of peers who have entered into that setting (higher education) lead to graduation into a new social state. This process replicates the rites of passage. Even these, however, were eliminated for continuing education participants—exactly the milestones necessary to accomplish transition. (Pitman, 1986, pp. 125-126)

The observations and reflections of Lewis (1988a, 1988b), Mezirow (1978, 1981) and other researchers cited resonate with our findings in the field. Without exception, our respondents perceived themselves as confronting barriers and as juggling many roles. The need for support, unambiguous approval, and practical assistance was voiced over and over. Finally, there was abundant evidence that most if not all women were slowly, painfully, necessarily undergoing a radical perspective transformation. For the most part they had received an uncritical organic meaning perspective from their culture which dictated that children and spouses come first, while mothers and wives defer and sacrifice. They were moving toward a self-conscious contractual relationship in which they were beginning to say, "I am important, too; I also must grow; I serve you best if I serve myself as well."

Lewis (1988a) noted that reentry women feel pulled in several directions by the conflicting demands from work, family, friends and community. They frequently experience opposition. Our research suggested that rites of passage are among the coping behaviors women are developing to maintain existing relationships and avoid conflict. In our opinion, Lewis' insistence that programs aiding reentrants must somehow be "incorporated into a visible substructure" (p. 13) can be effectively operationalized through a species of ritual.

Mezirow (1978) argued that perspective transformation is an important element in adult education. Women have acquired from their culture a meaning perspective which is often an uncritical organic relationship which hinders their return to higher education. They need to gain a "self-consciously contractual relationship with individuals, institutions, and ideologies" (p. 108) that can only happen through taking the perspectives of others who have a more critical awareness of the psycho-cultural assumptions. Moving participants to another point of view, to a different interpretation of their culture and to a new level in their society, is one of the major functions of rites of passage. Intelligently crafted ceremonies could assist in the formulation of a new meaning perspective that eases the arduous journey of the reentry woman and her family to the day she is vested with her degree.

Lewis (1988a, 1988b) offered many practical suggestions for institutions of higher learning to facilitate reentry, although she did not present them as rites *per se*. They in fact function as rituals to the extent that these activities legitimate the steps the returning woman is taking, mark the passage, ease the loss for those who depend upon her, enlist support, and help her manage her manifold duties. Among Lewis' recommendations were: special days for reentry recruits, featuring peer counselors; orientation classes designed for returning women, alternated through an entire quarter to address their changing concerns; and an open door policy that encourages their family and friends to visit the classroom.

A newer challenge for higher education is to aid returning women in the development of family rituals. Exploring the concept with them is a beginning. Counselors who work with this population could discuss some of the findings from this research, as appropriate, with their clients. Support groups could critique the findings and in the course of the discussion share their own experiences. "How to" manuals may emerge. In the end, of course, it is entirely up to each student and her family to fashion or not to fashion idiosyncratic rites of passage. The respondents reported that the university's rich tradition of ceremony speaks to them. Adult educators would do well to expand existing rituals and devise new ones so as to involve the family of the reentry woman, the group which accompanies her the most closely through the transition and whose understanding and support she needs most.

REFERENCES

Beck, E. (1990). Auditor's report. In N. P. Redding, *Rites of passage among reentry women: From the perspective of adult education.* (Doctoral dissertation, The Ohio State University, 1990). *Dissertation Abstracts International, 51,* 2240A.

Bogdan, R. C., & Biklen, S. K. (1982). *Qualitative research for education: An introduction to theory and methods.* Boston: Allyn and Bacon.

Ekstrom, R. B. (1972). Barriers to women's participation in post-secondary education, a review of the literature (RB-72-49). Princeton, N.J.: Education Testing Service. (ERIC Document Reproduction Service No. ED 072 368)

Eriksen, J. P. (1990). Academic counselors' perceptions of adult learners in higher education. (Doctoral dissertation, The Ohio State University, 1990). *Dissertation Abstracts International, 51,* 2237A. University Microfilms No. AAC 903 1061)

Fortes, M. (1962). Ritual and office in tribal society. In M. Gluckman (Ed.), *Essays on the ritual of social relations* (pp. 53–88). Manchester: Manchester University Press.

van Gennep, A. (1960). *The rites of passage.* (M. B. Vizedom & G. L. Coffee, Trans.). Chicago: University of Chicago. (Original work published 1908)

Gluckman, M. (Ed.). (1962). *Essays on the ritual of social relations.* Manchester: Manchester University Press.

Howell, R. S., & Schwartz, H. (1988). Community-based training for reentry women in non-traditional occupations. In L. H. Lewis (Ed.). *Addressing the needs of returning women* (pp. 65–77). San Francisco: Jossey-Bass.

Katz, J. (1976). Home life of women in continuing education. In H. S. Astin (Ed.), *Some action of their own: The adult woman and higher education,* (pp. 89–105). Lexington, MA: Lexington Books.

Lewis, L. H. (1988a). Ingredients of successful programming. In L. H. Lewis (Ed.) *Addressing the needs of returning women* (pp. 5–17). San Francisco: Jossey-Bass.

Lewis, L. H. (1988b). Extending an invitation to returning women. In L. H. Lewis (Ed.). *Addressing the needs of returning women* (pp. 95–109). San Francisco: Jossey-Bass.

Lincoln, Y. S., & Guba, E. G. (1985). *Naturalistic inquiry.* Beverly Hills: Sage.

Mezirow, J. (1978). Perspective transformation. *Adult Education, 28*(2), 100–110.

Mezirow, J. (1981). A critical theory of adult learning and education. *Adult Education, 32,*(1), 3–24.

Pitman, M. A. (1986). Continuing education for women—Checkmate? *Educational Horizons, 64,* 123–126.

Rice, J. K., & Meyers, S. (1989). Continuing education for women. In S. B. Merriam & P. M. Cunningham (Eds.) *Handbook of adult and continuing education* (pp. 550–568). San Francisco: Jossey-Bass.

Safman, P. C. (1988). Women from special populations: The challenge of reentry. In L. H. Lewis (Ed.). *Addressing the needs of returning women.* San Francisco: Jossey-Bass.

Tarule, J. M. (1988). Voices of returning women: Ways of knowing. In L. H. Lewis (Ed.), *Addressing the needs of returning women.* (pp. 19–33). San Francisco: Jossey-Bass.

Wallis, C. (1989, December). Onward women!, *Time Magazine,* pp. 80–99.

Winnick, C. (1977). *Dictionary of Anthropology.* Lanham, MD: Littlefield, Adams.

Evaluation Criteria

1. What is the foreshadowed problem and how clearly is it stated? Is it reformulated later on, after some initial data have been collected?

There really is no "foreshadowed problem" in this study. The authors proceed with a more specific question: Have certain "rites of passage" been developed to help women who are coming back to school cope with conflicting roles and to help them take on new perspectives? (The authors' answer is given in the first paragraph of the article, which is unusual.)

2. Is the conceptual and theoretical framework for the study clear? How well does the literature review argue for the importance of the current research?

The authors present three fundamental concepts: "rites of passage," "coping and accommodation strategies," and "perspective transformation." Each is examined in some detail. The authors argue that all of these concepts apply to the challenges facing reentry women. Their implicit argument is that if "rites of passage" does indeed describe the experiences of these women, and helps them to make important life transitions, then perhaps ways could be found to refine and expand these experiences.

3. What are the biases and preconceived ideas of the researcher? How are these dealt with in the study? Is the researcher well prepared to complete the study?

Unlike many other ethnographic studies, the biases and preconceived ideas of the researchers are clear. They already know what they hope to find. Further, we are told that the "principal researcher" is a reentry woman herself. Both of these suggest a high potential for bias. The article's references reveal that it is a condensation of the first author's doctoral dissertation.

Discussion Questions

1. What are the advantages to having a clear idea of what you're looking for in an ethnographic study? The disadvantages?

2. The article gives several definitions of "rite of passage." Which make the most sense in this setting? How closely do later examples of "rituals" fit these definitions?

3. What specifically are the potential sources of bias here? How troublesome do you think they are? In what ways are these sources of bias also potential *strengths* of the study?

4. Is the method of selecting participants clear and appropriate to the foreshadowed problem? How well are the participants and sites described?

Participants were solicited for the study through various means; criteria and methods of final selection are not revealed. Characteristics of the participants as a group are not described, either. We do not learn the *number* of participants until the "data analysis" section. We also are not told anything about the setting of the study, presumably a large university campus.

5. How involved is the researcher in the setting being observed? Would this involvement affect the behavior of the participants?

The principal researcher is intimately familiar with the setting, and as a reentry woman herself, is able to identify fully with the other participants: "[the researcher] did not appear to them as an outsider but as a participant *herself*" [emphasis added]. While this likely did not affect the participants' behavior as students, it almost surely affected the nature and quality of their responses to the researcher.

6. If appropriate, are multiple methods of data collection utilized? What was the duration and intensity of data collection?

The authors list four sources of data: interviews, field notes, the researcher's reflective journal, and participant observation. Closer inspection reveals, however, that the only *primary* source of data was interviews; it is unclear whether "participant observation" took place separately from the interview. The number of times each participant was interviewed is not given, nor is the number, length, or context of other observations. The authors imply that the amount and intensity of data collection varied from participant to participant. Only one person, the first author, collected the data.

4. Which of the omissions just mentioned do you consider to be the most serious? Why?

5. To what extent will an interviewer's identification with participants likely affect his/her rapport with them? His/her ability to remain neutral with regard to the content of the participants' responses?

6. The authors note that one of the uses of the reflective journal, in addition to helping make meaning of the data, was to "question the guidelines of the experts' methodology when the real situation did not seem to conform to textbook descriptions." What do you suppose the authors mean by this?

7. Are issues of credibility directly addressed by the researchers? How, and how effectively?

The authors address four issues of "trustworthiness": credibility, transferability, dependability, and confirmability. The authors contend that the first was established by "prolonged engagement," the second by "detailed description," the third by an external audit which found that the researcher had conducted the research "in conformity with generally accepted qualitative research principles," and the fourth by the use of a "peer debriefer," who conducted a cross-examination of the authors' interpretations. While use of an audit aids the study's credibility, the methods or findings of the peer debriefer, including the nature and extent of any divergent findings, are not provided. There is also no mention of any member-checking. These omissions, plus the admitted predispositions of the researchers and the fact that only one of them collected the data, do not build a strong case for the study's credibility.

8. Are the findings presented clearly? Are the data sufficiently detailed to allow a rich description? Are results accompanied by illustrative quotes and specific instances?

The article relies primarily on short quotes to buttress points the authors wish to make. As a result, the reader never gains a sense of who these participants were, or how their comments fit into a larger context. Each substantive point is, however, accompanied by at least one illustrative quote.

9. Do conclusions and interpretations follow logically from the results presented?

The conclusions the authors draw, for example, that "the entire curriculum forms a single rite of passage," require a considerable inferential leap. The authors do not indicate just how the college curriculum "develops an emotional state which facilitates bridging the gap between the old and the new," at least in a

7. The authors include "dependability" and "confirmability" as criteria for assessing trustworthiness. Do these terms relate to internal or external validity, as defined in this chapter?

8. Space for detailed context building and storytelling is limited in a journal article. How could the authors have made better use of the space they had, in your view?

9. What concepts other than "rite of passage" could have described the experiences detailed in this article?

way which is unique to reentry women. Remarkable by its absence is the participants' reference to the most obvious rite of passage, graduation. The first author, undeterred, fills in the missing data with a brief account of her *own* graduation ceremony.

10. Is sufficient detail provided to discern which parts of the study might be applicable to other settings? To which contexts is the study transferable?

Since the setting of the study is never described, transferability to other settings (at least on the basis of this article) is almost impossible. Reentry women, however, might well recognize feelings and experiences similar to their own, and gain comfort from the idea that what they are going through may be considered a "rite of passage."

10. If you are a woman reentering higher education, to what extent can you identify with the kinds of rituals and ceremonies described here? How well does the article help you understand your own experience?

How Does the Textbook Contribute to Learning in a Middle School Science Class?

Marcy P. Driscoll   Mahnaz Moallem   Walter Dick   Elizabeth Kirby

The Florida State University

❧

This study took an in-depth look at the natural use of the textbook in a middle school science classroom. Whereas previous research has concentrated primarily on what students learn when they read segments of text and the extent to which teachers use textbooks in class, this study examined how the teacher and students used the textbook during instruction and with what effect. Observed during a 3-week unit of instruction were an experienced teacher and an eighth grade class. Data on textbook use were also collected through a student questionnaire, student and teacher interviews, and "text checks" to see whether students were using their books at home as claimed. Results indicated that the textbook was used predominantly as a dictionary, probably because vocabulary learning was emphasized in instruction and assessed on the unit test. In addition, the textbook employed virtually no instructional strategies to support higher level objectives stated in the chapter, but the teacher did provide learning guidance (without, however, using the textbook) for tacit objectives that she held related to problem solving. Implications of these findings for the future role of textbooks in instruction are discussed.

INTRODUCTION

In recent years, textbooks have been the focus of public interest and controversy. Most often, concern is expressed over the content and comprehensibility of texts, as in, for example, the presentation of evolutionary theory in biology textbooks. Sinatra and Dole (1993) found problems of both content coverage and explanatory coherence in science texts that impeded student understanding of evolution.

Recommendations for textbook design have been forthcoming, but they have predominantly derived from this interest in student comprehension of text material. As Glynn, Andre, and Britton (1986) wrote in their introduction to a special issue on the design of instructional text, "our growing knowledge of the processes underlying text comprehension should guide our efforts to design effective texts" (p. 247). In this vein, Armbruster (1986) recommended that content area textbooks should be designed to help readers access both textual and content schemas. Chambliss and Calfee (1989) suggested, on the basis of their cross-cultural comparisons, that science textbooks should be schematically rather than taxonomically organized in order to promote better comprehension and integration of information. Sinatra and Dole (1993) argued that biology texts must provide enough textual and explanatory coherence to enable students to reject existing preconceptions about evolution. Finally, Garner (1992) examined the "seductive detail" effect, in which students tend to remember interesting details from textbooks instead of the important concepts and principles they are supposed to learn.

Driscoll, Marcy P., Moallem, Mahnaz, Dick, Walter, and Kirby, Elizabeth. (1994). How does the textbook contribute to learning in a middle school science class? *Contemporary Educational Psychology, 19*(1), 79–100. © 1994 Academic Press, Inc. Reprinted with permission of Contemporary Educational Psychology and Marcy P. Driscoll.

Most of these studies, however (and we have cited only a few for illustrative purposes) were conducted from a micro-level perspective focusing on how and what students learn from a textbook when they are asked to read sections of it. Yet very little is known about how textbooks are used by teachers and students in classrooms. Do students actually read their textbooks? How do teachers incorporate the use of textbooks into their instruction? What *do* textbooks contribute to effective instruction in school classrooms?

Publishers typically prepare textbooks with an eye toward covering the traditional topics of the subject matter, while at the same time incorporating unique features that will outsell the competition. Few publishers view this as a process for creating *instructional* materials. Rather, they see it as creating *teaching* materials, leaving the accountability for teaching effectiveness to teachers.

Recent efforts have been undertaken to study the role of textbooks in instruction, most often, it appears, in science education where textbooks are viewed as *the* major influence on instruction (Yore, 1991; Renner et al, 1990). Some of these efforts have paralleled the micro-level studies cited earlier. Alvermann and her colleagues, for example, have been concerned with how science texts can be constructed or augmented to effect conceptual change in students (Alvermann & Hague, 1989; Alvermann & Hynd, 1989; Hynd and Alvermann, 1986; see also Guzzetti, Snyder & Glass, 1992). Other researchers have been similarly concerned with the emphases of science texts on "the finished product of 'scientific fact' " (Stinner, 1992, p. 2) and the consequent low level of science textbook questions (Pizzini, Shepardson & Abell, 1992).

In those studies with a broader focus, investigators have primarily examined how *teachers* use texts (Yore, 1991; Gottfried & Kyle, 1992; Mitman, Mergendoller, & St. Claire, 1987; Stodolsky, 1989), and they cite as important the need to study texts "in the complex, natural instructional climates in which they function" (Mitman et al., 1987, p. 32). Following the call for more observational studies of text materials in science education, Gottfried and Kyle (1992) conducted a microethnographic study of textbooks in six biology teachers' classrooms. Three of these teachers had been identified as "textbook-centered" whereas three used multiple references in their classrooms. Gottfried and Kyle sought to determine whether style of textbook use was related to a teacher's ability to achieve "desired state" biology education criteria (Harms & Yager, 1981).

Although Gottfried and Kyle collected extensive observational and interview data, no clear picture of textbook use emerged because they coded data to reveal only the extent to which teachers used a single textbook or multiple references. Then they developed composite profiles of a textbook-centered vs. multiple reference classroom in reference to actual and desired state biology education. Gottfried and Kyle concluded that "regardless of textbook orientation, the majority of teachers in [the] study appear[ed] to function as passive, uncritical technicians who are ready and apparently willing to disseminate knowledge in an authoritarian tradition" (1992, p. 46).

If this is an accurate picture of what teachers do in science classrooms, what can we conclude about the effectiveness of the instruction? At this point we still know little about what students do with their textbooks or what they actually learn from them. Nor is it clear how what *is* learned relates to the instruction that has taken place, mediated by the student, the teacher, and the textbook. In this study, we began with the general question, how does the textbook contribute to learning in the complex, public school environment in which it functions? Then, in order to narrow the breadth of the question and make it more manageable within the context of a single study, we chose to investigate the use of the textbook in a single middle school science class. In keeping with Salomon's (1991) call for *systemic* research, we sought to provide an in-depth picture of the interacting influences within the instructional environment on student learning.

METHOD

Site Selection and Description

The study took place in an eighth grade science class taught by a science teacher with over 25 years of teaching experience. The school is located in a lower to middle class region of a moderately sized city in the Southeastern United States. It has a racially heterogeneous population of students (white, black, and Hispanic) in grades 5–8; approximately half of the students participate in the school's free lunch program. In the particular class that served as the case for this study, there were 18 students—8 boys and 10 girls; 8 black students, 2 Hispanic students, and 8 white students. The students were characterized by the school as slightly below average in achievement and motivation.

The criteria on which we based our selection of the school and teacher included the following: (a) the school must be situated in a location where textbooks are likely to be used (i.e., where they have not been supplanted by the use of computers and other sophisticated technology which might be characteristic of a wealthy school); (b) the grade level must be high enough that textbooks are commonly used as a means of instruction, but not so high that specialized books may be preferred to standard textbooks; (c) the subject matter must be one in which textbooks constitute a standard means of instruction; and (d) the teacher must be experienced and recognized as a good teacher. In essence, we sought to begin our research program with what could be reasonably deemed a "typical" case of textbook use in the classroom.

Prior to the beginning of this study, we conducted a pilot study using an exploratory case study design (Yin, 1989). We observed the same teacher in an eighth grade science class of 27 students. The pilot study provided us with information about logistics of the field site that helped us to refine our data collection procedures. Results of the study also enabled cross-case comparisons with the present study which helped to strengthen the reliability and validity of observed findings (Goetz & LeCompte, 1984).

Design and Data Sources

This study, like the pilot, was an in-depth case study investigating the use of the textbook in a middle school science classroom. The question of how the textbook contributes to what students learn in this setting is compatible with a case study design because it focuses on contemporary events outside the control of the researcher (Yin, 1989) and within a bounded system (Stake, 1988). In other words, "what is being studied is the case" (Stake, 1988, p. 256)—in this study, the science class—and what we seek to understand is the complex, dynamic system in which the textbook plays an important role.

Using a variety methods (including observations, interviews, surveys, and document analysis) to collect data from multiple sources (the teacher, the students, and the textbook) provided us with the means for generating a description and possible explanations of the textbook's role in learning. Although we initially took "learning" to mean "student achievement of chapter objectives," we acknowledged from the outset that the teacher could have other instructional goals to which we should pay attention if they emerged.

Data Collection

Data were collected for the duration of an entire instructional unit, which, for the unit selected, consisted of three weeks. The teacher recommended that we select a period of study that avoided school holidays (Christmas and spring break) and came before the school's standardized testing period. In order to make sure an entire unit of instruction was covered, we were limited to the months of February and March during the spring semester, and within this period, the teacher suggested that we select the unit on Light and Lenses. For this unit, the teacher covered Chapter 9 in the students' textbook, *Physical Science* (Harcourt Brace Jovanovich).

Observations. With few exceptions, the same two researchers functioned as nonparticipant observers in the class every day for 3 weeks. The class met for 50 min immediately before lunch and immediately after the teacher's planning period. It was not uncommon for the researchers to find the teacher in the process of setting up for the class when they arrived, and they frequently stayed to talk with the teacher after the class was over.

On the first day of the study, the researcher observers were introduced by the teacher as "people from the U." This seemed to be sufficient information for the students, because they ignored the researchers after a few initially curious glances. The researchers used the "focus questions" below to record what was happening to the textbook at every moment:

- What does the teacher do to initiate text use in class?
- What is the activity involving the textbook?
- What are the students doing with the text? Is everyone doing the same thing?
- How do worksheets/overheads relate to the text?
- Do all students have a book? Who does and who does not?
- Where do the students appear to keep their books?
- What shape are the books in? Are they covered? Do the students write in them?
- What does the teacher say about text use outside of class? What directions/assignments/advice does she give?
- What do the students say about their out-of-class text use?
- Does the physical environment of the classroom relate to text use, to facilitate or impede it?

Field notes that included both descriptions and the researchers' reflections about the observations were subsequently entered into the data management system of HyperQual, a Macintosh-based software program for recording, sorting, and analyzing qualitative data.

Student Questionnaire. We revised the student questionnaire used in the pilot study to focus exclusively on students' perceptions of their textbook use and what they thought of the textbook. So, in 17 questions of structured and open-ended formats, we asked such things as, How often do you take your book home (every night, every time there is an assignment, occasionally, almost never)? What sections of your science textbook (e.g., section objectives, text information, photographs, or skill activities) do you like or find helpful? How do you use the textbook to prepare for a chapter test? By what source (teacher, textbook, notes, other students) do you think you learn the most? In your science class, is what the teacher teaches the same as the information in the textbook (yes, no, the teacher only teaches us the important information from the textbook), and What would an ideal textbook be like in your favorite course?

We administered the questionnaire at the beginning of one class period during the first week of observations.

"Text Checks". Text checks were conducted on the only two occasions that the teacher specifically assigned chapter reading to be done outside of class. The purpose of the checks was to determine the accuracy of students' perceptions of their textbook use (i.e., did they actually take their books when they said they did). Therefore, the day after each reading assignment, we asked students to respond to three questions on a half-sheet of paper that we passed out: (1) Were you in science class yesterday (Yes, No)? (2) Have you opened your science textbook since yesterday's class (Yes, No)? and (3) If you answered "yes" to #2, what did you do with your textbook?

Although this was still a self-report measure on which students could respond inaccurately, we think it unlikely that they did so. For one thing, the checks were unexpected and students were asked to respond as soon as they came into class, before they had a chance to really think about what we were doing. For another, they evinced so little interest in our presence that there is no reason to believe they would care enough to misrepresent their use of the textbook.

Interviews. In addition to the observations, student questionnaire, and text checks, we collected information in informal student and teacher interviews about their perceived use of the textbook. Of the teacher, we asked such questions as, What role do you cast the textbook in when planning your instruction? How do you direct students to use their books? etc. The teacher interviews took place nearly every day either after class during the lunch period or before class during the teacher's planning period. In many cases, our questions probed points that were suggested from the observations.

Of the students, we asked questions that followed up on their responses to the questionnaire (e.g., you indicated you were a "book person"; what does that mean to you?) or that elaborated on something the teacher had reported (e.g., What does the teacher mean by "book people"? Why does she say that in class?). Over the course of 2 days, during the second week of observations when a substitute teacher was present, we selected students at random to interview. In the time allowed, we were able to interview half the students in the class.

Document Analysis. We examined the textbook chapter that was the subject of instruction during this study for its pedagogy and relationship to its accompanying unit test. Specifically, we analyzed the degree of alignment among the objectives stated in the textbook chapter, the pedagogical support for these objectives in the textbook chapter, and the test items used to assess achievement of the objectives on the unit test.

Student Performance. Finally, we collected student performance data. At the end of the 3 weeks, the teacher administered the 30-item unit test that came with the curriculum series. In accord with the teacher's directions, students answered the first 27 items and then chose one of the remaining 3 items. There were 10 multiple choice items, 5 matching items, 5 completion items, 7 items labeled "application/critical thinking," and 3 items labeled "writing critically." It was from among the three "writing critically" items that students were to select and answer only one.

Data Analysis

Our general strategy for data analysis consisted of organizing the data around three separate descriptions: (1) how the teacher used the textbook in her instruction, (2) how the students used the textbook for learning, and (3) how the textbook itself related to the content and assessment of instruction (Yin, 1989). According to Yin, "a descriptive approach may help to identify appropriate causal links to be analyzed—even quantitatively" (1989, p. 108). The process we followed was twofold. First, the quantitative data were aggregated and included in an extensive data base, together with field notes of observations, transcripts of interviews, individual responses to the student questionnaire, individual responses to the "text checks," individual scores on the unit test, a copy of the textbook chapter, results of the document analysis (linking each unit test item with the information supporting it in the textbook chapter and a related objective, if appropriate), and research memos written during data collection and analysis. Then, a qualitative analysis was undertaken which involved an iterative process of reading and rereading pieces of evidence, coding the different sources of data, and finally matching them across sources in order to bring them to bear on the questions of interest.

The purpose of the resulting descriptions is to suggest tentative explanations for what was observed and tentative answers to the guiding question, How did the textbook contribute to learning in this class? These are presented and discussed in the remaining sections of the paper.

RESULTS AND DISCUSSION

The Classroom and the Textbook

In order to create the context within which to interpret our specific findings, we describe in this section the classroom, the textbook, and the general flow of instruction as we viewed it for 3 weeks. The classroom was obviously one used for science, because a large poster of the

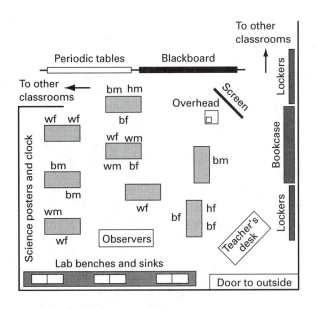

Periodic tables Blackboard

To other classrooms →

To other classrooms

bm hm

bf

Overhead

Screen

wf wf

wf wm

wm bf

bm

bm

bm

wf

wf

bf

hf

bf

wm

wf

Observers

Lab benches and sinks

Science posters and clock

Lockers

Bookcase

Lockers

Teacher's desk

To other classrooms ↑

Door to outside

Figure 1. A schematic diagram of the classroom showing the customary seating arrangement of the students and observers. m, male; f, female; w, white; b, black; h, hispanic

periodic table hung next to the blackboard, and lab benches with running water occupied the back wall. Along another wall were bookshelves containing general references (encyclopedia, dictionary) as well as science books, and student lockers flanked this bookcase. Students sat at tables (usually 2–4 at each one), which were arranged at angles to face the overhead projector and screen in one corner of the room near the blackboard (see Fig. 1 for a schematic diagram of the classroom showing the customary seating arrangement of the students and observers).

Students were allowed to sit at any table of their choosing, but once they chose a spot, the teacher preferred that they keep it for an extended period of time. As a consequence, students tended to sit in the same seats throughout the study. On a few occasions, the teacher moved a student to another location who was interfering with the work of classmates. Only once during this instructional unit did the students go to the lab benches and that was to fill test tubes with water for a demonstration directed by the teacher.

Chapter 9 of the textbook, Light and Lenses, consisted of three sections, each listing objectives and key vocabulary words that were to be learned in that section. There were eight objectives for the chapter, with two or three of these pertaining to each section (see Table 1). The general goals of the instruction were for students to describe the processes of light, the different theories proposed to explain the nature of light, how light travels through different media (e.g., convex and concave lenses, water, air), and how light rays are affected by mirrors.

Along with ample white space, the chapter also contained diagrams and photographs on every page. After every few paragraphs were bulleted questions asking about information presented in those paragraphs, and at the end of each section were questions labeled "reading critically" and "thinking critically." In shaded areas set off from the rest of the chapter (and usually occupying a half to a full page) were biographies of the scientists responsible for theories about light, skill activities, and investigations that students could carry out on their own or with the help of the teacher. Finally, at the end of the chapter were an end-of-chapter summary, science quiz, and list of references for additional reading.

In our initial discussions with the teacher about the textbook and this unit, she expressed dissatisfaction with the book, saying, "I wish we [the school district] hadn't selected it." She also commented that she was still learning the book and was not very familiar with the topic we were about to observe. Therefore, she thought she might follow the text somewhat more closely than she would have for other topics. This comment recalls the findings of Wilson and Gudmundsdottir (1987), whose case study of a social studies teacher revealed that the teacher "relied most heavily on the textbook when he knew little about the topic to be covered" (p. 49). However, the results of our pilot study showed this teacher's style of textbook use to be very similar to what we observed during the present study, even though the textbook and lesson were different.

TABLE 1. Chapter Objectives

Chapter Section	Objective
One	1.1 **Describe** how light travels and **state** the speed at which it travels through a vacuum.
	1.2 **Use** the ray model to find out how the intensity of light varies with distance.
	1.3 **Discuss** the theories that have been proposed to explain the nature of light.
Two	2.1 **Describe** the processes by which the direction of a light ray can be changed.
	2.2 **Compare** the light rays that emerge from a convex lens when a source of light is at various distances from the lens.
	2.3 **Explain** what is meant by the *focal length* of a lens.
Three	3.1 **Describe** the difference between a real image and a virtual image.
	3.2 **Explain** the properties of images formed in a plane mirror.

Instruction on Chapter 9, Light and Lenses, commenced toward the end of the class period on Tuesday, March 12, with the teacher directing students to open their textbooks to the chapter. Standing next to the overhead projector, she asked, "What are we going to talk about in this chapter?" After a student chorus of "light, models of light," she listed on a transparency the vocabulary words for Section 9.1, which also appeared on the first page of the textbook chapter, and asked, "Where do we get the meanings of the words?" She emphasized that these new words were very important for the students to learn and ended the period by telling students to "read section one in Chapter 9 and identify the meanings of the new words."

Over the next 3 weeks (altogether 13 days of instruction plus 1 day for assessment), a daily class routine developed in which the teacher opened the lesson with a brief review of vocabulary words or topics covered the previous day. She asked frequent questions and often wrote notes on an overhead transparency. In general, her teaching style could be described as "highly interactive" and "lively."

During 8 class periods (or 62% of the time used for instruction), the teacher made some reference to the textbook, but this did not mean that students necessarily opened or referred to their books. Throughout the period of study, the number of students who even brought their books to class ranged from 3 to the whole class (18). On most days, approximately half the class had books in evidence.

On 3 of the days during which the teacher made some reference to the textbook, she assigned questions (from the text and/or written on a transparency) that students were to answer in writing. They could refer to their textbooks for these assignments and they generally did so. In fact, it was on these days that the students were most actively engaged with their textbooks. The teacher collected the assignments for the purpose of recording a grade, but she also discussed them in class when she returned them the next day. On two separate occasions amounting to 31% of instructional time (March 15 and March 25–27), the teacher conducted demonstrations and experiments, during which time the textbook was neither referred to by the teacher nor used by the students. Over one 3-day period (March 19–21), a substitute teacher was present, who showed films one day and had students work on a written assignment the other two days. On Friday, March 29, the teacher administered the unit test.

The Teacher's Use of the Textbook

Two general findings emerged with respect to the teacher's use of the textbook in this study: (1) for this teacher, the textbook was the predominant source of instruction, and (2) the teacher used the textbook primarily to teach information, vocabulary, and study skills, while she used other means for teaching problem solving. Let's examine the evidence for each of these findings.

Consistent with other research suggesting that textbooks are the dominant influence on science instruction (Yore, 1991; Renner et al., 1990), the teacher in this study used the textbook chapter as the foundation for her instruction. For one thing, she began instruction on the unit with a reference to the textbook ("Please find in your book Chapter 9 . . .") and assigned students to read section one of the chapter for homework. Throughout the course of instruction on light and lenses, the teacher worked systematically through the chapter, regularly using or referring to the textbook. The following chronology of activities, excerpted from fieldnotes, shows the progress of the class through the unit of instruction.

March 12 "Please find in your book chapter 9 . . ." (*instruction on this unit commences*)

March 13 "Eyeball that first section. Tell me something important about light." (*she is reviewing what was supposed to have been read*)

March 18 "Now open to page 202." (*The teacher begins a discussion of a question in the first section review that students were to answer.*)

March 20 Assignment on board and also transparency:
- Answer 2 questions on p. 205 (*inserted questions in section two of the chapter; 'what is reflection?', 'what is diffuse reflection?'*)
- Answer 2 questions on "reading critically" on p. 208 (*this is in the section two review. It's unclear, there are 3 questions in this part; the substitute says do 2 of 3*)
- Then define 1. real image
            2. virtual image
            3. farsightedness
            4. nearsightedness
- Draw a sketch of the eyeball; label the parts (*on p. 213 in section three of the chapter*)

March 22 The teacher checks to see whether all students have done their assignment on Wednesday and Thursday.

March 27 Going through the parts of the human eye in the text . . . "If you have not read this section (*section three*) in the book, we are not going over every little detail that can be read in the text."

March 28 "A lot of you need to go to the summary. Be sure to go over vocabulary. You cannot use notes or books during the test."

March 29 *After answering several quick questions, the teacher administered the unit test.*

The teacher clearly expected students to bring their textbooks to class every day, as can be seen in this admonishment on a day when few students had brought their books and an in-class assignment required their use: "It's getting old, guys, reminding you to bring these books." She also expected students to have read sections of the text before discussing them in class:

I'll tell them things in advance that we're going to be covering and I expect them to have read it.

The teacher's reasons for relying on the textbook became clear in our interviews with her. In addition to her relative unfamiliarity with the topic, which exerted some influence, she commented:

I use the textbook a lot more than I would if I had a lab. I don't have any hot water. I don't have any gas. I don't have any student stations. So we have to rely on the textbook and things that we can do that require none of these things. You follow the textbook, that's about it.

The teacher also believed that students' lack of prior knowledge or preparation in science led to greater use of the textbook:

I use the book a lot more than I would [in the advanced classes]. I go over things in the book a lot more, because that's something they've got in their hand.

I use the textbook in [basic or regular] classes probably a lot more than I do in my two advanced classes. The regular classes, they need "Look on page so and so. See the picture."

Finally, the teacher had students use their textbooks in class to answer questions that might otherwise have been for homework, because she recognized the futility of assigning homework.

> …and it bothered me to no end to assign homework and four-fifths of them not do it. Now if they'll start it in class, we've been a lot more successful. If they start it in class, they will tend to finish it at home or the next morning early. But if I wait till the end of class and give them something, they just about are not going to do it, or what they can do in the morning while I'm calling role.

As for *how* the teacher made use of the textbook in her instruction, the following excerpts from our observations best exemplify her approach.

> She asks students, "What can we do to learn these words?"
> Students answer:
> • we look at the text and in the back of the book
> • we look for definitions in the dictionary
> The teacher emphasizes, "Your task is to read section one in Chapter 9 and identify the meanings of the new words."
> The teacher asks Rose to read from text vocabulary, then Gena, then Carlos. She indicates two key terms—lens and mirror.
> "If you're a book person, open your book to p. 205" (*to go over two questions on refraction*). "Now, Ben, don't read it. Tell me." The teacher asks for key words (e.g., bending) and reviews on the overhead, refraction (bending light rays through a medium).

Two points are evident from these examples. First, the teacher stressed vocabulary learning and she used the textbook to support this goal. She drew attention to vocabulary words in the margins of the text, she listed on overhead projections terms students were to look up in the chapter, she gave assignments that consisted of defining terms, and she asked questions in class such as, "What does lux mean?" or "What is diffuse reflection?" She also directed students to look up words in class (e.g., "Look up refraction"). In fact, on only 2 of

13 days of instruction did the teacher *not* make some mention of vocabulary words to learn.

Why did the teacher consider vocabulary so important to learn? There appeared to be at least two reasons, having to do with the teacher's basic beliefs about science and her judgment of the students' prior knowledge of science vocabulary. According to the teacher, "we're so vocabulary specific in a science class"; yet she finds that many students lack sufficient vocabulary for middle school science.

> We were talking in . . . my last science class about chlorophyll the other day. They had no concept of chlorophyll. Just didn't know. And yet, that's one of the things that an elementary student should know.
> . . . another problem we have at the middle school is very, very little science is taught at the elementary level. And when they come to us in sixth grade, . . . the previous background—it's not there.

The second point about the teacher's use of the textbook that is evident from our observations is her emphasis on students' acquiring study skills. She frequently reminded students to look for key words when reading, to "eyeball" when looking for specific answers to questions, and to paraphrase to check their own understanding. She also reported that every 6 weeks or so, she goes over the parts of the textbook (table of contents, captions, glossary, etc.) and reminds students to use such strategies as highlighting, looking for underlined words, and reading the chapter summary when studying for a test.

> About every 6 weeks I remind them. Now glossary—all the textbooks have those. Math has 'em, language arts has 'em, most of 'em do now. Index, table of contents, I'll say "Look up in the table of contents, we're fixin' to start unit 6. Find it and turn to that page." But at the very first of the year we go through the book like a reading inventory and we work through and they have a little worksheet that says "What is the caption under the picture?" and it's amazing how many of them don't know what a caption is.

Teaching students to use their textbooks as a dictionary or reference source is consistent with the teacher's own view of the text as a resource. On several occasions, she mentioned that she thinks of the book as a resource, to her as well as to the students. She herself uses activities and information from other books if the text is lacking in an area that is covered on the unit test or that she considers important. For example, she spent one class period discussing what can go wrong with a person's eyes. Although identification of parts of the eye was covered in the textbook, diseases of the eye were not. Her purpose for discussing them, the teacher described to us later, was to relate the abstract concepts of science to students' daily lives and to prompt them to have their own eyes checked on a regular basis.

Finally, although the teacher required students to answer a total of three out of a possible eight critical reading questions, which supported the higher level objectives in the chapter, she tended to use means other than the textbook for facilitating problem solving in students. It is important to note that students had difficulty answering some of these critical reading questions, a possible reason for the teacher assigning so few of them. Consider, for example, the following exchange between the teacher and students as the latter attempted to answer a question about how long it takes for light to travel a certain distance.

> The teacher tries to help students answer one of the questions in Reading Critically. "What is the formula for the time?" Keith reads aloud from the text at his table. The teacher writes on the blackboard how to figure time. $t = d/v$ (v is speed). She gives an example. She reminds students that they are doing a lot of work for answering this question.

It is also true that few of the questions included in the chapter required problem solving on the part of students. Rather, most were likely to promote retention of facts or learning of vocabulary. For example, of 16 questions inserted in the text, half began with the phrase, "what is (are) . . .," and three-fourths could be answered by a single fact stated in the textbook. Typical instances include: "What are light rays?" "What is a lux?", "How fast does light travel in a vacuum?" and "What causes nearsightedness?" In addition, 30 practice test items found in the science quiz at the end of the chapter were true-false, multiple choice, completion, and short answer questions that in 80% of the cases called for recall of facts or vocabulary. These results are consistent with those of Pizzini et al. (1992), who found that lower level questions accounted for 78.8% of all textbook questions in two science curriculum series.

Perhaps as a consequence of these low-level questions as well as her desire for more hands-on activities (recall her comments about the lack of laboratory facilities), the teacher included two laboratory activities in this instructional unit which came from sources other than the textbook. In one, which the teacher said she had found in another book, students were to record observations and generate hypotheses when they examined words printed in red or black ink through a test tube filled with water. In the other, the teacher used a light box and various lenses and mirrors to demonstrate what happens to light when it passes through a lens or bounces off a mirror. The teacher learned this lab, she said, in a summer workshop for in-service teachers where the activities were demonstrated.

In summary, then, the teacher used the textbook during about two-thirds of her instructional time, but mostly as a means of facilitating acquisition of scientific vocabulary and general study skills. Less than one-third of instructional time was devoted to problem solving activities, and these did not involve the use of the textbook.

Students' Use of Their Textbooks

Two questions are of particular interest with regard to students' use of their textbooks: (1) to what extent did they actually use their books? and (2) when they *did* use their books, what did they use them *for?*

In answer to the first question, students in this eighth grade science class appeared to take their cues largely from the teacher. When the teacher reminded them to bring their books to class, approximately half of them did so, but it took her prompting again for them to open their books to appropriate pages or sections during class. These prompts were often accompanied by the phrase, "if you are a book person," which students told us was the teacher's way of reminding them of what to do if they felt they learned best using the book:

> At the beginning of the year, [the teacher] talks about different ways people can learn. Learning from the book is one way. Then, throughout the year, she reminds people about what to do if they learn in a particular way.

If only "book people" were expected to refer to their books on a routine basis in class, how many did this include? On the student questionnaire, only three students reported that they learned best from the textbook, whereas seven students reported that they learned best from the teacher. The remaining students were evenly divided in their opinions that the handouts or other students helped them learn best.

Evidence for the students following the teacher's lead can also be seen from their responses to other items on the questionnaire, which confirmed our observations and the teacher's impressions. When asked whether the teacher teaches the same information as in the textbook, for example, students (15 of 18) overwhelmingly said, "the teacher only teaches us the important information from the textbook." When a new chapter is started in class, about two-thirds of the students reported reading some of the chapter or the first section, which is what the teacher generally assigned. This finding was consistent with how often students reported taking their textbooks home; slightly more than 60% said that they take their books home "nearly every night" or "any night that I have an assignment to complete."

The same proportion of students (61%) reported on the "text checks" that they had in fact taken their books home both times the teacher gave a reading assignment to be completed outside of class. But they also confirmed

in interviews the teacher's statement that whatever reading is done in the text is more likely to occur in class:

> I will read the book and do the assignment only in class. I don't take the book home. I don't know why, but I don't.
> The teacher tries to make sure there is time to do assignments in class, because half the class won't do them for homework. Then, when they don't, the whole class ends up reviewing anyway.

Also as the teacher expected, some students had difficulty understanding the textbook. One student reported that "some parts of it about a specific subject sound the same and I cannot find the answer for the question," while another thought the "ideal" textbook "wouldn't have as much work." Finally, students tended to pay as much attention to the teacher as to the textbook, because "at least one question on each test is about something covered in class that was not in the book."

As for what students do with their textbooks when they do use them, observations revealed that students used their books in class mostly to answer questions and look up vocabulary words. As indicated in the previous section, the teacher gave assignments that consisted of answering questions in the text, and she asked questions in class that could be answered with reference to the text. When students were asked about the components of the textbook that they liked or found helpful in learning, "skill activities," "inserted questions," and "photographs" ranked highest, while "biographies" and "investigations" ranked lowest (see Table 2). However, for no component did any more than two-thirds of the students indicate using it, and 12 out of 15 components were reported used by less than half the class. This suggests, once again, that students tended to follow the cues of the teacher; they paid attention to those components of the textbook (primarily the inserted questions) to which she directed their attention.

It came as a surprise to us, however, that skill activities was reported as the most used textbook component. In the Light and Lenses

TABLE 2.   Components of the Textbook as Students Reported Using and Liking Them

Textbook Component	Percent of Students
Skill activities (2)[a]	67%
Inserted questions (16)	60%
Photographs (21)	53%
Captions (26), text information, new science terms (14)	47%
Science quiz (1)	40%
Diagrams (13)	33%
Objectives (8), reading critically (7 q's), thinking critically (8 q's), end-of-chapter summary (1), references for additional reading (3 refs)	27%
Investigations (1)	20%
Biographies (1)	7%

[a] The number in parentheses represents the number of times each element appeared in the textbook chapter.

chapter, there are two such activities and both require application of concepts learned during the chapter. Given the difficulty students experienced solving problems during this unit, it seems unlikely that they actually tried the skill activities at home. Rather, it is more likely that, in checking 'skill activities' on the questionnaire, students may have been expressing their preference for doing activities in class. They clearly enjoyed the laboratory activities that were done in class, and in describing her "ideal" textbook, one student said, "It would have activities and I would like to do the activities."

In summary, then, students read their textbooks only when prompted by the teacher to do so, but even their reading tended to be directed toward answering specific questions, either in the book itself or raised by the teacher.

Textbooks and Effective Instruction

Although a picture of textbook use in this science classroom is emerging, little has yet been said about the role of the textbook in effective instruction. In other words, how did the textbook contribute to what students learned in this class? In order to answer this question, we must examine both what students did learn and how this was influenced by the textbook in the overall instructional system.

To begin with, students learned more than what was measured on the unit test, but that provides a point of departure. Two-thirds of the items on the test assessed factual knowledge or vocabulary learning (e.g., matching correct terms to definitions or writing the correct term in a statement of its definition or a fact about it). Three items (10%) required the use of a rule (e.g., how long would it take a beam of light to travel 9.0×108 m?), and four items required identification of a concrete concept (e.g., focal length, virtual focus). The essay item (students were to select one of three questions) called for explanation of some phenomenon (e.g., nearsightedness).

Scores on the unit test ranged from 9 to 25 out of 28 items, and the average score was 16.6 (standard deviation = 4.9), which is just over 59% correct. This is surprisingly low considering what seemed to us as inordinate repetition of test-related information in class. According to the teacher,

> I figure—who it is—Joe Stanchfield says you gotta hear or see something seven times before it even begins to be yours. So I figure if they copy it down, if they read it up there [on the overhead], maybe they'll hear me say it, and they read it in the book. That's four. And I've also started using a lot of things in here such as group work.

As previously discussed, the textbook also included pedagogical support for the vocabulary and facts that were assessed on the unit test.

Why the students performed so poorly on the test, then, is a matter for some conjecture.

The teacher mentioned on several occasions the lack of student prior knowledge in science, but she also thought that unit tests were sometimes too difficult for her students. In one interview, for example, she mentioned having to rewrite test items:.

Question: The questions are too difficult or the language is too difficult?
Answer: Yes!

On the unit test administered by the teacher in this study, items ranged in difficulty from .30 to .90 with a standard deviation of .23, which suggests substantial variability in student performance across items. Anticipating this result, the teacher told us that she normally counts in-class written assignments in the computation of students' grades in order to avoid having many of them fail. In addition, students indicated that she sometimes allows them to use their textbooks when taking units tests.

What else students learned during this period of instruction is difficult to say with confidence, because no other formal assessment was administered. Did students acquire more effective study skills? Perhaps. They were at least aware of the different parts of a textbook and the teacher's efforts to assist them in learning how to study. One student commented on being able to use the textbook during tests that "you learn how to use the book." The teacher also mentioned that the students' grades were improving over time, which could be taken as an indication of better study skills or increased knowledge of science. In either case, the fact that students' grades have improved is likely to enhance, from the teacher's point of view, the importance of the textbook for learning.

Did students learn to solve problems related to this unit of instruction? The answer is less clear than whether they acquired study skills, but what indicators exist cast doubt that they did. Student performance on the concept and rule items on the unit test, for example, was lower than the mean score, with fewer than half the students, on the average, answering these

items correctly. Moreover, only two students answered the essay question satisfactorily. However, the teacher clearly viewed the process of learning to solve problems as something to be addressed over a long period of time:

> You can't just set out equipment, give 'em a piece of paper and say this is the plan, do it. You can't do it. Now you might can start out the beginning of the year and start training them. You can do it with them and the next time they do a little bit less with your help and [a little more on their own] …But you've got to start out with a lot of structure …

By the time in the school year that this study was conducted (March), students followed directions for activities without much guidance from the teacher, but it is less clear that they understood the reasons for their actions. And what problem-solving skills they might be acquiring probably did not come from their use of the textbook. As the teacher viewed the difference between herself and the textbook,

> I can answer questions. I can clarify, and I can word it differently, too. You read the textbook and if you don't understand that one sentence, there's nowhere else to go to say it differently.

Finally, it is worth noting that document analysis revealed little congruence between the objectives stated in the textbook chapter and either the unit test items or the instructional events included in the chapter. According to Gagné (1985), for instruction to be effective, certain events must be included to facilitate specific, internal processes of learning. These "nine events" have been synthesized from research on learning and are designed to support such learning processes as encoding, retrieval, transfer, and so forth. Effective instruction also requires coherence among goals students are expected to attain, what is actually taught during instruction, and what is assessed by performance measures (Gagné, Briggs, & Wager, 1992; Dick & Reiser, 1989; Tuckman, 1988).

Although only three of the eight objectives (1.1, 2.1, and 3.1; see Table 1) can be clearly classified as knowledge oriented, evidence has already been presented that the instructional events included in the textbook supported mostly knowledge acquisition and that the test measured mostly knowledge acquisition. At best, then, the instruction delivered by the textbook had the potential to be effective mostly for learning of factual knowledge, despite its claim that students should be able to attain higher level objectives after completing the chapter.

GENERAL DISCUSSION

So how did the textbook contribute to learning in this middle school science class? The study reported here provided an in-depth look at the natural use of the textbook in one science classroom. Although we cannot claim that our results show how textbooks are used in all classrooms, or in all subject areas, or at all levels of education, we do believe that they are probably not unique to this one class. And these results raise, in our opinion, some significant issues concerning the design, selection, and potential use of textbooks.

The first, and perhaps most important, can be phrased as a question: What role *should* textbooks play in effective instruction? Before an answer to this question can even be offered, however, we must decide what it is that we want students to learn.

The textbook examined in this study stated objectives that can be categorized as ranging from knowledge (e.g., state the speed of light through a vacuum) to analysis (compare the light rays from a convex lens when a source of light is at various distances from the lens) on Bloom's (1956) taxonomy. However, it provided instructional events in support of primarily factual learning, which was also assessed by the accompanying unit test. Perhaps the objectives reflect what textbook authors, state department officials, and presumably the public at large want students to achieve. In Florida, as may be true in other states, textbooks are adopted partly on the basis of how closely they match the state skills and competencies defined by the Department of

Education. It is conceivable, then, that publishers include objectives that will satisfy state adoption committees without careful regard to whether the textbooks actually facilitate the achievement of those objectives.

The teacher in this study, too, held a range of instructional goals for students—from learning the definitions of concepts to solving problems to studying effectively for a test—and she varied her instruction accordingly. Her primary use of the textbook, however, and consequently that of the students, was as a reference tool for looking up facts and definitions of vocabulary, which were then what students tended to get right on the unit test.

This emphasis on vocabulary learning was partly a function of the low prior knowledge possessed by these students. Not knowing prerequisite concepts needed to comprehend the text accounts for why the students might approach the text as a dictionary and why the teacher encouraged this use (cf, Armbruster and Nagy, 1992). In addition, however, using the text as a reference tool was consistent with both the teacher's view of the text as resource and her interest in facilitating good study habits. In other words, the more students practiced looking up information in the text (for whatever reasons), the better they would become at this skill. Together, these results suggest two problems for textbook designers: how to effectively handle low prior knowledge among students using a particular text and how to best facilitate information search and retrieval.

This brings us back to the question of what purpose textbooks *should* serve in instruction. Should they provide the goals for instruction along with the appropriate instructional events necessary to achieve those goals? If the answer is yes, then our results support those of Sinatra and Dole (1993) and Pizzini et al. (1992) in suggesting that textbook publishers must undertake considerable revision of (at least) science textbooks to improve their instructional effectiveness. Instructional events and unit tests must be brought more in line with instructional objectives, and field testing should be conducted to assure appropriate levels of difficulty and ascertain the effectiveness of the textbook in facilitating goal achievement.

If, on the other hand, the textbook should be considered as one of many information resources for teaching and learning, as Cunningham, Duffy, and Knuth (in press) have argued, then other implications for textbook design and use emerge. According to the recently articulated constructivist view of teaching (see, for example, discussion in the May and September, 1992, issues of *Educational Technology*), instructional activities, including those in the textbook, must support an active process of knowledge construction in learners. To this end, researchers have proposed situated learning (Brown, Collins, & Duguid, 1989), anchored instruction (Cognition and Technology Group at Vanderbilt, 1990), and others. As these authors have also demonstrated, new interactive technologies have made possible simulations, microworlds and extensive databases to support the activities they propose. Interestingly, according to the *Social Studies Review* (Winter, 1991), Texas has now become the first state to adopt a videodisk-based curriculum in elementary science.

Where this leaves the textbook is not entirely clear. Students will listen to the teacher and each other, will consult other information sources besides the textbook, and will build their own understandings, for better or worse. It would be difficult to claim from this study, however, that the students were engaged in active knowledge construction of the sort that constructivists want the textbook to support. There were few resources in the classroom available to these students *besides* the textbook and teacher, and given their general SES level, it is unlikely many additional resources would have been available to them at home. In addition, it seems likely that students responded to the "hidden messages" of the textbook, teacher, and test regarding what is important to learn in science. Fact learning was emphasized and assessed, and so facts were what students primarily learned.

For the textbook to play a more effective role in supporting active knowledge construction, it should be conceived as part of a total instructional system, where the role of each component in the system is identified. The textbook may, for example, suggest sources of information to study or be tied into a larger database. It may suggest exploration strategies or contain worked out examples. It may become a handbook more than a textbook. Certainly, to effectively support knowledge construction in a reasoned way, it must present multiple perspectives on a topic rather than authoritatively stated, bald facts. Whatever the future role of textbooks, however, we must consider what goals are considered desirable for learning and how these may best be facilitated. We must also consider how best to facilitate teachers' understanding of the roles textbooks can play in instruction. In the words of our teacher,

> When an intern comes in, they'll come in and we'll provide them with the textbooks. Well, they don't know what to do with them. To get ready [for student teaching], they'll come in and say, "We're supposed to come in and spend a day with you and then we'll be back in two weeks." Fine, but if they don't know what to do with the textbook to get ready to use the textbook, they're wasting their time.

REFERENCES

Alvermann, D. E., & Hague, S. A. (1989). Comprehension of counterintuitive science text: Effects of prior knowledge and text structure. *Journal of Educational Research, 82*(4), 197–202.

Alvermann, D. E., & Hynd, C. R. (1989). Effects of prior knowledge activation modes and text structure on nonscience majors' comprehension of physics. *Journal of Educational Research, 83*(2), 97–102.

Armbruster, B. B. (1986). Schema theory and the design of content-area textbooks. *Educational Psychologist, 21*(4), 253–268.

Armbruster, B. B., & Nagy, W. (March, 1992). Vocabulary in content area lessons. *The Reading Teacher, 45*(7), 550–551.

Bloom, B. S. (Ed.) (1956). *Taxonomy of educational objectives: The classification of educational goals. Handbook I. Cognitive domain.* New York: Longman.

Brown, J. S., Collins, A., & Duguid, P. (1989). Situated cognition and the culture of learning. *Educational Researcher, 18,* 32-42.

Chambliss, M. J., & Calfee, R. C. (1989). Designing science textbooks to enhance student understanding. *Educational Psychologist, 24*(3), 307-322.

Cognition and Technology Group at Vanderbilt. (1990). Anchored instruction and its relationship to situated cognition. *Educational Researcher, 19,* 2-10.

Cunningham, D. J., Duffy, R. M., & Knuth, R. A. (In press). The textbook of the future. In C. McKnight (Ed.), *Hypertext: A psychological perspective.* London: Ellis Horwood Publishing.

Dick, W., & Reiser, R. A. (1989). *Designing effective instruction.* Englewood Cliffs, NJ: Prentice-Hall.

Gagné, R. M. (1985). *The conditions for learning.* (4th ed.) New York: Holt, Rinehart and Winston.

Gagné, R. M., Briggs, L. J., & Wager, W. W. (1992). *Principles of instructional design,* 4th ed. Fort Worth: Harcourt Brace Jovanovich College Publishers.

Garner, R. (1992). Learning from school texts. *Educational Psychologist, 27*(1), 53-63.

Glynn, S. M., Andre, T., & Britton, B. K. (1986). The design of instructional text: Introduction to the special issue. *Educational Psychologist,* 21(4), 246-251.

Goetz, J. P., & LeCompte, M. D. (1984). *Ethnography and qualitative design in educational research.* Orlando, FL: Academic Press.

Gottfried, S. S., & Kyle, W. C., Jr. (1992). Textbook use and the biology education desired state. *Journal of Research in Science Teaching, 29*(1), 35-49.

Guzzetti, B. J., Snyder, T. E., & Glass, G. V. (1992). Promoting conceptual change in science: Can texts be used effectively? *Journal of Reading, 35,* 642-649.

Harms, N. C., & Yager, R. E. (Eds.) (1981). *What research says to the science teacher* (Vol. 3). Washington, DC: National Science Teachers Association.

Hynd, C. R., & Alvermann, D. E. (1986). The role of refutation text in overcoming difficulty with science concepts. *Journal of Reading, 29,* 440-446.

Mitman, A. L., Mergendoller, J., & St. Claire, G. (April, 1987). *The role of textbooks in middle grade science teaching.* Paper presented at the Annual Meeting of the American Educational Research Association, Washington, D.C.

Pizzini, E. L., Shepardson, D. P., & Abell, S. K. (1992). The questioning level of select middle school science textbooks. *School Science and Mathematics, 92*(2), 74-79.

Renner, J. W., Abraham, M. R., & Grzybowski, E. B. (1990). Understandings and misunderstandings of eighth graders of four physics concepts found in textbooks. *Journal of Research in Science Teaching, 27*(1), 35-54.

Salomon, G. S. (1991). Transcending the qualitative-quantitative debate: The analytic and systemic approaches to educational research. *Educational Researcher,* August–September, 10-18.

Sinatra, G. M., & Dole, J. A. (April, 1993). *Textbook presentations of evolutionary biology: Issues impeding comprehension and learning.* Paper presented at the Annual Meeting of the American Educational Research Association, Atlanta, GA.

Social Studies Review. (Winter, 1991). A Bulletin of the American Textbook Council, No. 7.

Stake, R. E. (1988). Case study methods in educational research: Seeking sweet water. In R. M. Jaeger (Ed.), *Complementary methods for research in education.* Washington, DC: American Educational Research Association.

Stinner, A. (1992). Science textbooks and science teaching: From logic to evidence. *Science Education, 76*(1), 1-16.

Stodolsky, S. S. (1989). Is teaching really by the book? In P. W. Jackson and S. Haroutunian-Gordon (Eds.), *The 88th NSSE Yearbook.*

Tuckman, B. (1988). *Testing for teachers.* San Diego: Harcourt-Brace-Jovanovich.

Wilson, S. M. & Gudmundsdottir, S. (1987). What is this a case of? Exploring some conceptual issues in case study research. *Education and Urban Society, 20*(1), 42-54.

Yin, R. K. (1989). *Case study research,* revised edition. Newbury Park: Sage Publications.

Yore, L. D. (1991). Secondary science teachers' attitudes toward and beliefs about science reading and science textbooks. *Journal of Research in Science Teaching, 28,* 55-72.

Evaluation Criteria

1. What is the foreshadowed problem and how clearly is it stated? Is it reformulated later on, after some initial data have been collected?

The foreshadowed problem is stated clearly in the last paragraph of the Introduction:"How does the textbook contribute to learning in the complex, public school environment in which it functions?" The authors do not reformulate the question, although they do delimit it to a middle school science class. Note how, in the general discussion, the study's results led to *another* foreshadowed problem.

2. Is the conceptual and theoretical framework for the study clear? How well does the literature review argue for the importance of the current research?

The framework for the study—a single case study design—is quite brief, and lacks a strong theory base. The central argument made by the researchers is that, while "micro" studies have looked at the effect of particular textbooks as treatments, and broader studies have examined how teachers use texts, little is known about how *students* use texts and to what effect. The essence of the authors' argument is that the study is important because it has not been done before.

3. What are the biases and preconceived ideas of the researcher? How are these dealt with in the study? Is the researcher well prepared to complete the study?

It is difficult to tell what the researchers' preconceived ideas might be. Since their purpose is to discover how students use textbooks in this class, they appear to be open to whatever they might discover, and indeed they express "surprise" occasionally at what they have found. The authors do seem critical of some of the teaching methods used (e.g., citing an "inordinate repetition of test-related information in class"), and seem dismayed at the low level of student performance. No information is

Discussion Questions

1. Does the foreshadowed problem seem clearer or more meaningful when it is stated later, after the literature review, rather than earlier, as in the other articles contained in this chapter?

2. The review says a lot about what has *not* been studied. Is this sufficient justification for the current research?

3. In many articles you find citations of authors' previous works in the References section. A large number of self-citations may enhance the authors' credentials, but it may also indicate that the authors have already made up their minds about what "should" be going on. Which argument do you find more persuasive?

given about the authors of the study, only one of whom (Dick) is listed in References, so their credentials are impossible to determine.

4. Is the method of selecting participants clear and appropriate to the foreshadowed problem? How well are the participants and sites described?

As the foreshadowed problem was stated in general terms, it was up to the researchers to select a classroom that might be considered "typical" of textbook use. The site selection criteria are clearly stated, as are the characteristics of the selected classroom, and it is left up to the reader to determine how "typical" the selected classroom is.

5. How involved is the researcher in the setting being observed? Would this involvement affect the behavior of the participants?

Clearly, the researchers were observers, not participants. The authors note that the students virtually ignored them in class, but there are no independent data confirming this.

6. If appropriate, are multiple methods of data collection utilized? What was the duration and intensity of data collection?

The multiple methods used in this study constitute a major strength. Two researchers engaged in systematic observation of the classroom, using low-inference "focus questions" to record their data. Other methods included a student questionnaire; "text checks" on the veracity of student self-report; informal student and teacher interviews; the degree of "alignment" among textbook objectives, text material, and test items; and student performance data. Data collection lasted for three weeks, covering one instructional unit.

7. Are issues of credibility directly addressed by the researchers? How, and how effectively?

4. Do you think the researchers were successful in obtaining a "typical" case, or is it likely that this is not a typical case and will not be representative of other classes?

5. How inconspicuous do you think the researchers really were? How likely is it that the students' behavior was affected by the presence of the researchers?

6. Does three weeks seem long enough to collect sufficient detail to reach credible conclusions?

7. Does it seem like experimenter bias could influence the analysis of observations or interviews? Are you satisfied with the credibility of the data analysis procedures?

Aside from a brief reference to the use of a pilot study to "refine data collection procedures" and "enable cross-case comparisons," issues of credibility are addressed only indirectly, through a presumed triangulation in which "pieces of evidence" were "matched across sources."

8. Are the findings presented clearly? Are the data sufficiently detailed to allow a rich description? Are results accompanied by illustrative quotes and specific instances?

As is typical of much qualitative research, the Results and Discussion section of this study is rather long. This detail is needed, however, as it helps us understand the setting of the class—which is especially important given the authors' intention to examine a "typical" classroom. The classroom diagram is a helpful touch, as are the student and teacher quotes and the excerpts from the researchers' notes. All add an air of credibility to the study. Notice that the results are summarized by major question and not by data source; this makes instances of triangulation easier to find.

9. Do conclusions and interpretations follow logically from the results presented?

Throughout their presentation of results, the authors gradually portray how the teacher used the text and how students "followed the cues of the teacher," resulting in their reading only what and when the teacher told them to. This evolving picture of learning largely by rote leads logically to the conclusion that the textbook played little if any role in students learning problem-solving skills. The authors then launch into a general discussion about the role that texts *should* play—a remarkable extrapolation from a single case, "typical" or not.

10. Is sufficient detail provided to discern which parts of the study might be applicable to other settings? To which contexts is the study transferable?

8. In summarizing the results, quantitative summaries are provided (e.g., frequencies and percents). Are these appropriate in a "qualitative" study? Do they help us understand what is happening in the classroom?

9. What conclusions would *you* draw from the data presented in this study?

10. Early in the article, the authors acknowledge how differently textbooks are used, depending on the subject matter. Do you think that the findings of this study are transferable only to science classes in middle school? Why or why not?

The case is sufficiently detailed to allow any classroom teacher in a similar setting to judge the transferability of these findings. There is also enough detail here for teachers to reflect on their own use of textbooks, and to ask themselves how, if at all, they might use them differently.

Chapter 5 _____

Action Research

All of the studies reviewed in the previous chapters, both quantitative and qualitative, have a common goal: To expand the existing knowledge base about an educational problem or issue. Their intention is to generate insights that may be useful in other settings.

Sometimes, however, research has another purpose entirely. An empirical study may be undertaken in order to help make decisions about specific problems in specific settings. Generalizing beyond the setting is at best a secondary consideration.

Two kinds of research fall into this category, and each can take any of the methodological forms (quantitative/qualitative, experimental/nonexperimental, etc.) shown in Figure 1-1. What distinguishes these forms of research from others is not *how* the research is done, but *why*. **Evaluation research** is undertaken expressly to help determine the worth of a particular educational program, and to help inform decisions about whether to continue or change that program. **Practice-based research** (or teacher research, classroom research) is undertaken by educational professionals in their own practice settings for the purpose of better understanding their work and how to improve it. Both evaluation and practice-based research are variants of what is called "action research"; some specific action in the form of changes in policy or practice is expected to occur as a result of the inquiry. The basic differences between action research and more "traditional" research are summarized below:

	"Traditional" Research	Action Research
Purpose	Conclusion	Decision
Context	Theory	Practice
Standard	Truth	Usefulness

The *purpose* of traditional research is to draw conclusions about the nature of the world; the purpose of action research is to go a step further and ask, "So what if anything should change?" Whereas in a traditional study researchers might examine the correlation between class size and pupil achievement in order to draw conclusions about the relationship between these two variables, in an action research study, researchers might assess the effects of class size on school achievement to help a local school board develop appropriate policies on maximum number of students allowable per classroom.

The *context* of traditional research is theory. In most quantitative research, specific research questions follow from more general theoretical propositions, and in most ethnographic research, theory is built inductively from case studies. In action research, however, theory plays a distinctly secondary role. Key research questions derive from practice: How effective is a local Head Start program in increasing school readiness among disadvantaged children? How can a teacher modify her behavior so as to motivate underachieving students in her third-grade classroom? While the results of action research may often have theoretical implications, the focus is on the tangible and the here-and-now.

The principal *standard* by which traditional research is evaluated is the extent to which it helps reveal "truth." The standard for action research, on the other hand, is much more practical: Does it provide information that helps inform decision making? For example, a traditional study of the impacts of modular scheduling on student achievement would be most concerned with the credibility of the data and the internal and external validity of the design. An action research study, while not discounting the importance of scientific credibility, would be relatively more concerned with the extent to which these data help lead to optimal scheduling policies.

One might conclude from the above that action research is less academically rigorous than the kinds of research presented in previous chapters. Not necessarily. It is true that designs with strong internal validity are hard to find in action research, simply because the opportunities for experimental control are few or unavailable. This may be why a lot of action research uses qualitative designs, which are flexible, emergent, and better able to capture complexity and contextual nuance. In fact, in many ways the criteria for good action research pose greater challenges. Not only do action researchers need to pay attention to the general criteria governing all educational research, they also need to consider the consequences of their findings. As action research is intended to facilitate change, researchers in this realm cannot afford simply to conduct their study, write up their results, and move on. They also need to consider the implications of their data for the policy or practice context. It is not enough, for example, for the evaluator of an adult literacy program to find that certain groups appear to benefit from the program while others do not. The evaluator must also be sensitive to the ways in which the data from the study will be used; information that is used to help make value judgments— about what is and is not effective—has both political and ethical overtones.

Thus, one of the best ways to identify action research in the literature is to look for value-laden terms in the title and/or research question. For example, instead of "Did the educational intervention raise standardized test scores?" an action research question would be, "Was this program *effective* in *improving* educational performance?" Discriminating between the two *forms* of action research is largely a matter of focus: In evaluation research the study is being done to help make difficult *policy* choices, such as whether a program should be retained, changed, or replaced by another. Evaluations are thus often conducted by outside experts. In practice-based research, the focus is on the improvement of educational *practice,* and the researchers are usually the practitioners themselves.

All of the above suggest that special criteria are needed for reviewing action research. A study could be sound methodologically but useless (or worse, misleading) for decision making. Conversely, a study could have major methodological flaws and still provide useful information.

Criteria for Evaluating Action Research[1]

1. Does the research provide accurate information about the practices studied? (This is similar to the credibility criterion in traditional research.)

2. Does the research serve the needs of a given audience?

3. Is the research realistic, frugal, and diplomatic?

4. Has the research been conducted legally and ethically? (applies particularly to evaluation research)

---

[1]Adapted from *Standards for Evaluations of Educational Programs, Projects, and Materials,* by the Joint Committee on Standards for Educational Evaluation. New York: McGraw Hill, 1991.

Effects of Curriculum Alignment versus Direct Instruction on Urban Children

George Brent   Nicholas DiObilda
Rowan College of New Jersey

❧

ABSTRACT

The city of Camden, New Jersey, received a Follow Through grant to implement the direct-instruction model in one of its elementary schools. The standardized achievement test scores of Grade 2 pupils who experienced the direct-instruction model were compared with the scores of pupils who experienced traditional basal programs. The traditional programs were aligned with the standardized Comprehensive Test of Basic Skills (CTBS) used by the district. An additional factor included in the evaluation was the effect of student mobility on achievement. The achievement of mobile students was compared with the achievement of stable students. Finally, stable students were given an additional standardized test, the Metropolitan Achievement Test (MAT), to assess the effects of the programs independent of the aligned curriculum. The results indicated that (a) the direct-instruction students did as well as the aligned students on the CTBS, (b) the achievement of stable students was generally higher than that of mobile students on the CTBS reading subtest, and (c) the direct-instruction students were superior in mathematics on the MAT subtest.

Camden, New Jersey, is an economically depressed community with a population of approximately 87,000 persons. It is a city that has suffered shrinking financial resources, a middle-class exodus, decaying physical facilities (including schools), and a growing population of poor minority children. Approximately half the families receive welfare, and about 60% of

Camden's children live in poverty, the highest percentage in the nation (Kozol, 1991).

The Camden School District administrators felt that elementary-grade standardized test scores of its students were too low. In an effort to raise standardized test scores, Camden school officials aligned the curriculum of elementary school programs in reading, mathematics, and language arts with the skills measured by the Comprehensive Test of Basic Skills—Form U, Level D (CTBS) (Harris, 1981), which is the standardized test used by the district.

Curriculum alignment was achieved by listing the skills of the standardized test and comparing them with the skills listed in curriculum objectives and curriculum materials. Where disparities occurred, the curriculum was revised. Teachers were trained to implement the revised curriculum. A timetable for meeting objectives was established. The academic year was divided into quarters, and specific curriculum objectives were addressed in each quarter. Supervisors provided assistance and guidance in helping teachers teach content related to the quarterly objectives. All elementary schools in the district used an aligned curriculum except Davis School, the one chosen to participate in Follow Through.

Follow Through

Follow Through, created in 1967, is a federally funded program designed to extend the benefits of Head Start in providing education, health, and social services to low-income children. Reauthorized by Congress in 1986 (Hawkins, 1986), Follow Through provides funds to im-

Brent, George, and DiObilda, Nicholas. (1993). Effects of curriculum alignment versus direct instruction on urban children. *The Journal of Educational Research, 86,* 333-338. Reprinted with the permission of the Helen Dwight Reid Educational Foundation. Published by Heldref Publications, 1319 Eighteenth St., N.W., Washington, DC 20036-1802. Copyright © 1993.

plement and evaluate programs that provide promise in improving the educational achievement of low-income children. The city of Camden received a Follow Through grant in September 1988 to implement the direct-instruction model in Davis Elementary School.

Direct instruction is a unified system of instruction and materials that forces many changes in traditional classroom practices (Gage, 1985; Gersten, Carnine, & White, 1984). New instructional materials that are introduced to the classroom are designed according to a clearly defined set of principles, for example, analysis of the objectives in order to form teachable component concepts and sets of concepts, identification of preskills, and selection and sequencing of examples. Teacher guides include highly structured scripts that entail positive reinforcement and immediate corrective feedback. Extensive teacher training is required to implement the program fully.

A major evaluation of Follow Through models completed in 1977 (Englemann, Becker, Carnine, & Gersten, 1988) revealed that the direct-instruction model was effective in promoting beginning academic achievement. The direct-instruction programs in reading, mathematics, and language arts appealed to Camden school personnel because of their documented success in other Follow Through projects with similar students. Other perceived advantages included high structure in the curriculum, increased time on task, and extensive teacher training.

Various elementary schools in the Camden school system began partial implementation of the direct-instruction model's program in reading in the early 1980s. Evaluations revealed that the program was more effective in promoting reading achievement than traditional basal reader programs were (Brent, DiObilda, & Gavin, 1986; Brent & DiObilda, 1985–86). The Follow Through grant provided resources to fully implement direct-instruction programs in reading, mathematics, and language arts in Davis Elementary School for Grades K to 3 for a period of 3 years beginning September 1, 1988, and ending June 30, 1991.

At first, the teachers at Davis School were fearful that their pupils' standardized test scores would fall if they did not follow the aligned program. However, they were assured by the principal and assistant superintendent that they would not be required to meet the district's quarterly objectives. The teachers' supervisors were also instructed to allow teachers to follow the direct-instruction curriculum. A special direct-instruction coach was assigned to help teachers implement the direct-instruction programs. The Follow Through project allowed the district to assess the effects of an aligned versus an unaligned curriculum on reading, mathematics, and language arts achievement as measured by the district's chosen standardized test, the CTBS.

All the teachers were part of the effort to raise standardized test scores by aligning the curriculum. However, the test scores from the CTBS may contain a systematic bias that artificially raises the performance of all students and permits only generalizations to similarly aligned programs. To solve that problem, another standardized test, the Metropolitan Achievement Test Survey Battery (MAT) (Prescott, Balow, Hogan, & Farr, 1985) was given to "stable" students in both programs. Stable students were those students who had been continuously enrolled in their program for at least 2 years.

The MAT was administered 2 weeks after the CTBS, with only 1 month's prior notice to the pupils or the classroom teachers. The MAT results permitted generalizations about the performance of stable pupils in each program and a more valid comparison to national norms and to programs that do not specifically teach to the test. The MAT was not administered to mobile students because of the additional cost and the fact that the stable students' performance provided a more accurate portrayal of how students who had the full benefits of each program compared with the national norms on an independent standardized test.

A second question regarded the effect of both experimental and control programs on mobile students, that is, students who move from school to school annually and therefore do not have continuity in their academic lives.

Approximately 20% of the U.S. student population moves each year (Lash & Kirkpatrick, 1990). In New Jersey, the average mobility rate is 18% per year (New Jersey State Department of Education, 1989). In Camden, the overall rate is 33%. In Davis School, the overall mobility rate is 44%, and in the control school, it is 41%.

Recent studies indicate that mobility has a disruptive effect on the academic achievement of urban students (Ingersoll, Scamman, & Eckerling, 1989; Schuler, 1990). The present study assessed the effects of student mobility and stability on achievement. Additionally, we examined interactions between the instructional program and student mobility.

METHOD

Setting

Two urban elementary schools (K through 5) participated in the Follow Through project—one as an experimental school, the other as a control school. Students in Grade 2 were selected for this study because they constituted a cohort that experienced at least 2 full years of instruction in their respective programs. Davis School adopted the Oregon direct-instruction model for kindergarten in the 1988–89 school year. The program was fully implemented in 1990 and 1991. The other school maintained the conventional program in mathematics, reading, and language arts, which had been used in the school for at least 10 years and was aligned to the 1981 version of the CTBS (Harris, 1981).

The two schools were a mile apart. They served similar neighborhoods and were similar in the demographic and racial composition of their students. Approximately 45% were Black, 45% were Hispanic, 7% were Asian, and 3% were Caucasian. In each school, approximately 60% of the children had participated in Head Start or a similar preschool program. For the second grade, the average class size was 25 students in the Davis School and 21 students for the control school. The average attendance rate for each school was 90%. Although the overall mobility rate for both schools was ap-

proximately 45% annually, it was much higher for students included in the experiment, because the mobility rate was cumulative. The cumulative mobility rate for the 2 years of the project was 77% for the direct-instruction students and 70% for the control students.

Subjects

There were 99 second-grade students in the direct-instruction classrooms, including 23 stable students who had been in their program for at least 2 full years and 76 mobile students. There were 90 second-grade students in the control classrooms who received traditional reading, mathematics, and language arts instruction. These 90 students included 63 mobile students and 27 stable students who had been in the program for at least 2 years.

Materials

Several direct-instruction programs were used in the project. For reading and language arts in kindergarten, the students used Distar. In Grades 1 and 2, they used *Reading Mastery I* and *Reading Mastery II* (Englemann & Bruner, 1983) for reading instruction, and *Reasoning and Writing, Levels A, B, and C* (Englemann, Davis, Arbogast, & Silbert, 1991) for language-arts instruction. For mathematics instruction, the students used prepublication versions of *Connecting Math Concepts* (Englemann & Carnine, 1992). The direct-instruction model was not fully implemented during the first year of adoption because teachers were not accustomed to the programs and needed training. Most of the start-up problems were solved by the second year of the project, and the programs were fully implemented.

In the control school, students used the *Ginn Basal Reader Series* (Clymer & Venezky, 1982), the *Holt Math Series* (Nichols, et al. 1981), and Harcourt Brace Jovanovich's *Language For Daily Use* language-arts series (Strickland, 1983). Students used the books in each basal series intended for their grade levels. Within classes in the control school, students were divided into ability groups for reading instruction, but they were taught mathematics and language arts in whole classes. A similar grouping procedure was used in the direct-instruction classrooms.

Procedure

In early April, students in both schools were given the CTBS as a regular part of the school standardized testing program. The test yields 12 scores: total reading, word recognition, vocabulary, comprehension, total language, mechanics, expression, spelling, total mathematics, computation, mathematics concepts/applications, and total battery.

Two weeks later, the MAT was administered to stable students in both programs. The MAT yields 8 subscores and 4 total scores. The subscores are identical to those of the CTBS except that the MAT also includes a problem-solving subscore.

RESULTS

CTBS

We used a 2 × 2 (Program: Direct Instruction vs. Traditional Instruction × Mobility: Mobile Students vs. Stable Students) analysis of variance to analyze each total score and its component subscores. Normal curve equivalent scores were analyzed, and means were converted to percentile ranks. Means, standard deviations, and F values for the CTBS scores are presented in Table 1.

For main effects, the direct-instruction students scored significantly higher than did the traditional students on mathematics computation. Also, stable students scored significantly higher than did mobile students on total reading, word attack, vocabulary, comprehension, and total battery. There were no significant differences in the total language scores of two of its components, mechanics and expression, nor was there a significant difference in the total mathematics scores.

There were also three significant interactions related to vocabulary, spelling, and mathematics concepts. A post hoc test using Tukey's

HSD procedure revealed that the stable traditional students scored significantly higher than did the mobile traditional students on vocabulary and spelling. On mathematics concepts and applications, the stable traditional students scored significantly higher than did the traditional mobile students and the stable direct-instruction students.

An examination of the means for all groups reveals a similar pattern of significant differences. The pattern shows a similar level of achievement for both direct-instruction stable and mobile students. The stable traditional means are similar to both direct-instruction groups. However, the mobile traditional students' means are lower than their stable counterparts and both direct-instruction groups.

MAT

MAT results for stable students only are presented in Table 2. The table reveals that the direct-instruction stable students scored significantly higher in total mathematics and two of its subscores, computation and mathematics concepts. The means for the MAT subscores are lower than the means for the CTBS subscores, but they are near or above the 50th percentile.

DISCUSSION

Program Effects. On the CTBS, the direct-instruction group scored significantly higher on mathematics computation than did the traditional basal mathematics group. However, there was a significant interaction favoring the traditional stable students over their mobile counterparts in the control group and the stable students in the direct-instruction group. Evidently, the direct-instruction program is more effective in developing computational skills at Grade 2. However, the traditional mathematics program led to higher achievement on mathematics concepts for stable students in that program. The CTBS results for mathematics concepts indicate that higher test scores in a traditional mathematics program are dependent upon not only

TABLE 1.   Grade 2 CTBS Results for 1991

| | Group | | | | F^a | | |
| | Direct Instruction | | Control | | | | |
Subtest	Stable $n = 23$	Mobile $n = 76$	Stable $n = 27$	Mobile $n = 63$	P	M	I
Total reading					0.22	6.38*	2.68
M	71	66	77	54			
SD	19	20	20	18			
Word attack					2.69	5.72*	1.47
M	73	67	71	52			
SD	16	17	18	18			
Vocabulary					0.09	5.38*	4.78*
M	62	62	76	51			
SD	19	19	21	19			
Comprehension					1.32	5.14*	0.52
M	74	66	72	56			
SD	17	19	16	18			
Total language					1.22	2.41	1.10
M	74	71	74	59			
SD	19	19	17	21			
Spelling					0.84	2.80	4.27*
M	63	64	69	49			
SD	20	17	15	19			
Mechanics					2.59	2.73	2.82
M	87	87	88	74			
SD	17	17	20	22			
Expression					0.35	3.19	0.50
M	58	52	58	45			
SD	16	16	15	19			
Total mathematics					1.30	0.98	0.58
M	88	87	87	81			
SD	14	19	21	18			
Computation					5.22*	0.22	0.58
M	91	88	82	83			
SD	14	18	18	17			
Mathematics concepts					1.21	2.31	7.26**
M	68	74	85	66			
SD	19	20	19	18			
Total battery					0.59	4.63*	2.82
M	77	75	81	62			
SD	17	19	20	18			

Note. NCE means were converted to percentile rank means for this table. Standard deviations are NCE units.
[a]*F*-value annotations: P = program main effect; M = mobility main effect; I = interaction.
*$p < .05$; **$p < .01$.

TABLE 2. Grade 2 MAT Results for 1991 for Stable Students

	M	SD	F
Total reading			0.00
DI[a]	51.3	16.39	
Control	51.0	18.57	
Word attack			0.05
DI	53.1	18.82	
Control	50.3	23.61	
Vocabulary			0.08
DI	49.0	15.57	
Control	46.3	17.95	
Comprehension			0.09
DI	51.0	16.41	
Control	53.7	15.86	
Total language			1.03
DI	54.2	17.32	
Control	43.7	17.89	
Spelling			0.08
DI	60.5	19.84	
Control	57.2	21.41	
Language			1.18
DI	49.0	16.80	
Control	38.5	16.51	
Total mathematics			7.30**
DI	75.6	15.56	
Control	49.5	19.21	
Computation			8.61**
DI	75.9	16.40	
Control	48.4	18.07	
Mathematics concepts			10.13**
DI	77.9	18.20	
Control	48.4	15.32	
Problem solving			0.60
DI	61.0	11.78	
Control	53.2	21.39	
Total battery			1.68
DI	61.2	17.39	
Control	47.5	18.08	

Note. NCE means were converted to percentile rank means for this table. Standard deviations are NCE units.
[a]DI group, $n = 23$; control group, $n = 27$.
**$p < .01$.

curricular alignment but also stability in the program.

A startling contrast is provided by the MAT results. Recall that the MAT was given only to stable students in both programs. The direct-instruction means were significantly higher than the traditional means for both computation and concepts. The contradiction of the CTBS and MAT standardized test results suggests that the CTBS results were more dependent on the aligned mathematics curriculum (traditional) and that the direct-instruction program led to more generalized abilities, for at least computation and mathematics concepts.

Mobility. The analysis of variance for the CTBS scores also revealed a significant main effect for the mobility factor. Stable students scored significantly higher than did mobile students on word attack, vocabulary, comprehension, total reading, and total battery. It appears that reading ability is more affected by continuity of instruction than is mathematics or language abilities.

An examination of the means for the four groups indicates that mobility was more detrimental to those in the traditional programs than to those in the direct-instruction programs. In every subscore mean, there was little difference (no more than 6 percentile points) between the direct-instruction mobile and stable students. However, there was a substantial difference between the mobile and stable traditional students. The differences ranged from 16 to 25 percentile points. The differences were large enough to create a significant interaction for vocabulary and spelling ability in which the stable traditional students scored significantly higher than their mobile counterparts did, but not higher than either direct-instruction group. The evidence adds further support to the conclusion that reading achievement in the traditional program is dependent upon continuous instruction in that program, whereas the direct-instruction program may minimize the effects of mobility. That is, for reading ability, the basal reader groups took 2 years of continuous instruction to attain approximately the same level of performance as the direct-instruction mobile students.

The means presented in Tables 1 and 2 show a success story for both programs. On all measures, for both the CTBS and the MAT, the means were near or surpassed the 50th percentile. Both programs were successful in promoting student achievement. Because the traditional curriculum was aligned with the standardized test, we expected satisfactory levels of achievement on the test given by the district. Satisfactory levels of achievement also occurred with direct instruction, which was not specifically aligned with the test. Apparently, the direct-instruction program leads to levels of achievement similar to those in a traditional program that is adjusted for the skills included on a standardized test.

The standardized test performance of the students in the traditional programs may be affected by the program itself, the alignment of the curriculum with the test, the establishment of quarterly objectives, and monitoring of adherence to those objectives by supervisory staff. Traditional programs used in urban settings may require those characteristics to improve student achievement. The lower performance of the mobile traditional students indicates that urban schools may need to give mobile students more attention to compensate for the discontinuity of their schooling. Increased attention may take the form of better record keeping and prompt transference of the records from the sending school, more extensive diagnostic evaluation of academic abilities upon entering a new school, and supplementary instruction on components of the traditional program thought to affect subsequent achievement.

In contrast, the performance of the direct-instruction students may be most affected by proper and complete implementation of the program itself. Curriculum alignment with a standardized test and quarterly objectives may be unnecessary to achieve satisfactory standardized test performance with the direct-instruction program. Also, mobile students who enter the direct-instruction program at the beginning of a school year might not have to use extensive diagnostic testing and supplementary instruction. Finally, it may be unnecessary to revise a

reading, language, and mathematics curriculum when a district changes or updates its standardized test. Curriculum revision can become driven by other forces that compel a district to change the content or materials of instruction.

CONCLUSIONS

Our results indicate that the direct-instruction programs are as effective as traditional programs that are aligned with a specific standardized test. When a different independent test, the MAT, was used to assess the effects of instruction for stable students only, the direct-instruction program in mathematics led to significantly greater achievement.

As measured by the CTBS, student mobility has a negative effect on student achievement, especially in reading. Stable students scored significantly higher than did mobile students on all measures of reading achievement and on the total battery. Furthermore, mobility interacts with the program for vocabulary, spelling, and mathematics concepts in that mobile students in the traditional program take at least 2 years to attain the same achievement level as the mobile direct-instruction students. The results of this study suggest that student mobility is a major reason for lower achievement among urban children of low socioeconomic status.

REFERENCES

Brent, G., & DiObilda, N. (1985-86). Direct instruction in an urban school. *The Reading Instruction Journal, 29,* 2-5.

Brent, G., DiObilda, N., & Gavin, F. (1986). Camden direct instruction project. *Urban Education, 21,* 138-148.

Clymer, T., & Venezky, R. (1982). *Ginn reading program.* Columbus, Ohio: Ginn and Company.

Englemann, S., Becker, W., Carnine, D., & Gersten, R. (1988). The direct instruction follow through model: Design and outcomes. *Education and Treatment of Children, 2,* 303-317.

Englemann, S., & Bruner, E. (1983). *Reading Mastery I.* Chicago: Science Research Associates.

Englemann, S., & Bruner, E. (1983). *Reading Mastery II.* Chicago: Science Research Associates.

Englemann, S., & Carnine, D. (1992). *Connecting math concepts.* Chicago: SRA/McGraw-Hill.

Englemann, S., Davis, K., Arbogast, A., & Silbert, J. (1991). *Reasoning and writing, Levels A, B, C.* Chicago: SRA/McGraw-Hill.

Gage, N. L. (1985). *Hard gains in the soft sciences: The case of pedagogy.* Bloomington, IN: Phi Delta Kappa.

Gersten, R., Carnine, D., & White, W. A. T. (1984). The pursuit of clarity: Direct instruction and applied behavior analysis. In W. Heward, T. Heron, D. Hill, & J. Trap-Porter (Eds.), *Focus on behavior analysis in education* (pp. 38-57). Columbus, OH: Merrill.

Harris, J. (Ed.). (1981). *Comprehensive Test of Basic Skills.* Monterey, CA: CTB/McGraw-Hill.

Hawkins, A. (1986). *Human Services Reauthorization Act of 1986.* House of Representatives, 99th Congress, 2nd Session, Conference Report. (ERIC Document Reproduction Service No. ED 277451)

Ingersoll, G. M., Scamman, J. P., & Eckerling, W. D. (1989). Geographic mobility and student achievement in an urban setting. *Education Evaluation and Policy Analysis, 11,* 143-149.

Kozol, J. (1991). *Savage inequalities.* New York: Crown Publishers.

Lash, A. A., & Kirkpatrick, S. L. (1990). Classroom perspective on student mobility. *The Elementary School Journal, 91,* 177-191.

New Jersey Department of Education (1989). *School Report Card,* Trenton, NJ.

Nichols, E., et al. (1981). *Holt mathematics.* New York: Holt, Rinehart and Winston.

Prescott, G., Balow, I., Hogan, T., & Farr, R. (1985). *The Metropolitan Achievement Tests-MAT6 Survey Battery* (6th Ed.), San Antonio, TX: Psychological Corporation.

Schuler, D. (1990). *ERS Spectrum, 8,* 17-24.

Strickland, D. (1983). *Language for daily use.* Orlando, FL: Harcourt Brace Jovanovich.

Evaluation Criteria

1. Does the research provide accurate information about the practices studied?

By traditional standards, the design of this study is extremely weak. Because the study is essentially a pre-experiment, comparing student performance in two schools with no experimental controls, threats to internal validity are rampant. How are we to know, for example, that any differences observed are due to the instructional strategies ("curriculum alignment" vs. "direct instruction") and not to inherent differences in the two schools or their students? A closer examination, however, reveals that dismissing the study for internal validity reasons would be premature. First of all, the two schools studied have comparable demographics. Second, the tests administered are both highly reliable and, for the purposes of this study, reasonably valid. Third and most important, students taught by

Discussion Questions

1. Despite the apparent usefulness of the data collected in this study, would you still be concerned about drawing inappropriate conclusions regarding the "effectiveness" of direct instruction? Why or why not?

the "direct instruction" method performed just as well as, and in some areas better than, students in a comparable school who had been taught to the test. In a traditional research study, findings of "no significant differences" are generally not regarded with much interest, particularly with experimental designs as weak as this. But because this was an evaluation study, looking specifically at the effectiveness of direct instruction, finding comparable (and in math, perhaps superior) performance by the "direct instruction" students lends credibility to the argument that direct instruction presents an effective alternative.

2. Does the research serve the needs of a given audience?

The article is unclear about whether all those affected by the evaluation were identified and their information needs addressed. It would be unfortunate if the full evaluation of the "direct instruction" program did not include measures of student, teacher, and parental satisfaction.

3. Is the research realistic, frugal, and diplomatic?

While many criticize the use of standardized tests as measures of instructional effectiveness, student performance on these tests has obvious political importance. No new way of teaching is likely to get far if students do not do well on them. Thus the research reported in this article is sensitive to the politics of the situation, and realistic in scope. The design was practical, and disruption of normal practice was kept to a minimum. The one additionally imposed measure, the MAT, was given to provide a benchmark to national norms. Whether or not the study was "frugal" (i.e., whether the evaluation produced information that justified its cost) is difficult to tell from this article; that question can only be answered by the relevant decision makers.

2. If you were an administrator with Camden School District, how useful would you find these results? Explain.

3. Who are the relevant decision makers in this situation? How well do you think their information needs were satisfied?

4. Has the research been conducted legally and ethically?

There is no evidence here of any conflict of interest (i.e., no evidence that the researchers have any "stake" in the findings), or that there were any legal or ethical concerns. Neither students nor teachers were put at risk by their participation.

4. Create a scenario for an evaluation study of "direct instruction" in which this standard would be violated.

Improving the Grades of Student Athletes: A Study of Attitudes, Expectations, and Academic Performance

Henry Davis   Jim Guthrie
Highland Springs (Virginia) High School

INTRODUCTION

The Highland Springs Community

With its roots going back to 1891, Highland Springs High School is located about nine miles east of downtown Richmond, Virginia. This high school, and in particular its athletic program, has traditionally been a focal point in the community. The character of Highland Springs has been molded out of the agricultural traditions of the nineteenth century, which have now given way to the lifestyle of a modern, predominantly blue collar community.

Demographic changes in the school population have been significant. Whereas the school population in 1982-83 was 56% white and 43% black, the ratio in 1987-88 was nearly even with 49.4% black, 49.3% white and 1.3% Asian and Hispanic. The present figures are 65% black, 34% white, and 1% Asian and Hispanic. The school population reflects national trends with almost a third of the students living in single parent homes, and many living with other relatives or moving from one parent to another. Due to a slowdown in industrial growth, coupled with shifts in school zones and population centers, the school population is decreasing. From an enrollment of 1,951 and a staff of 175 in 1976, the student population decreased to 1,450 with a staff of 130 in 1987-88. At present the enrollment stands at 1,151 with a faculty of 92.

It is also true to say that although community involvement and interest in the school's athletic program is higher than in neighboring schools, these too have waned somewhat.

The Research Topic

As two teachers of mathematics in a high school with a strong sporting tradition, both having more than a passing interest in sports (Jim is the soccer coach), we have from time to time discussed the academic performance of our students. In particular we have been concerned with trying to find ways to optimize the performance of our student athletes.

In our discussions we raised and discussed several questions about student athletes in general. Some of these questions were as follows:

> Do student athletes value athletic performance over academic performance?
>
> Do student athletes expect special treatment in the classroom?
>
> Do student athletes have special goals?
>
> Do student athletes perform better academically in season, or out of season?
>
> Are student athletes more pressured than other students?
>
> Do student athletes have special needs?

We decided to gather information from student athletes, their parents, their teachers, coaches and administrators. We also decided to analyze their academic records.

THE INSTRUMENTS

Questionnaires

Questionnaires were developed and designed for student athletes, the parents of student athletes, and for teachers, including administrators and coaches.

Davis, Henry, and Guthrie, Jim. (1996). Improving the grades of student athletes: A study of attitudes, expectations, and academic performance, pp. 1–20. Reprinted with the permission of the Metropolitan Educational Research Consortium.

The questionnaire for student athletes contained questions about study habits, academic performance, time spent on athletic activities, parental involvement, future goals, and demographic details.

The questionnaire for the parents of student athletes contained questions about their preferences, their attitudes towards their children's athletic and academic activities, and the aspirations they hold for their children in these areas.

The teacher survey asked for rankings on a Likert scale about the perceptions that teachers had concerning attitudes, needs, and expectations of student athletes, among other topics.

Structured Interviews

Interviews with predetermined questions were conducted with teachers, including coaches and administrators. Some of the questions sought responses about their perceptions of the attitudes, needs, academic performance, and goals of student athletes, and opinions on how the student athletes could be motivated in the classroom.

Interviews with groups of two to four student athletes were also carried out using the same set of questions.

The questionnaires and interview questions are included as an appendix.

QUESTIONNAIRE RESULTS

Student Athlete Questionnaire

About 250 questionnaires were distributed to student athletes, mainly through coaches, and 66 responses were received. Of the 66 respondents 32 represented the school in a single sport and all the others represented the school in 2 or more sports. The following table gives the relative percentage of respondents representing the school in each of the various sports.

Football	23%
Track*	17%
Soccer	14%
Basketball	13%
Baseball	10%
Volleyball	8%
Wrestling	5%
Softball	4%
Tennis	3%
Gymnastics	2%
Golf	1%

*Track includes Cross Country.

These percentages are also presented as a circle graph in the appendix.

Of the 66 respondents 50 or 76% chose academic excellence as being more important than being an outstanding athlete, and 10 or 15% chose being an outstanding athlete as more important. Two said both were equally important and 4 gave no answer.

The responses on the number of hours spent on their sports outside of the school day, on a daily basis were as follows:

No. of Hours	No. of Students
Under 1 hr	2
1 hr	3
1-2 hrs	4
2 hrs	8
2-3 hrs	11
3 hrs	12
3-4 hrs	6
4 hrs	7
4-5 hrs	7
5 hrs	3

Three respondents did not indicate a time.

The responses on the number of hours spent on academic work outside of the school day, on a daily basis, were as follows:

No. of Hours	No. of Students
Under 1 hr	8
1 hr	15
1-2 hrs	12
2 hrs	10
2-3 hrs	4
3 hrs	3
3-4 hrs	4
4 hrs	7
4-5 hrs	1

Two respondents did not indicate a time.

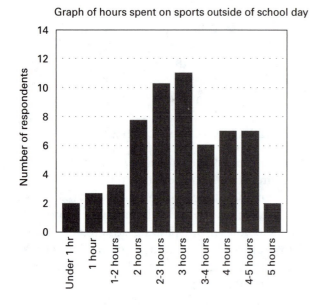

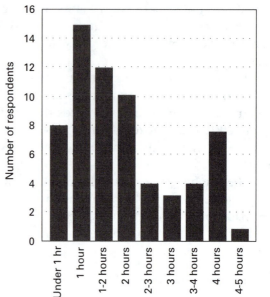

Figure 1.

For purposes of comparison, bar graphs of these two sets of hours are shown in Figure 1. It is interesting to note that the graph of the number of hours spent on sports peaks at 3 hours while the graph of the number of hours spent on academic work peaks at 1 hour.

Of the 66 respondents, 52 or 79% answered that they intended to continue sports after high school, and 13 or just under 20% said they would not. One respondent gave no indication.

Sixty-two (62) of the respondents or 94% answered that they intended to continue academic studies after high school and 3 or about 4.5% said they would not. One respondent gave no indication.

Of the 66 respondents, 25 or 38% answered that it was their goal to become a professional athlete, and 3 said maybe. Out of these, 15 of them or nearly 23% thought it was a realistic goal. Those indicating that it was not their goal to become a professional athlete numbered 37 or 56%. Of the 25 "yes" responses, 15 were of black ethnic origin, and 8

were white. The gender makeup of the 25 positive responses was 21 male and 4 female.

The 66 respondents rated their athletic talents and skills on a scale of 1 to 5, with 5 being the highest as follows:

Rating	No. of Respondents	Percentage
1	1	1.5%
2	3	4.5%
3	14	21.0%
4	36	54.5%
5	11	17.6%

On a similar scale, the 66 respondents rated the level of parental support for their sporting ambitions as follows:

Rating	No. of Respondents	Percentage
1	3	1.5%
2	5	4.5%
3	16	24.2%
4	8	12.1%
5	34	51.5%

Of the 66 respondents, 57 or 86% indicated that their parents pushed them to perform better in academics as opposed to sports, 5 or 7.6% indicated both, 2 or 3% indicated neither, and 2 gave no responses.

Forty-one or 62% of the respondents said their academic performance was better than their athletic performance, 17 or about 26% said their athletic performance was better, 4 thought both were equally good, and 4 gave no response. Of the 17 who thought their athletic performance was better, 12 had indicated that it was their goal to become professional athletes. Further, 7 out of that 17 were from football, 5 from baseball, and 2 were from basketball.

On the question of whether they performed better academically in or out of their sporting season, 35 or 53% indicated out of season, 25 or just under 38% indicated in season, 5 indicated neither, and 1 gave no response.

Asked what was their overall academic grade, the responses were as follows:

Overall Grade	No. of Respondents	Percentage
A	5	7.6%
B	32	48.5%
C	20	30.3%
D	3	4.5%
F	4	6.1%

Asked for their opinion as to which area, sports or academics, gets more support from the school, 38 or almost 58% of the 66 respondents indicated sports and 25 or nearly 38% indicated academics. One indicated equal support for both while 2 gave no response.

Asked for their opinion as to whether athletes should be required to perform well academically, 60 or 91% answered yes, five answered no and one gave no response. They were also asked to explain why, and 20 or one-third of those answering "yes" cited either eligibility requirements for participating in high school sports or requirements for entering college. Another 20 cited future security and 6 of those specifically mentioned "in case of injury."

Asked if the school should do more to promote their athletic talents, and to explain their answers, 40 or nearly 61% answered yes, and 20 or about 30% answered no. Amongst the yes answers, the reasons varied widely and no particular tendency was indicated. Those answering no, gave no reason.

Questionnaire for Parents of Student Athletes

Among the parents of student athletes there were 33 respondents.

All the parents indicated that they would prefer their son or daughter to perform better in academics rather than in sports.

From the 33 respondents 31 or 94% indicated that their son or daughter studied outside of school hours during their sporting season. The number of hours per day spent on study during the season, as reported by parents is as follows:

Number of Hours	Number of Students
1 hour	5
1-2 hrs	6
2 hrs	3
2-3 hrs	5
3 hrs	5
3-4 hrs	0
4 hrs	2

Of the 31 parents answering the question, 3 gave no indication of the number of hours, 1 said not enough, and 1 said less than out of season (Figure 2).

Of the 33 respondents, 29 or 88% indicated that they pushed their son or daughter to study during their sporting season (two changed the word "push" to "encourage") and 4 responded negatively.

Of the 33 respondents, 20 or about 61% indicated that they pushed their son or daughter to attend practice during their sporting season, 11 or 33% indicated that they did not push their son or daughter to attend practice, and two gave no response.

In response to the question as to whether they wanted their son or daughter to become

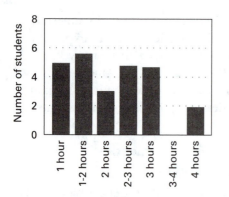

Figure 2. Hours per day spent studying, during sports season, as reported by parents.

a professional athlete, 12 parents or just over 36% answered yes, 14 or 42% answered no, three answers could be interpreted as maybe, two said they would support their children's choice, and two gave no response. Of the 14 positive responses, five cited football and three cited basketball.

Of the 33 respondents, 28 or 85% wanted their son or daughter to pursue a professional career not in sports. This means that many parents indicated that they wanted for their children both a professional sporting career and a professional career not in sports. A wide range of professions were cited and there was no dominant trend.

Asked for their opinion about which area, sports or academics, gets more support from the school, 25 of the 33 respondents or nearly 76% said academics, 5 or 15% said sports, and 3 gave no indication.

All of the 33 respondents expressed the opinion that athletes should be required to perform well academically, and 13 or 39% of them cited future security as a reason. Six (6) or 18% stressed the need to be well rounded, and only 3 or 9% mentioned that very few succeed to become professional athletes.

Of the 33 respondents, 17 or nearly 52% thought that the school should do more to promote athletic talents, 10 or 30% did not think the school should do more to promote athletic talents, and 6 did not express an opinion. The

area in which people wanted the school to do more, was helping to expose the athletes' talents and skills to college recruiters.

Teacher Survey

There were 52 respondents to the teacher survey, and these included eight coaches. The survey required the respondents to express their degree of agreement or disagreement with 14 statements on a scale of 1 to 5, with 1 indicating "strongly disagree" and 5 indicating "strongly agree." The numerical responses were averaged and graphed in Figure 3.

In response to a question asking what the county (i.e., the school district) could do to assist the teachers in their work with student athletes, 14 (including three coaches) or 27% mentioned instituting SAT prep/counseling/tutoring programs, by providing money for such programs. Thirteen (13) or 25% mentioned putting in place more rigorous standards and monitoring with respect to academic performance of student athletes.

From the coaches there were some strongly articulated individual opinions:

1. Hire qualified coaches who are nationally accredited.
2. Give some special consideration to allowing extra time for homework when away games are involved.
3. Teachers must be willing to "work with" coaches.

The responses of the coaches to the question of what they did to monitor the academic performance of their student athletes, in general addressed checking up on grades and keeping in regular communication.

INTERVIEWS

Teacher Interviews

The general interpretation of the term "Student Athlete" among the teachers interviewed was a student who took on the additional activities of representing the school in a sport. Some

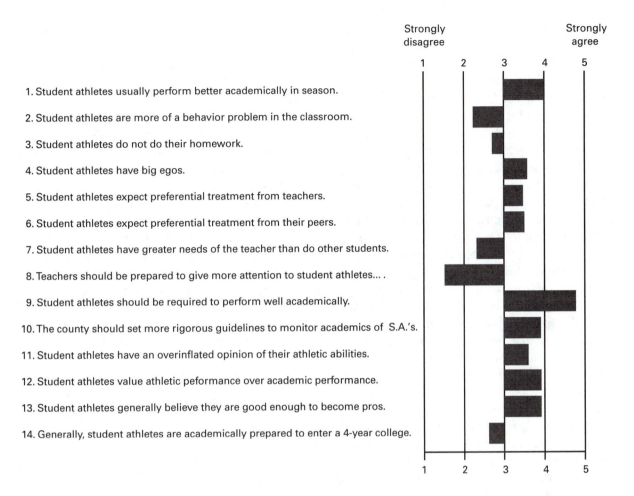

Figure 3.   Teacher survey results.

teachers took the step of stressing that student athletes were students first, who were also athletes, particularly because there were academic criteria for eligibility.

While the teachers did not think that there were noticeable physical differences between student athletes and other students, they did agree that student athletes were individuals who had made the choice to participate in sports as representatives of the school.

While teachers were very cautious about conceding that the school had any special responsibility to student athletes over and above its responsibility to other students, all teachers were sympathetic to the idea of being willing to make reasonable concessions with respect to deadlines when late practice sessions and away events were involved. The opinion was strongly expressed that student athletes should be made aware, through some sort of support system, of the necessity to be academically prepared for life after sports.

Focusing on the classroom teacher, the teachers interviewed, while reaffirming the idea of no preferential treatment, recognized the need for the classroom teacher to work along with coaches in helping the student athlete to efficiently structure his school activities to achieve an equitable balance. The classroom teacher it was felt was strategically positioned to set and require the high expectations that will help them to succeed both in academics and athletics.

The interviewees did not believe that the needs of student athletes should be seen as different from the needs of other students. They did however, consider it necessary that teachers should be sensitive to the special situation of student athletes, since there were considerably more demands on their time, albeit by their own choice. The view was repeated that efforts should be made to impart to student athletes, early in their high school career, time management and study skills.

Without exception, the teachers interviewed thought that the great majority of student athletes, particularly the younger underclassmen, had an unrealistic view of their future after high school. They usually believe that they are destined for fame and fortune in professional sports. Reality only sets in for some of them by the time they become seniors.

When asked how they thought teachers could motivate student athletes outside of their particular sporting season, there was both tacit and overt agreement that it was more difficult to motivate them after the sporting season was over. A number of suggestions were made, but the one most often repeated was for teachers to show interest in and support for the sporting activities. Also strongly emphasized was the need to establish and maintain communication and genuine relationships with the athletes year round. Another suggestion was to consistently maintain and remind the athletes of high expectations. Some of the teachers who had been at Highland Springs High School for many years, rued the continuing breakdown of relationships over the years. Relationships between students and parents and teachers and the community were becoming more and more fragmented as everyone was getting more busy with more and more paperwork to the detriment of the more basic needs. The school community needed to reestablish a network of mutual support for each other.

The consensus among those interviewed was that the school community expected our athletes to always win. This "win at all times" mentality was seen as less than desirable. It was felt that criticism and derision particularly from their peers when our teams did not win tended to be overly harsh. This coupled with dwindling attendance at sporting events put unwarranted and undesirable pressure on the student athlete, who were the ones making the extra effort for the benefit of the school.

The general view of the student athlete at Highland Springs High School, as expressed by those interviewed, was that they were students who had made a conscious choice to go the extra mile for the school, usually to fulfill some individual purpose or need. These were students who needed to be guided along realistic paths. They needed to be made aware of the opportunities and challenges that awaited them on their chosen paths. They needed to be helped in budgeting their available time in order to achieve balanced success. They needed to be taught how to channel their competitive drive to become equally competitive in the classroom.

Student Athlete Interviews

Student athletes were interviewed in groups of 2, 3, and 4, using the same set of questions used with the teachers.

For the most part they did not feel that they were noticeably different from other students, but the opinion was expressed that there was something almost intangible about them that their peers and other people their own age could recognize. The real difference about student athletes, they all asserted, was that they made the choice to participate. They did concede that some Student Athletes did think they deserved privileges, but on the whole they would prefer to be treated the same way as other students.

The Student Athletes did not believe that either the school as a whole or teachers in particular had any special responsibility towards them, over and above their responsibilities to other students. They emphasized that students should not get any special treatment simply because they were athletes. They all however, expressed the opinion that some consideration be given to some extended time for homework assignments, particularly for away events. They also felt that at times some special tutoring ought to be offered, or that special study halls could be set up for athletes, to compensate for classroom time missed through no fault of their own.

Some of the groups interviewed expressed the view that the school needed to keep all sports alive, not only the popular ones like football and basketball. Those athletes in the less popular sports felt that the school should provide better facilities for training, and more funding. Boosters, they said, should be for all sports, not just for football and basketball. They also said that trainers and coaches should be interested in developing the full potential of all participating athletes, and not just the best ones.

No significant suggestion was offered as to how teachers could motivate students outside of their sporting season. The suggestion was made however, that seasonal assemblies should be organized to speak to athletes about grades, and the importance of maintaining good grades in order to be eligible to represent the school.

The student athletes felt that what the school community expected from them was simply to win. If they did not win, they were ignored by the general public. If they did not win, they were derided, particularly by their classmates who generally showed little or no understanding for what they themselves might be feeling after a loss. When they did win, their peers would brag about them and soon forget.

When asked about pressure from the school community, the general response was that there was simply not enough support from the community to generate any significant pressure, except perhaps for football and basketball where the traditional supporters of the school demanded high expectations.

While a few of the students seriously expressed the goal of becoming professional athletes, most of them said it was not their goal, but that they would grasp the opportunity if such an opportunity arose. Most of them intended to continue to participate in sports after high school, either on the college level or just for recreation.

ACADEMIC RECORDS

The academic records of all the student athletes participating in football, basketball, baseball, soccer, and softball were analyzed. Grade point averages for the first, second, and third grading periods for the 1995-96 school year were calculated for all those athletes, and for purposes of comparison, the grade point averages for random groups of similar sizes were also calculated. The means of the grade point averages for each group were then calculated and are tabulated below. Also included in the table are the means of the grade point averages for all boys and all girls in the school.

Group by Sport	GPA for 1st 9 wks	GPA for 2nd 9 wks	GPA for 3rd 9 wks
Football	2.17	2.09	2.07
Random	1.91	1.66	1.75
Boys Basketball	2.05	2.10	1.99
Random	2.28	2.33	2.07
Baseball	2.35	2.32	2.32
Random	2.13	2.15	2.11
Boys Soccer	2.63	2.70	2.74
Random	1.59	1.78	1.60
Girls Basketball	2.85	2.26	2.15
Random	2.52	2.59	2.76
Girls Softball	2.86	2.43	2.67
Random	2.19	2.27	1.94
Girls Soccer	3.27	3.13	3.30
Random	2.40	2.06	2.03
All boys in HSHS	2.03	1.94	1.93
All girls in HSHS	2.40	2.27	2.33

The information from this table could be analyzed in many ways, but our focus was to see if student athletes performed better academically in season or out of season. For football, boys basketball, boys soccer, and girls soccer their GPA's were highest during the season. In baseball, girls basketball, and girls soccer their GPA's were highest in the first grading period, and this was in keeping with the overall pattern schoolwide. In football and basketball we are able to see that the GPA's fell after the season was over.

RECOMMENDATIONS

After carefully reviewing and discussing the information gathered, we came up with the following recommendations:

- We recommend that the school institute a pre-school session on time-management for all student athletes and their parents.

- We recommend that the school institute a pre-season assembly for all student athletes in each sport, using a motivational speaker focusing on time-management and study skills.

- We recommend that the school appoint a resource person to monitor each athletic season's student athletes for the entire school year, with particular responsibility for (a) monitoring grades and classroom performance, and (b) making students aware of NCAA requirements.

- We recommend that funding be provided to put in place special tutorials and study halls for student athletes during their sporting season.

- We recommend that a concerted effort be made to impart the above mentioned time-management and study skills to student athletes during their 9th grade year.

- We recommend that monitoring of student athletes' grade for eligibility be mandatory for every 9 week grading period, instead of only during the athletic season.

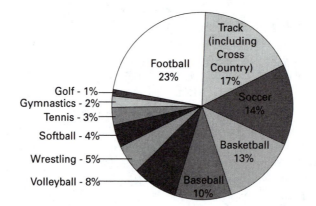

Circle graph showing percentages of student athlete respondents representing HSHS in the various sports

APPENDIX
STUDENT ATHLETE QUESTIONNAIRE

1. In what sport(s) do you represent your school? _____
   _____
   _____

2. Which is more important to you?   Academic   Being an
                 (Circle one)   Excellence   Outstanding
                                              Athlete

   Why?

   _____

   _____

   _____

   _____

3. How many hours outside the school day
   do you spend on your sports?   _____

4. How many hours outside the school day
   do you spend on academic work?   _____

5. Do you intend to continue sports after high school?   YES   NO
                                                (Circle one)

6. Do you intend to continue academic study after high school?   YES   NO

7. Is it your goal to become a professional athlete?   YES   NO
   If yes, do you think this is a realistic goal? _____
                           Name the sport _____

8. On a scale of 1 to 5, with 5 being the highest,
   rate your athletic talent and skills. (Circle one)   1   2   3   4   5

9. On a similar scale, rate the level of parental
   support in your sporting ambitions. (Circle one)   1   2   3   4   5

10. Do your parents push you to perform better
    in sports or in academics? (Circle one)   SPORTS   ACADEMICS

11. Which is better? (Circle one)   Your   Your
                                   Academic   Athletic
                                Performance   Performance

12. When do you perform
    better academically? (Circle one)   In Season   Out of Season

13. What is your overall academic grade? (Circle one)   A   B   C   D   F

14. In your opinion, which area gets more
    support from the school? (Circle one)   SPORTS   ACADEMICS

15. In your opinion, should athletes be
    required to perform well academically? (Circle one)   YES   NO
    Explain why _____

    _____

    _____

    _____

16. Should the school do more to promote
    your athletic talents? (Circle one)   YES   NO
    If so, what? _____

    _____

    _____

    _____

GENERAL INFORMATION

17. What is your age? _____

18. What is your grade level? (Circle one)   9   10   11   12

19. What is your gender? (Circle one)   MALE   FEMALE

20. What is your ethnic origin? (Circle one)   Black   White   Other

Thank you for your cooperation!

Please complete and turn in this questionnaire this week.

QUESTIONNAIRE FOR PARENTS OF STUDENT ATHLETES

1. In which area would you prefer your
   son to perform better? (Circle one)   Sports   Academics

2. In which area would you prefer your
   daughter to perform better? (Circle one)   Sports   Academics

3. Does your son/daughter study outside of
   school hours during the sporting season? (circle one) Yes   No
   If so, how many hours per day? _____

4. Do you push your son/daughter to study
   during his/her sporting season? (Circle one)   Yes   No

5. Do you push your son/daughter to attend
   practice during his/her sporting season? (Circle one) Yes   No

6. Do you want your son/daughter to
   become a professional athlete? (Circle one)   Yes   No
   If so, in what sport? _____

7. Do you want your son/daughter to pursue a
   professional career, not in sports? (Circle one)   Yes   No
   If so, in what field? _____

8. In your opinion, which area gets more
   support from the school? (Circle one)   Sports   Academics

9. In your opinion, should athletes be
   required to perform well academically? (Circle one)   Yes   No
   Explain why _____

   _____

10. Should the school do more to promote
    athletic talents? (Circle one)   Yes   No
    If so, what? _____

    _____

TEACHER SURVEY

Are you an Athletic Coach? (Circle one)   Yes   No

Please read the following statements carefully and indicate your level of agreement on the scale provided. If you have no opinion circle the X.

	Strongly disagree				Strongly agree	No opinion
1. Student athletes usually perform better academically in season.	1	2	3	4	5	X
2. Student athletes are more of a behavior problem in the classroom.	1	2	3	4	5	X
3. Student athletes do not do their homework.	1	2	3	4	5	X
4. Student athletes have big egos.	1	2	3	4	5	X
5. Student athletes expect preferential treatment from teachers.	1	2	3	4	5	X
6. Student athletes expect preferential treatment from their peers.	1	2	3	4	5	X
7. Student athletes have greater needs of the teacher than do other students.	1	2	3	4	5	X
8. Teachers should be prepared to give more attention to student athletes than to other students.	1	2	3	4	5	X
9. Student athletes should be required to perform well academically.	1	2	3	4	5	X
10. The county should set more rigorous guidelines to monitor the academic performance of student athletes.	1	2	3	4	5	X

	Strongly disagree				Strongly agree	No opinion
11. Student athletes have an over-inflated opinion of their athletic abilities.	1	2	3	4	5	X
12. Student athletes value athletic performance over academic performance.	1	2	3	4	5	X
13. Student athletes generally believe they are good enough to become professional athletes.	1	2	3	4	5	X
14. Generally, student athletes are academically prepared to enter a four-year college.	1	2	3	4	5	X

15. What could the county do to assist teachers in their work with student athletes? _____

_____

_____

_____

_____

_____

_____

_____

_____

_____

For Coaches only.

16. What do you do to monitor the academic performance of your student athletes?

_____

_____

_____

_____

_____

_____

_____

_____

_____

TEACHER INTERVIEW QUESTIONS

1. What is your interpretation of the term "Student Athlete"?

2. In your opinion, how is the student athlete noticeably different from other students?

3. In your opinion, what are the responsibilities of the school to the student athlete?

4. In your opinion, what are the responsibilities of the teacher to the student athlete?

5. How do the needs of student athletes compare to the needs of other students in the classroom setting?

6. How do you think student athletes view their future after high school?

7. In what ways can teachers motivate student athletes outside of their particular sporting season?

8. What do you think the school community expects from student athletes?

9. In what ways does the school community put pressure on the student athlete?

10. How can the teacher help the student athlete to excel in the classroom?

11. What is your general view of student athletes at H.S.H.S.?

Evaluation Criteria

1. Does the research provide accurate information about the practices studied?

The purpose of this research, undertaken by two high school teachers, was to bring some data to bear on the longstanding belief that student athletes are less motivated and do less well in their schoolwork. The accuracy of these data varied. The response rate for the student athlete and parent questionnaires was low, and thus inferences are of dubious value. The response rate from the teacher questionnaire is better (about 56%). Most of the narrative focuses on interviews with student athletes and teachers, and both groups provide some apparent insights, including a few surprises. The problem is that there is no way for the casual reader to know how much of what is reported reflects the authors' own biases. This suggests that action research is most useful as a point of departure for further reflection and discussion.

2. Does the research serve the needs of a given audience?

Yes, almost by definition. Practice-based research is designed and carried out to serve the needs of practitioners themselves. As teachers concerned about the academic progress of their student athletes, the authors formulated questions that they (and other teachers at that school) were most interested in, and collected data accordingly. As the findings have policy significance, however, in retrospect it probably would have been wise to discern the information needs of administrators at that school as well, and bring them into the process.

3. Is the research realistic, frugal, and diplomatic?

This study was done on a shoestring budget, and so the principal cost was the time of the investigators, which was considerable. While their attempt to collect data from so many sources is commendable, they probably

Discussion Questions

1. What can practitioner-researchers do to pursue information of interest without letting bias get in the way? How well are the authors' conclusions backed up by the evidence? Are you troubled by the lack of a literature review in this article?

2. Even though this study was done strictly to meet information needs of teachers in this high school, what value (if any) does the study have for other teachers and schools?

3. Given the highly labor-intensive nature of practitioner research, it is important to use time as efficiently as possible. If you had been one of the two teachers conducting this research on student athletes, how, if at all, would you have used your time differently?

spent too much effort for the value of some of the information they obtained.

4. Has the research been conducted legally and ethically?

From all appearances, yes, although no safeguards are noted.

4. In-house studies are vulnerable to findings that are potentially embarrassing to others in the school. Do you detect any such findings in this study? What can researcher-practitioners do when this happens?

Index